To PETE & Roc ♡

OUR SACRED hONOR,
defend THE oppressed !
Your FRiEND

Reds Holmey

July, 2007

The Lemon Dance

Tell Fidel El Rojo is Coming

by

Reds Helmey

Savannah, Georgia
2000

Reds Helmey
The lemon dance, tell Fidel el rojo is coming

ISBN 0-9703232-0-4

1. Robert M. Helmey, 1969 — airplane hijacking. 2. Biography.
3. Savannah, Georgia

Library of Congress Control Number 00-092545

Copies of this publication may be ordered from R. M. Helmey, 1012
Wilma Street, Savannah, GA 31410. Cost: $29.95 cost of the book plus $3.50
shipping. If you are a resident of Georgia, please add 6% sales tax.

The Lemon Dance

Tell Fidel El Rojo is Coming

Dedication

This book is dedicated to my wife, Maxine.

And to some wonderful and irreplaceable friends who had faith to believe I could write: Herman Kleinsteuber, Rose Chance, Bobby Herndon, Bess Ramsey, Mike and Ronda Ruth, Louise Sebastion, Tony Cela.

And to the writer's group, Zona Rosa.

And to my editor who said, I am not being picky, I want your book to be a success — Stephanie Jackel.

With special thanks to the following:

117th AC&W Squad, Georgia Air National Guard

Dog Company, 10th Infantry Battalion, USMCR

5th Rifle Company, FMF, USMCR

11th and 13th Special Forces Group, USAR

Local #96 International Association of Heat and Frost Insulators and Asbestos Workers.

Thomas G. 'Short Man' Corley, a true friend, and his mother, who will always be remembered as a lady of character and charity.

And to the memory of Arthur 'Nick' Bougas.

And to the loving memory of my mother, Freda Waters Helmey.

Prologue

United Flight 459, this is Havana. Go ahead.
I have an armed passenger in the cockpit.
He wishes to send a message.
And what is the message?
He wishes to inform Fidel Castro of his pending arrival.
Is that the exact message, 459?
Negative. The exact message is: Tell Fidel that El Rojo is coming.

On January 11, 1969, I told my wife that I was involved in a conspiracy to assassinate Fidel Castro, that I'd been given the green light to detour an aircraft to Cuba. "If everything goes all right, I'll be back in four to six months," I said. "If I don't make it, pray for me. After I arrive in Cuba, you will be given $250,000 by a Special Agent of the local FBI."

The ride to the airport that night in Captain Tommy Close's old Buick didn't seem real. I felt as if I had no power over what was going on. It was as if I had done this before.

"Tommy, it's critical to President Johnson that Castro be assassinated before Richard Nixon takes office Wednesday."

Message is received. United 459, you are cleared to land at Jose Marti. Use runway on East-West direction.
All right, Havana. Will use East-West runway.
You are coming up now on the downwind tangent.
Please begin descent at rate of 500 feet per minute.
Roger, Havana.
You will taxi to the main terminal and unload. Do not stop on runways or taxiways. Proceed immediately to terminal. Passengers will be escorted to the terminal and

taken to Havana. Crew will answer questions and will
cooperate with Cuban authorities. Armed passenger will be
taken into custody as soon as he arrives. Please inform us
now of his name.

Havana, the name of our passenger is Robert McRae
Helmey.

Description, please.

About six foot three, 230 pounds, has red hair and stocky
build.

The United Captain is worried, and his biggest worry is me.
I had come into the cockpit with a gun in my hand, and now I'm
sitting in the observer's seat directly behind him. To reassure
him, the engineer, and the co-pilot that I mean them or their
passengers no harm, I keep up a casual conversation. At one
point during our flight, I even ask the engineer to hold the pistol
for me.

A squall line on the aircraft's radar is far to the east of us.
"We won't have any problem getting around it," the pilot assures
me.

Now the lights of Havana are clearly visible from the
cockpit, even through the low cloud cover, like sequins over dark
cloth. The lights of the runway stretch beneath us as though
some giant has laid out a gleaming path, a double row of greenish
pearls to guide us. The pearls keep coming and it seems we are
going faster and faster. Now the wheels touch the concrete of the
runway, and I feel the tell-tale thud as the Boeing 727 settles
down. The engines whine as they slow the weight of the aircraft,
and I am on the ground.

I rise from my seat while the plane is still rolling toward the
terminal. "Son, are you sure you want to do this?" the pilot asks
me.

"Yes, this is what I have to do," I say, handing him the pistol.

I open the door of the cockpit and step into the cabin. A
stewardess stands in my way, and I touch her arm.

"Bless you, sister. I"ll take care of this."

Now the aircraft has stopped on the ramp in front of the terminal, and the engines have ceased. At the doorway of the plane, I see that the Cuban ground crew has not yet rolled the ramp up to the door. I sit on the door threshold, then jump ten feet to the ground. After landing on the concrete surface, I walk toward the Cuban soldiers with my hands held high in the air. As I do so, I look back to the jet's red, white and blue colors for the last time.

Introduction

Eleven months later, on that November day in 1969, the weather in Savannah was beautiful. It was crisp and clear. Thanksgiving was just eleven days away. Cuba was behind me now. The fear of the unknown was being replaced by the reality of what was before me. Still, I had a lot to be thankful for. I was finally to face a judge and jury who would decide whether I would serve a minimum of 20 years, or, as some people liked to remind me, be made an example of and face the death penalty. I knew my life would never be the same, regardless of the verdict.

For some ten months I had been in prison, mostly in Cuba. As unclear and tragic as things appeared to be at the time, that's where my life had really begun changing.

Standing outside my attorney's office, I remembered those uncertain days and nights in solitary confinement at Havana's G2 prison. The cell was the size of a small bathroom. It was a black hole, that reminded me of a tomb. The lights and water were controlled by the whim of the Cuban soldiers. Walls were covered in blood, smells were nauseating, putrid. Shots rang out in the night. The sounds of human cries came to haunt me. When the cell door opened, there was that fear of the unknown. Yet I had learned much about myself. I thought of death. The very beliefs that had shaped my world were shaken to the core, and I was left doubting all my previous values.

During the sixties, the assassinations of John F. Kennedy, and later his brother, Bobby Kennedy, and Dr. Martin Luther King had ripped at the fabric of Western society. During the Viet Nam War, young Americans were coming home in body bags while hippies and yippies indulged in psychedelic drugs and rock festivals. In the midst of this turmoil, I had still been a believer in guns, guts, and America, but now I was having to question some of those beliefs. What had seemed a solemn obligation ten months earlier now had no meaning. I felt I had abandoned the principles that I once had been willing to die for. Now these principles seemed senselessly patriotic, even jingoistic.

My body wanted to quit, but my spirit wouldn't let it. I had lost 70 pounds on prison food that consisted mainly of black beans and rice, if I got anything at all. I was a prisoner accused of being a counter-revolutionary and a CIA agent by my G2 interrogators. They reminded me that Che Guevara had been captured in Bolivia with the help of the CIA and the Green Berets, that the go-ahead to murder him had been given by the CIA and the Bolivian High Command.

The walk from my attorney's office at the Georgia State Bank Building to the Post Office Building, housing the Federal Courtroom where my trial was to begin, took a little longer that day. Standing just outside the bank's main entrance was bank president Max Herring. Some years earlier we had worked together at the Telephone Company and had become close friends. I had even been an usher in his wedding. During all the years that I had known him, everyone called him Pee-Wee. Now that he was president of the bank, he preferred to be called Mr. Herring or Max. I knew that was good business etiquette, but I made the mistake of calling him Pee-Wee that morning.

"Good morning, Pee-Wee."

"Morning, Reds," he said with a strained look on his face.

"Pee-Wee, I need a few thousand to pay my lawyer," I said in a joking manner.

Glancing back, as he scrambled to open the bank door, he said, "Reds, after the verdict come talk to me," a troubled look on his face. It was then that I realized things would be different even if I were found not guilty.

I'd heard most of the stories going around Savannah. Some people believed I was drunk, on drugs, or just crazy as hell. Others believed that there really was an assassination plot on Castro, and I was part of it. A few believed all of the above. Now a jury was going to hear the evidence and decide my future.

I was charged with kidnapping and hijacking a United Air Lines Boeing 727 aircraft to Cuba on January 11, 1969. The jury would hear other testimony from the crew of the aircraft, the FBI and several psychiatrists, including Dr. Corbett H. Thigpen, co-author of the book, *The Three Faces of Eve.*

My defense would be that I was temporarily insane at the time of the hijacking. There would be other testimony of a possible CIA-FBI conspiracy.

"Was patriotism a factor? Could it have been a burning hatred for Communism that motivated him? Many who knew him believed that this was the driving force," read an article in the *Savannah Morning News* dated Jan.16, 1969. "'Reds just had his own way of doing things sometimes,'" the article went on quoting one of my friends. "'In a way, I'm glad he did it because I know his intentions were good. He simply took that step that no one else would dare take. That's Reds.'"

The Government had the burden of proof beyond a reasonable doubt. I entered the court room and sat at the defense table.

The marshal called the court to order: "All rise. This court's now in session, the Honorable Alexander A. Lawrence, Judge, United States District Court, presiding."

I was asking myself the same questions that I had been asked over and over. Why had I hijacked that aircraft to Cuba? If I was part of a conspiracy, what happened? Castro was still alive and kicking. Had the CIA used some new 'hypnotic drug' or other method of control that was not traceable back to them? But why? Had head injuries triggered an irresistible impulse to do something that I felt had to be done? That seemed to be the unanimous conclusion of the psychiatrist and an easy way for them to explain it all away.

The only thing I was certain of without a shadow of a doubt was that on January 11, 1969, I had believed that I was playing some part in a CIA operation that involved executive action at the highest level.

Part One

THE CHILD

The Child is Father of the Man
William Wordsworth

The Child

My mother said I was a "Depression baby," and I can remember my folks talking about hard times, Mr. Hoover, W.P.A. and the CCC camps. Things must have been really bad during those years. The '20's and '30's, I had no idea how it must have been, except for what they had to say. I recall every time food was left on my plate, they would give me a lecture on how the "Chinese people" were starving to death. I didn't know who the Chinese people were, but I was convinced not to leave any food on my plate.

When I was eight years old, my grandmother announced to the family that my mother's sister, Betty, was going to Pearl Harbor. "Why?" I asked. She explained that Betty had married a sailor and his name was G.P. "When sailors are real good, don't cuss or drink alcohol, Uncle Sam sends them to Pearl Harbor," she added.

I wasn't too sure about sailors, and I didn't know I had an uncle named Sam. But if there was no cussin' or liquor drinkin' at Pearl Harbor, it must be a real fine place.

Mom's brother, Robert, had just bought a brand new Chevrolet, and he volunteered to take his sister the 2500 miles to San Diego. So Mother, Betty, her child Little Harry, and Tootie Trapani, a friend of Mother's, all squeezed into Robert's '40 Chevy coupe for the trek. They did make it there and back, although the stories about their visit to Tijuana, Mexico, were never entirely clear to me. But yes, Betty and Little Harry did make it to Pearl Harbor to be with G.P. the sailor.

The following year my sister Saundra, six, died of leukemia. My parents told me she had gone to be with Jesus. I had heard good things about Him in Sunday School, but it didn't help. Her death left a void that was never filled in my life.

On Sunday, December 7, 1941, my parents and I went to the 11 o'clock service at the Lutheran Church of the Ascension in Savannah. Mother said that she couldn't go back to the church in Garden City because it held too many memories of my sister. On the ride to Central Junction for Sunday dinner with my grandparents, I switched the car radio on. "We interrupt this program to bring you a special news bulletin. The Japanese have just bombed Pearl Harbor! I repeat, the Japs have just bombed Pearl Harbor ... stay tuned to this station," said the announcer excitedly.

"Oh! Betty, Betty," cried mother. "Those dirty Jap bastards have finally done it."

"Freda, calm down and lemme hear the news."

"Mac, I can tell you what's going on, those slant-eyed devils have started the war. I knew my sister shouldn't have married that damn sailor," she shouted hysterically.

"Mama, don't cry, it'll be O.K.," I said.

The trip to Gongie (grandmother) and Papa Waters' house passed fast that day. When we arrived, I can remember everyone talking and saying bad things about the Japs, how they were sneaky and yellow. I was curious about who the Japanese were. Uncle Billy cleared it up for me. "Slanted-eyed people like the Chinese." They must be hungry and bastards, too, I thought. Billy and I walked to Mr. Kicklighter's store to meet some of his buddies. At the store the big boys talked, and the rest of us listened.

That day I was convinced that the Japanese would be in serious trouble if Billy and Tot Michael ever got into the war, and they were talking about joining up as soon as possible. I wanted to go with them, but Billy said I was too damn young.

A P-40 Fighter airplane passed overhead going toward

Travis Air Field. Tot Michael looked up. "One day I'll be flying one of those," he said, pointing his finger toward the sky.

I don't know if he ever flew a P-40, but he did fly P-47's during the war and was awarded the Distiguished Flying Cross.

Uncle Billy joined the Navy and became the coxswain of a LCVP (Landing Craft Vehicle Personnel). He fought at Okinawa in one of the bloodiest battles of the war. Under heavy fire, he landed U.S. Marines ashore in the landing craft he had named the *Amazing Grace.*

Savannah's Union Station sounded like the Farmer's Market on Saturday night when Aunt Betty returned from Pearl Harbor. The loudspeakers were blaring out information, and that added to the excitement. Rows of oak benches were filled with people, most of them in uniform. The whole female Waters clan was there. Gongie, the matriarch of the bunch, was keeping us together like a mother hen watching over her chicks. All of us were anxiously awaiting Betty and her children's arrival. I wanted to see if my cousin Harry's hair really was redder than mine, as my Aunt had written in her letters to my mother. I was so keyed-up that I tripped over some baggage as we passed through the doors entering into a great metal and glass shed that covered the tracks and platforms. I could hardly hear because of the train engines. When I saw this big metal box with an American flag draped over it, I shouted, "Gongie what's that?"

"One of our boys who paid the price for our freedom."

I spotted Betty first. "There she is! There she is!" I shouted. Betty was carrying little Harry in her arms. Harry's legs hung down from Betty's side. There were bandages on both of his knees. I ran to meet them. The Waters were the most melodramatic bunch of people on earth, and this night was no exception. Gongie was so excited she was jumping up and down, hugging strangers or anybody else that would stand still.

"Where's Saundra?" Betty shouted.

Gongie put her arms around Betty and whispered. The

euphoria turned to tears.

That night at Central Junction Aunt Betty told the clan about the attack on Pearl Harbor. She graphically described with her hands how the Japanese airplanes had bombed and machine-gunned the water works near their house. She swore you could count the teeth of the Japanese pilots as they roared overhead. We saw the scars on little Harry's knees where she had dragged him while they were fleeing.

"G.P. was aboard the *USS Regal,* and they didn't even have any live ammunition. Hell! They threw potatoes at those bastards with the red zeroes on the wings," she said, excitedly.

Could those bastards be that hungry, I wondered? Then she said something that made us realize how close the war was. "We gotta dig bomb shelters in our backyards before those yellow buzzards bomb us."

All my mother's brothers had joined the Navy: Robert, Earl, and Billy, my hero and teacher. Man, was I was proud of them. If only I could've gone with them. I asked my mother why Dad hadn't signed up like her brothers. She told me that he was too old. I didn't understand that because I knew Uncle Earl was older than my dad. When I asked about that, she explained, "Earl volunteered." Then she said, "The Helmeys don't volunteer or take orders from anybody."

After thinking about her assessment of the Helmeys, and hearing bits and pieces of their conversations at the Sunday get-togethers, I knew she was right. They didn't think much of anybody who would join the military. I can still hear what they had to say about soldiers. "The only reason they sign up in the first place is 'cause they need somebody to tell'em what to do. They're lazy and got lead in their asses."

I didn't want to listen to that stuff. I knew my uncles on the Waters side were good men and didn't have any lead in their ass. I never told my dad about my feelings, but I was ashamed for anybody to know how he felt about the boys who were fighting and dying for our freedom.

After all the bad things I'd heard the Helmeys say about the military, it left me confused that my grandparents had named all their sons after famous generals like Lee, Sherman, and Bonaparte.

The Helmey side of my family lived on a farm in Effingham County, an hour's ride from Savannah. They were Salzburgers, descendents of Austrian-German Lutherans who had fled Europe in the 18th century because of religious persecution. The Salzburgers were the most hard-headed, hard-working, determined people God ever created. Gongie Waters always said that she understood why the Pope ran their asses out of Germany. Unlike the Waters side of my family, they showed little affection and didn't hug or kiss. Good people, but as different from the Waters as black and white. My Scotch-Irish and German blood didn't mix well.

We moved to Savannah. Mother believed that Garden City had too many things that reminded her of Saundra. Dad said he wanted to be close to his new business. They never agreed on anything, not even the weather.

In the city things really changed for me. I didn't get shipped off to relatives or friends of the family for weekends or summers, as in the past. We moved to an apartment house that the Trapanis owned. It was just across Perry Street from my dad's auto repair shop. Up until that time in my life, I hadn't seen too much of Mother or Dad except on the Sunday trips to the Helmey Farm. Mother told me Dad was always busy making a living for us. I never knew what her excuse was, except that she was sick a lot. I had a hard time trusting my mother, especially when I knew that she had been taking pills, which was most of the time.

"Son, your mother had so many complications during your birth that she almost died," Gongie explained. "The doctor told her not to have more children. She didn't listen to him, and Saundra was born by Caesarean section." After Gongie told me that, I felt guilty about even being born.

I saw more of Dad since his garage was just across from our apartment. Now I could go to him when mom didn't cook and get money or he'd take me to eat at a cafe. That was great because she couldn't cook anyway. At times I believed she was trying to starve me to death. Nobody seemed to understand why I was so skinny, but I sure did.

The Savannah Theater was just across the street from our apartment — a whole new world opened up for me. From the time I saw the movie "Wake Island," I wanted to be a Marine. Popcorn became my main meal, and John Wayne my main man. At school, studies took a back seat because I was too busy selling war bonds and stamps. I was the School Treasurer, and it was my job to take up the stamp money, go to the bank, and buy stamps for the war effort. That seemed more important to me than reading, writing and arithmetic.

The Lutheran Church of the Ascension was just three blocks from our Perry Street apartment. My dad attended only the Sunday church service, but I went to both Sunday School and the regular service. I asked 'The Chief,' as I now called Dad, "Why do I have to go to both Sunday School and the regular service?"

"Boy, because I said so!" That settled that.

He should have told Mother the same thing, because she didn't go at all. She professed to be a Baptist and didn't like the music in the Lutheran Church. She thought Lutherans were in pain when they sang hymns.

After studying Luther's Small Catechism, I didn't think Martin Luther sounded like a person who should have a religion named after him. However, Pastor Lynn struggled with my hard head until I was confirmed a Lutheran.

I was ten years old the spring of 1943 when we moved to a predominately Irish-Catholic neighborhood. It was nice to be living in a house again. I had my own room and didn't have to sleep in the same one with my parents anymore. The first kid I met in the neighborhood was Bubber Feus. I'd stopped at Tim's Ice Cream parlor on Waters Avenue to eat a little cream when he came in the door. "Boy, don't you go to the Lutheran Ascension Church?" he blurted out.

The way he said it ticked me off, but I knew I needed all the help I could get in my new surroundings. "Yeah," I said. Then I asked him where he lived.

"On 41st Street," he said. We only lived a couple of houses from each other. Bubber and I were to become life-time friends. He said he was also Lutheran.

Grayson Stadium was a short distance from my home on 42nd street. At night I could see the lights of the stadium from my bedroom window. They were like a giant magnet drawing me. Baseball, football, and other things now took the place of war movies and John Wayne.

There were other heroes for me to ponder. The night "Joey Chitwood's Thrill Circus" came to Grayson Stadium, I found out about another kind of hero, the dare-devil stunt man from whom I got the message that taking a risk was a rip-snorter and good. I was a quick study from then on. Joey jumped six cars and a bus in an old Ford that night.

The next day I tried to jump 42nd Street on a modified Western Flyer bicycle. I used a jar of Vaseline to grease the flyer. Then I removed the fenders and anything else that might slow it down. Bubber and another friend, Ed Ike, whom I had just met, worked on getting Coca-Cola crates and boards for the ramps. I had never let anybody know this, but Uncle Billy had given me his "Bicycle Brand" jockey strap when he joined the Navy. He said I'd grow into it some day. I also had his old football helmet and leather jacket. When I came out of my house dressed for the big jump, Bubber said, "Man, you look good." Then he handed me a rabbit's foot.

Rows of live oaks down both sides of the street formed a canopy overhead. All the preparation and activity had drawn curious on-lookers. The problem was to have a clear shot, with no cars interrupting, so I could get up enough speed to make the jump. Soon we had enough people to stand at the intersections of the two blocks needed to reach a speed right for the feat.

I waited for the signal from Bubber. "Go!" he yelled from the ramp. I didn't have a speedometer on the bike, but everybody said I was doing over 50 mph when I hit it. The engineering angle of the ramp must have been wrong. As well as I can remember, and from the reports of the bystanders, I did three end-over-ends, touching the moss-covered limbs of the trees. I landed with my head in the sewer drain on the opposite side of 42nd Street.

When I came to, I knew the helmet and leather jacket had helped, but Billy's strap saved what was more important. After inspecting what was left of the bike, we found moss in the wheels, and I knew I had flown with the eagles that day. That event brought out a new me and was a turning point in my life. Now I knew how to get attention, no matter the cost. I gave Bubber his rabbit's foot back.

The day President Roosevelt died at Warm Springs was a sad one. Everyone said he had taken us out of the Depression. I recall the day in April when he was buried. We Boy Scouts wore our uniforms to school. Gongie Waters said it didn't seem fair for God to take him after all that he had done for America. She added, if He had to take someone, it should have been his hussy of a wife, Eleanor.

I finished Junior High by the skin of my teeth. It was August 6, 1945; President Harry Truman told the world about the bomb which we had just dropped on Japan on a city named Hiroshima.

Broughton Street was a sea of people, as it had been four years earlier when I had heard my mother cry, "Betty, Betty, Betty." This day there were young and old people — soldiers, sailors and marines. Some were dancing, others hugging and kissing, some crying, some drinking and some just looking on. They all had one thing in common, shouting: "The war is over!

The war is over!"

Gongie only cooked fried chicken when the preacher was coming or when something special had happened. After dinner she showed us snapshots of Billy at Pearl Harbor.

"My little Willie is on the way home," she proclaimed. It was then I knew we had won for sure, and that my teacher, Billy, was on the way home.

Mother was sure I needed more discipline, and military school was just the place to get it. I knew she was wrong. The only thing I needed was for her to learn how to cook something besides macaroni out of a box. It was hard to believe my parents agreed, but on that they did. What I really needed was for them to listen to me just a little, I thought. But they had too much going on in their lives at the time to even listen to each other. They decided that Benedictine Military School in Savannah was just what I needed.

But I knew that Gongie would listen to me and help me. She asked why I didn't want to go to Benedictine. "First of all," I responded, "it's military and no girls go there."

She laughed. "Bobby, didn't you know your Uncle Billy went there." She went on to explain that Billy would be going back to B.C. to graduate because the war had cut short his senior year in high school. After she told me that, it didn't take long for me to agree to go.

I couldn't think of any place in the world I'd rather be than with Billy. After all, he had just won a war, and I had always wanted to wear a uniform. But I was scared the Helmeys would think I had lead in my ass, too. I asked Gongie if she knew why the Helmeys felt like they did about the military. She explained it this way: "The Helmeys don't like the military because they can't start out as generals." My military adventure was about to begin. The girls would have to wait awhile.

Maybe it was just me, but Uncle Billy seemed different. All the grown-ups said war causes people to do funny things. They were right because all Billy had on his mind was women, whiskey, and song. It was hard for me to believe that the Navy had really sent my uncle to Pearl Harbor. He cussed, drank beer, and chased women like a dog in heat.

I had passed Tommy's night club in Thunderbolt many times when thumbing to the beach. This time it was different. I was with Billy and some of his old Navy buddies. The juke box was loud, and the place was so smoky that you could hardly see anything or anybody. When the waitress asked my age, Billy said, "He's old enough. Give us Pabst Blue Ribbon all the way around the table, Pretty Thing."

She looked at my uncle for a moment before she spoke, "Honey, if he's that old, I'd love to take him home with me."

"Pretty Thing, you couldn't take it. He's got ten inches."

As she walked away laughing, she said, "Then he's not related to you, Billy Waters."

"Bobby, how'd you like some of that?" my uncle asked.

It was then I knew I was one of the big boys. I heard about things and places that nobody my age had ever heard, I thought. I looked at the beer in front of me and made the decision to go for it. After my sixth one, things started to get a little fuzzy. The world was in fast forward for me.

In the fall of 1946, I started Benedictine Military Academy as a freshman. The Roman Catholic priest who ran the school had a reputation for bringing out a young man's potential. But the only thing they brought out of me, at first, was the red ass, my stubborn streak. You had to call them "Father" and they went around dressed like your mother. Long black robes they called cassocks gave them the look of someone who was out of touch with the modern world. It mystified me that anybody would give up so much for God. But the cassock and collar were also the only things some had in common.

Father Alquin was my Latin and Ancient History teacher. I had to struggle with Latin, but he taught Ancient History with such passion that you believed he had lived in ancient Greece and

Rome. During Religion, the Catholic students went to Mass. Protestant, Jews and reformed Crackers went to the library to study. Usually we were unsupervised in the library.

"Mr. Helmey, would you please come into my office?" I knew something serious was on Father Alquin's mind. "Do you know what this is?" he asked.

"Yes Father, it's the box used to store chess pieces."

His face grew redder with each word I spoke. Then I remembered what I had done to that box. It had been a couple of weeks since I spotted it during study period. It had just looked like a plain old wooden box to me. That morning I decided to carve "Red" under the lid with my knife.

"Mr. Helmey, did you know this box is over 200 years old and is made of rosewood. The chess pieces are pure ivory."

I was looking for a way to escape. I knew what was about to happen. As I stood up, he sailed over his desk in a single leap with a drumstick in his right hand while his left hand grabbed me by the hair. Then he started pounding away with the oak stick.

"No! Father," I shouted, "I didn't know it was an antique box," as I covered my head with my hands.

"You red-headed monkey, I'll beat the red out of your ass," he growled.

After a few minutes, he cooled down. He hadn't really hurt me, but he had certainly gotten my attention.

"Sit down, Reds," he ordered.

"Father, you call me Reds — I don't understand."

"Because you're two different people," he answered. "Some days I see you as a nice young man. Then there's times when the devil is in you. You disarm people with your charm." Later he told me I should become a politician, but he wouldn't vote for me unless I converted to Catholicism. The name Reds stuck.

The only time I saw Billy was when we passed in the halls going to classes. "How's your hammer hanging, boy?" or "Boy, have you dipped your wick yet?" was all he would ever say. He was still my favorite uncle, but I knew I was on my own now. Billy had other things on his mind.

The R.O.T.C. program was the real test for me. My Helmey blood didn't want to yield at first. Then I found out my instructors didn't give a damn about my blood. It was my ass they were after.

My first squad leader was Sgt. Lewis Kooden. Louie was Jewish, and I know without a shadow of doubt he believed the name Helmey was not only of German ancestry but that I was a blood relative of Adolf Hitler.

A new word was added to my vocabulary: "demerit." Every demerit awarded you one half-hour of additional drill time, called "jugtime." I became a permanent member of the jug. I will always be thankful to Sgt. Lewis Kooden for teaching the first Helmey how to keep in step. To my surprise I was beginning to like the military. It was taking orders that gave me the problems.

That year I was awarded the Neatest Cadet Medal and promoted to the rank of Corporal. Military Science and Tactics became my favorite subject. I seemed to have a natural affinity for it.

The real struggle for me was Algebra. Public schools had not prepared me for parochial school math. Neither had life prepared me for the priest, Father Vincent, who taught it. Father Vincent was a big red-faced barrel-chested priest who had been attached to General Patton's 3rd Army during World War II. He looked like a rumpled black grizzly bear when he entered the classroom. I felt that he still believed he was in combat.

"Helmey, what does 'X' equal?" His voice boomed out in his Irish Boston brogue.

"I don't know, Father."

"I'll give you 100 for that answer because you're right. You don't know a damn thing about Algebra, Helmey. 'X' equals the unknown, and that's what you represent to me."

I don't know why, but he always seemed pissed off about something. Maybe he was like my Uncle Billy — the war had changed him. He kept my ass so uptight that I didn't learn anything about Algebra except 'X' equals the unknown that entire year.

Algebra and jug became a serious and embarrassing problem for me. I felt off track and dumb as hell in Algebra class, and jug was giving me a bad attitude.

I went to David "The Rat" Shoob for advice.

"No problem, Reds. All you need to do is join the band." They don't drill except on Friday. Monday through Thursday, they practice making noise in the band room."

"Rat, I can't play any musical instrument."

"Neither can anybody else in the band, Reds; just fake it until you make it. They have a shortage in the "E" flat alto section."

"O.K., what do I need to get Father Vincent off my ass."

"That's a hard one. But if you can get in Father Terence's class, he might be able to teach you something."

"Thanks, Rat."

Mr. Verhive, the band director, was a large strapping man. He spoke with a German accent. He loved cigars and seldom was he seen without one in his mouth.

"What instrument do you play, Mizter Helmey?" he asked.

"I've always wanted to play the "E" flat alto."

"Das goo'd, but do you play da horn?"

"Not exactly, but I've had music in junior high."

"All right Mizter Helmey, I let you try out."

Rat's advice paid off. I wasn't a full time member of the jug anymore. I was playing "blended music" with my E-flat bass tuba. I didn't sound so bad when I was drowned out by the entire band. Somehow he could always hear me over the other instruments. "No, no, Mr. Helmey, daz dee wrong note." Then he would come back to the tuba section and hand me his baton while he demonstrated how the note should sound on my horn. My mouthpiece always tasted like Mr. Verhive's cigar.

Just before St. Patrick's Day, Mr. Verhive called me into his office. "Mizter Helmey, dis is hard for me to ask of you, but voo'd you please transfer to the drum section?"

"You think I could do a better job on the drums, Mr. Verhive?"

"Vell, let's say I goat a very special job for you."

"What's that?"

"Transporting da' bass drum."

"I've never played a bass drum before."

"Oh, I don't vont you to play it, Helmey, I vont you to carry it for Mizter Greer to play in the St. Patrick's Day Parade."

As thousands watched, I carried it strapped to my back while Mr. Greer pounded the drum.

It was something George Powers said after the parade that got my attention.

"Reds, you've got to quit bein' everybody's clown. You let people pull your string — I guess you wanna be a nice guy."

I didn't want to believe him, but it gave me a lot of food for thought.

My main man, Uncle Billy, graduated and was accepted at Georgia Tech in Atlanta. The school year ended with my failing algebra.

Billy called to ask Mother if I could come to Atlanta for a week so we could spend some time together before he started Tech in the fall and I went to summer school. A lady friend of my Uncle Sherman was going to Chattanooga. She told me that she would be more than glad to drop me off in Atlanta.

When she picked me up, I noticed her perfume immediately. I knew it was some of that exotic stuff, "Midnight in Paris."

"Are you anything like your Uncle Sherman, Bobby?"

"Yes, ma'am, I'm a Helmey."

"How old are you?" she asked.

"Almost sixteen," I said, grinning.

"And, I'll bet you've never been kissed."

"No, ma'am."

She winked and said, "Maybe we can fix that."

It started raining just before we got to Macon. So we closed the car windows to keep the rain out. It was warm and humid. She told me to get the fan from under the front seat to cool us off. It had a picture of a swan on one side and the name Henderson Brother's Funeral Home on the other.

As I nervously gripped the wooden handle and started fanning her, she was unbuttoning her blouse.

"Bobby, you need to move closer with that fan, I'm about to burn up," she said, dropping her hand on my crotch.

"Yes, ma'am." I said trying to hide the bulge in my pants.

Then she pulled her skirt up so high that I could see her black drawers. "I'm so hot that I've gotta pull off the road and cool down," she said nervously.

She pulled off Route 80 at the next dirt road and parked under a large oak tree. Then she crawled over the seat into the back of the car. "Bobby, don't look, I gotta change into some cooler clothes," she muttered.

"No, ma'am, not me! I won't look."

By this time I was breathing hard and fanning for all I was worth. I made the mistake of looking in the rear view mirror. She was buck naked and rubbing her nipples with one hand and fingering her black hairy pussy with the other.

"Boy! Get in this back seat and fuck me before this thing explodes," she moaned, with her eyes closed.

It scared me, but I crawled over the back seat fanning and pulling off clothes at the same time.

She dropped me off at the bus station in Atlanta. Billy had been waiting for two hours and thought we had had car problems. I told him that the car had run hot a couple of times and we had to stop and let it cool down.

"Did she have the car repaired?" Billy asked.

"After Macon, we didn't run hot again."

"Well, I hope she makes it to Chattanooga. It sounds like something Sherman has worked on and couldn't fix."

"Billy, that's exactly what she said."

November 22, 1948

Dear Billy,

Sorry I haven't written you before now, but you know me. Your sister says we're just alike because we don't take anything serious. The week I spent with you knocking around Atlanta was great. It also was the week for a couple of firsts in my life. The first one happened on the ride up. I knew by the look on your face at the bus station that you never believed her car ran hot. You remember telling those stories at Central Junction before the war about Spanish Fly. Well, I think Uncle Sherman's girl friend got into some of that stuff.

The other I can thank you for, the ticket home on Delta. The DC-3 ride home was almost as exciting as the trip up. The one thing they both had in common was that they scared me a little, but I'm willing to try both again soon.   After all the advice you gave me about growing up I was ashamed to write this letter. I'm no longer at Benedictine. I got caught skipping school too many times. Father Bede kicked me out and told Freda that I needed more supervision. She's talking about sending me off to school. I guess that's the best way for her and the Chief to handle me and also some of their problems. I'll tell you about them later.

A friend of mine, George Powers, has been talking about joining the Marines. If I were old enough, I know that's what I'd do. If I get sent to military school, it will probably be good training for me to use at Parris Island when I do get to join the Marines.

My eye operation didn't turn out well. The left eye lid still droops and causes me to look like I've got a black eye. I get tired of explaining to people that I haven't been in a fist fight. It has caused a few scraps when they call me gimp eye. Well, I can't think of anything else to tell you, except I hope to see you Christmas.

Love you, Bobby

Part Two

HEROES

Who'er excels in what we prize
Appears a hero in our eyes.
Jonathan Swift

Heroes

There is a destiny that makes us brothers, none
goes his way alone. All that we send into
the lives of others comes back into our own.
Edwin Markham

The drive to Charleston, South Carolina, didn't take long that morning in early January, 1949. When my mother and I drove onto the campus of Porter Military Academy, it was like stepping back in time. The high brick wall that extended around the perimeter of the campus gave me the feeling I was inside an old fortress. Moss-covered oaks lined both sides of the drive that divided the parade ground from the school and main barracks buildings. Two brass cannons stood at the entrance to the sally port where the sign read "Headmaster."

I didn't want my parents to know I was glad to be leaving home. As unclear as things seemed to be at the moment, I was excited about a fresh start even if it meant being sent off to school.

The Headmaster was a short potbellied man who looked like he hadn't missed too many meals. He introduced himself to my mother as Mr. Elliot.

"Would you like to step into my office, Mrs. Helmey?"

My mother and Mr. Eliott went into his office while I waited on the outside. The whole time they were there, I saw cadets peering in the window at me. I knew I was getting sized up. After a few minutes the door opened and Headmaster Elliot asked me to step into his office. He welcomed me aboard and gave me a short sermon about being a Christian gentleman. I knew the speech was more for my mother than it was for me. I could read the man's face; he didn't look real to me.

"Do you have any questions, Mr. Helmey?"

"No, sir."

My mother and I stayed in the Headmaster's office while he went to complete the paperwork for my enrollment. It was one of the few times that she and I really talked. We both agreed that this was probably the best thing for me. I wanted to please both my parents and I didn't understand why I felt the way I did about them. I had always believed they never should have gotten married. Maybe they just had to.

After we said our good-byes, I walked Mother to the car and watched as she drove off with tears in her eyes.

"Report to the Orderly Room, Helmey," said Mr. Elliot.

The students at Porter were not only from the South but from all over the forty-eight states and even some foreign countries. The majority of foreign students were from the Caribbean Islands and Central America. Most of them were from Cuba's wealthy and powerful families.

My first roommate, Tommy Tokonaga, was an American of Japanese extraction from Columbia, South Carolina. After all that I'd heard about the Japs during the war, finding out that he was just like most of the guys I knew was refreshing. In fact, he'd give you the shirt off his back. Another myth that I had grown up with was that Greeks, Italians and Jews were all the same, and you couldn't trust any of them. Porter helped me put to rest a lot of the crap that I'd heard about the so- called foreigners.

The noise out in the hall was getting pretty loud. I asked Tokonaga what it was all about. He explained that Porter allowed an open forum for students to debate any issue that they wanted to as long as it was done within certain guidelines, such as no dirty language, fighting and that kind of stuff.

The student who was on the soapbox was from Costa Rica. He spoke in both Spanish and English at times. His facial expressions left no doubt how passionately he felt about the subject he was debating. He was knocking Cuban students for letting the United Fruit Company and other outside interests run their country.

"The only thing the Cuban Government runs is pimps and whorehouses, and Mafia is King in your country," he shouted. His discourse lasted until some of the Cuban students shouted him down, calling him a "Costa Rican Peasant" and "La Frutera."

I learned that debate was healthy and the democratic way of resolving differences. That year, I heard a lot of students who had a way with words, but none could match the bombastic oratory of the Cuban cadets.

The only bugle call I understood well was "mess call"; the others puzzled me as much as algebra.

We filed into the mess hall and stood before our tables. The blessing was said and the command "Seats!" was given. I was seated across the table from another Savannahian, Arthur Nicholas Bougas, known as "Nick the Greek."

"How ya like Porter, Cracker Boy?" Nick snapped.

"So far, things are great, especially the food."

He gave me a funny look and said, "Yeah, the bugler said you were strange as hell at times."

I chuckled at Nick's obvious ruse.

"You know, General Summerall is speaking at chapel this morning," he said.

"Who's he?" I asked.

"The General over at the Citadel," Nick answered.

When we filed into the chapel that morning, the brightness of the morning sun was dimmed by the brilliant colors in the large stained-glass windows. The student body was seated, and the organ played "Onward, Christian Soldiers."

Tommy leaned over to me and in a soft whisper said, "This chapel was a horse stable during the Civil War, and if you try, you can still smell the horse shit."

Then Colonel C.P. Walker, Professor of Military Science and Tactics, stepped to the rostrum to introduce General Summerall. He was dressed in the uniform of a World War II Cavalry Officer. Patton in all his glory was never decked out like Walker was that day. Every crease was razor sharp in his dress blouse and pink breeches. His cavalry boots and Sam Browne belt glistened. The ribbons and decorations on his chest shone like the stained-glass windows. As Colonel Walker introduced General Charles Pelot Summerall, I realized that he was the first general I had ever seen in the flesh.

I can't remember all that General Summerall said that morning, but I will never forget the words that hung with me.

"You young men are the future of this great nation. Without a strong and disciplined military force, this nation cannot stand. You must defend and protect the principles of God and country with your life if necessary."

It was at that very moment that I knew I had to be a soldier, and a genesis of what patriotism meant to me was born.

After chapel that morning, the comments that I heard were as different and varied as the cadets. Some were so motivated by his flag-waving speech, they vowed to make the military a career. While a few wanted to lead a second Confederate Army to victory, others believed all the old 'fart' wanted was to recruit some of the wealthier Porter boys for the Citadel. The bugle sounded for classes.

When I walked into Colcock Hall that first morning I was really uptight. I was having flashbacks of Father Vincent's class at Benedictine.

This time the teacher was a retired Rear Admiral, Admiral Charles M. Furlow, United States Naval Academy graduate. He was a wiry man with the energy of a whirling dervish, and right away you knew he was in charge. But under all his salty appearance he radiated an easygoing humor.

He was to kindle something in me that I would carry the rest of my life. Algebra would never be the same after the Admiral. I knew this man cared and that I was more than an 'X.'

Frank W. "Sonny" Seiler and I had grown up in the same neighborhood. We lived within a mile of each other, attended the same church, played ball at the same park, and had a lot of mutual friends. Still, Sonny was different. He always seemed to have a little more pedigree than most of the guys I ran around with. Oh, he was a good guy — but he could bitch like a banshee when he got mad and didn't get his way.

The hardest thing for me to understand about Sonny was his ambition to excel at whatever he did. His duties and responsibility as bugler at Porter were more than I could comprehend. Thirty-three times a day, at precisely the right minute, he had to blow a different bugle call. Which meant he had to catalog a serious amount of music in his head. Also, he had to get up before reveille and couldn't go to bed until he had blown taps. He had to comply with the same schedule as all the other cadets. It was no wonder I hadn't been able to talk with him much since I'd arrived.

As I waited for him to give the next bugle call, it all became clear to me — our pastor and Sonny's parents had talked with my mother and had planted the Porter seed. They were the ones who were instrumental in my being at this prestigious reform school. I wondered what Sonny had been sentenced for.

"Rose Eye Reds, it's good to see you. What 'cha think about this institution of higher learning?"

"If I learn the bugle calls, I'll make it, Sonny."

I'd forgotten about telling him the story of how I had injured my left eye. When I was nine years old, I had stuck a large rose thorn through my upper eyelid and it left me with a pronounced droop; also when the roses bloomed, the eyelid would swell until the eye closed. That was the first time anybody had ever called me Rose Eye Reds, and Sonny was a master at hanging nicknames on people that always seemed to stick.

I didn't mind Sonny calling me Rose Eye or anything else for that matter because he was my friend.

"Reds, you met any of the Savannah boys yet?"

"Yeah, Nick and Pete Bougas."

"There's several; one boy's mama runs a whorehouse on the Ogeechee Road. I named him 'Pussy Parker.'"

It didn't take long for me to realize that Nick and Pete knew their way around. They'd attended boarding schools since their parents were divorced early in their childhood. During the summer breaks they lived in Savannah with their father, who owned and operated the Silver Moon Bar & Grill in a predominately black section of town. They had learned their street savvy from helping him during the summer months.

Nick and I hit it off right away. We had a lot in common, especially when comparing our fathers and their taste in women. He told me the story about his father coming to this country from Greece during the First World War. During the crossing, his ship was torpedoed by a German U-Boat in the North Atlantic. He almost lost his toes because of the freezing water in the bilge of the life boat.

I then shared how my father had come to Savannah in a horse and wagon from Scuffletown. "Nick, he told me that he didn't have but thirteen cents in his pocket and all his ancestors came from Germany on a sail boat," I said, proudly.

"Reds, one of your fuck'n distant relatives was probably in that U-boat that torpedoed my Daddy's ship."

"I doubt that, Nick, the breed of Germans my daddy came from ain't been near the water since the crossing, not even to bathe. At least that's what my Grandmother Waters said."

My first Friday night at Porter, Nick showed me around Charleston. There was a strong nor'easter blowing as we stood looking out toward Fort Sumter from the Battery that night.

"Reds, you wanna drink of liquor?" Nick asked.

"A drink of what?"

Before I could get the words out of my mouth, he was handing me the half-pint of V.O. he had pulled out of his uniform jacket like a magician pulling a rabbit out of a hat. He took the bottle and said, "Ever been to a whorehouse?"

"One time, but it was just to make a delivery. My Dad repaired the madam's car — you know, Indian Lil's down on Indian and Fahm Streets."

"Well, tonight you're going to Charleston's red-light district — West Street."

"We must be going on credit," I said, grinning.

"Naw, we just lookin' tonight, but we could get lucky. Sometimes the old broads break down and give it up for us young stallions," Nick said, smiling.

"Sounds like we need some strong 'Trojan' rubbers."

On Monday, Colonel Walker announced to the Cadet Corps that President Carlos Socarras of Cuba was sending a member of his personal staff to review the cadets. The President wished to express his gratitude and appreciation to the Academy for training the future military leaders of his country.

Daily the band practiced "The National Hymn of Cuba."

I auditioned for a position in the E-flat tuba section, but like my efforts at Benedictine, I just couldn't make the cutting edge with the horn. However, my talent didn't go unnoticed, and I was given the honor of carrying the band guidon, which I'm sure Nick had something to do with since he was the Drum Major.

Finally, the big day arrived. All the Cuban cadets were excited, especially Cadet Lt. "Monk" Munoz, whose father was the colonel sent by their President. I found it hard to grasp how the Cuban cadets were so serious and showed such emotions about their national politics.

Curly Tabres and I had become close friends. He loved to show off his knowledge of Cuban and American history by giving me a daily history quiz.

"Reds, what's the name of my *Presidente?*" Tabres asked.

"Xavier Cugat," I said.

"Shit, Reds, you probably don't even know the name of your own President."

The campus was decorated with Cuban and American flags. The P.A. system was playing Sousa marches while the Cadet Corps prepared to pass in review. Colonel Walker welcomed Colonel Munoz to Porter and then asked him to speak.

"I speak on behalf of President Socarras and the people of Cuba. We would like to thank the Academy for providing military and academic training for our future leaders. Also, he would like to invite you to visit Cuba soon." The Colonel sounded more like an official of the Cuban Chamber of Commerce than he did a soldier.

The bugler sounded the Post call. The Adjutant walked at a fast half-step toward the center of the parade ground and smartly posted, reading the orders of the day and posting again.

Nick raised the baton, blew his whistle, and the band played something that was a mixture of the foxtrot and a tango. Supposedly, it was the "Himno de Bayano," Cuban National Anthem. Next, the order was given to fire the cannon salute.

"Boom! Boom!" The earth-shaking, ear-splitting sound of the cannons could be heard all over the city of Charleston. Every dog within earshot began howling and barking. Someone, either intentionally or unintentionally, had put too much black powder in the cannons. When the smoke from the gun powder cleared the air, the Cuban Colonel was standing in the V.I.P. seats fanning his overweight wife who had fainted.

After a short rest period, the ceremonies continued.

"Pass in review," ordered the commanding officer.

The Cadet Corps marched past the reviewing stand and sharply saluted the Cuban Colors.

Hartman, the Costa Rican, was relieved of his duties as Cannon Master; I never joked with Curley Tabres about Cuban politics again.

Every Monday after classes I'd stop at Batch Flythe's room and weigh myself. He had an old set of bathroom scales that everybody at Porter used. The room was pretty crowded, so I sat on a foot locker waiting my turn and listening to the conversation.

"Reds, you're putting on weight," Batch commented.

"He still looks pretty light in the ass to me," Buster Calmese said sarcastically.

"Yeah! And he's got a gimp eye too," added Jerry Ledbetter.

"You two Yankee cocksuckers can kiss my rebel red ass," I said fuming.

Before the next words came out of my month, Calmese and I locked up and the fight spilled out into the hall. A crowd gathered to watch the battle. Calmese was about 20 pounds heavier than I. It wouldn't have made any difference if he'd been King Kong. My only thought was to beat his fucking brains out — he and Ledbetter represented every bastard that had ever called me gimp eye or skinny.

After we tumbled down a flight of stairs still fighting, somebody yelled, "Capt'n Fat Daddy is on his way!" Everybody scattered. It was amazing how fast our tempers cooled down when we heard that. I ran up the stairs and Nick shouted for me to come to his room.

"Cool it, man. You're a quick-tempered fucker," Nick said. Jerry Ledbetter was in the room. Smiling, he extended his right hand to me.

"Reds, I'm sorry. I am a big mouth Yankee, and I apologize for wising off about your left eye. I also didn't know you were a friend of the Greek," he said, looking nervously at Nick.

"I didn't know you were so sensitive about your eye and your being skinny," Nick said, grinning.

"Attention in the room," Nick called out, as Captain "Fat Daddy" Christopher entered the room.

"What's going on in here and who was fighting in the halls a minute ago?" he said, loudly.

"Don't know anything about a fight, sir," I said.

"Mr. Helmey, you didn't have but one black eye yesterday. Now you've got two."

"Sorry, sir, I bumped into a door," I replied.

"Until you decide to tell me who was fighting, you're restricted to the barracks, Mr. Helmey."

I never knew who talked Fat Daddy into lifting my restriction, but I feel sure it was Nick or Sonny. I had become a firm believer that people would walk all over your ass if you didn't stand up and let them know you would fight. The pain of a few cuts and bruises didn't last near as long as the wound of being called a coward.

Admiral Furlow told me to stay after class. "We need to talk about a few things, Reds."

The thoughts of failing Algebra went through my mind.

"Did you want to see me, Admiral?" I asked nervously, after the other students had left the room.

He walked slowly back to my desk and sat directly in front of me, eyeball to eyeball.

"You believe it's important to know where you're going in life, Reds?"

"I haven't given it much thought, Admiral."

"That's obvious as hell. What do you want to do with the rest of your life?"

"I don't know, sir, maybe join the Marines when I'm old enough."

"Are you preparing for that day."

"No, sir."

"Then how in the hell do you expect to become a Marine?"

"I guess the Marines could train me."

"What do you think I'm trying to teach you algebra for?"

"Admiral, I don't see how algebra has anything to do with the Marines."

"Reds, that's your problem with algebra and everything else in your life you don't think is important. It's all about discipline and hard work, son. Would it be different if the Marines said you had to learn algebra before you could join?"

"Probably would, sir"

"In other words, you could do it if you wanted to. You remind me of the story of the mule that you can lead to water but you can't make him drink. I want you to listen to me. I really want to help you, but you've got to want to help yourself first. You have choices in life, it's all up to you. I could and should fail you, but I'm not. I'm going to give you one more chance. Next year, you're going to wish you had joined the Marines if I see you not trying to do your best. Do you understand?"

"Yes, sir! God bless ya, Admiral."

"Now, get out of here and have a good summer."

I shook his hand and saluted him. As I looked my report card over, I felt good, all my grades had gone up. So had my weight, by 20 pounds. When Tommy and I said our goodbyes, we thought it would be just for the summer. Little did we know it would be forty years before we'd have another conversation. I will always remember his gentleness and understanding manner. He was a stand up guy and a decent human being.

Tabares gave me his address in Havana and said, "Study your history, *mi amigo*, one day you will be glad you did."

"See you at the Ascension Sunday, Reds," Sonny shouted.

Nick promised he'd call when he got back to Savannah.

It was good to see my grandparents. I hadn't seen them since I'd gone off to school. I was glad they had moved from Central Junction to Savannah. It was only a 10-minute walk from our house on 42nd to their home on 37th Street.

When we finished our hugging and kissing, Gongie asked me if I had been behaving myself.

"Yes, ma'am. At Porter we have chapel every morning at St. Timothy's. It's a Christian gentleman's school."

"So have they been instructing you how to be Christian?" Gongie would have fainted if she'd known what I'd learned in the past year at that Christian school.

"I know that's right, but to be honest with you, they just leave that church stuff up to you," I answered.

"Bobby, you've been confirmed a Lutheran, gone to a Catholic high school, and now a Episcopalian school, and you still haven't any idea what a Christian is. It's not about church, son."

"You're right, Gongie. But I see most people talkin' one way and living another, most of them are so-called Christian gentlemen. So I guess I'm a little confused about the whole mess," I added.

"I love you son, but that doesn't give you any excuse." She smiled, "Bobby, I want you to go to church Sunday with me. I want you to meet some nice young ladies."

Gongie was seated in the choir, and the services had already started. As I walked down the aisle toward the front of the church I spotted my Grandfather, and I sat down with him.

The song leader said, "Please stand and turn in your hymnals to page 57 and sing all the verses of 'Amazing Grace.' As we stood to sing, my grandmother looked straight into my eyes. That few moments in time are indelibly etched into my heart. I felt something deep down in my spirit when I heard that song that I can't explain. Those words still echo today, *"A-maz-ing grace how sweet the sound, that saved a wretch like me!"* I tried to hide the tears, but Gongie saw them.

The preacher shouted so loud it shook the windows. The service at the Lutheran Church was so different. It seemed as though the preacher was directing his message at me.

His sermon was about a man named Joshua, and how a couple of spies were helped by a prostitute named Rahab. Most of what he said that day went over my head, but the message from the hymn, "Amazing Grace," would remain in my soul forever. My Grandparents never knew that I had overheard their conversations about the preacher's drunken binges throughout the years, and how my grandfather and other members would help him sober up. It was hard for me to understand his being their leader. They would forgive him and let him continue to preach and pastor the flock. I felt good about their compassion for him and mixed-up about how I felt.

During the summer of '49, I worked for the Chief at his Amoco station and garage. His bookkeeper was a young attractive single woman. I'd overheard some of the mechanics laughing about her and Dad fooling around. One day when a black mechanic and I went on a service call, he said he had caught my dad in the parts room, "Jammin' dat woman." At first I thought it was a joke, but after watching them playing around, it didn't seem so funny. I felt betrayed. I wished he were more like other fathers ... around, sometimes.

I spent a few weekends with Bubber Feus at his family's country house at Montgomery. Good ole Bubber hadn't changed, he was still my most faithful and trusted friend. Sonny, Nick, and I did a little shark fishing, off Tybee Island out in the Atlantic, and a lot of girl watching on the beach that summer of '49.

A few days before returning to Charleston for my senior year, I ran into the old B.C. friend who had given me the advice about folks pulling my string.

"Reds baby, I ain't seen ya around. Where ya been?"

"George, I'm in a military school over in Charleston."

"You still lettin' people yank your strings?" he said, smiling broadly.

"Nah, the string is gettin' shorter, my man. So, what's happenin' with you, George?"

"Man, I've been to amphibious training at Little Creek, Virginia, with the Marine Reserves. That's some serious shit. I'm joinin' the regular Marine Corps very shortly, Reds."

"Yeah, that's great, I wish I could go with you, man."

About that time Nick stopped to give me a ride.

"See you later, George. I'll always remember your advice. Take care of yourself," I said, as we drove away.

I never saw him again after that day. Now forty-five years have passed and there's a monument in Forsyth Park commemorating all those Marines from Chatham County, Georgia, who made the supreme sacrifice. Engraved on the Korean side of the monument is a line that reads: Matthew "George" Powers, Jr. PFC-USMC. *Semper fidelis, my friend.*

I was very disappointed to learn that Tommy Tokanaga wasn't returning to Porter. I found out from one of his close friends that he was seriously in love with a young lady in his hometown.

His parents had agreed to let him attend school in Columbia, South Carolina. Nine months later, it was obvious that it was true love and he had made the right decision. My new roommate was Jerry Ledbetter. We'd buried the hatchet and came to a good understanding. He never called me "gimp eye," and I never used "Yankee bastard" again.

Curley Tabares hugged me and said, "Man! I missed you. Did you study your history, my friend?"

"No, Curley, but I studied how Teddy Roosevelt and the Rough-Riders saved Cuba's ass from the Spaniards," I said.

"Well, *Rojo*, I've got one for you. Did you know during the American Revolution that Count Casimir Pulaski, a Polish cat, and a couple of hundred blacks from Haiti saved Savannah's ass from the British?"

"Man, that's bullshit, ain't no nigger saved Savannah."

I put most of my energy and effort into football. After being so skinny for years, I had something to prove. And the twenty pounds I had gained made me feel like a heavy-weight. I was now tipping the Toledos at one hundred-sixty-five pounds.

Coach Earl "Red" Bethea was a legend at Davidson College for his ability to kick a football. They called his punts "booming spirals." He also was good at getting the very best out of your ass, or he'd give that a booming spiral.

I almost quit football because of how much he sounded like my dad one day. We'd been running wind sprints and I really thought I'd been busting my hump.

"Helmey! Give me twenty extra laps around the field."

"For what, coach?" I yelled.

Then he said the magic words: "Because I said so!"

After running the laps, I was walking off the practice field. "Helmey, come here," he shouted. "If you wanna play on this team, you'd better adjust your attitude — I don't wanna hear 'for what' again. Tomorrow pick it up, or you'll be doin' laps until your he-hog-hangs-down."

I didn't say anything back to him, but just kept on walking. My mind was made up, I'd had it with him and his bullshit phrase, "Because I said so."

I was sitting at my desk looking out the window when Ned Thornhill and "Flip" Chevrier walked into the room.

"Reds, we need to talk with you for a few minutes. You got the time?"

Ned was Captain of the football team and a Christian gentleman, one of those Jack Armstrong types. Flip was the quarterback, but he didn't have a drop of Armstrong blood. They sat down at the desk and looked me directly in the eyes.

"Reds, we need you. Coach Bethea wouldn't push if he didn't think you needed it. Believe me, it's nothing personal. He just wants your best — that's his job and he's good at it," said Thornhill.

"Reds, you make a difference and the team needs you. Hell, there ain't no pass-defense against that jitter-bug step of yours in the end-zone," Flip said, grinning.

I felt ashamed and proud at the same time. I knew what had set me off, and I wasn't happy with myself for letting his words piss me off. On the other hand, it was the first time in my life anybody had told me that they needed me, and it felt good.

"I really appreciate you guys — the problem is me. I'm sorry, man! I'll be at practice tomorrow with a new attitude."

Before they left the room, Nick walked in. "What's all this shit about you quitting the team, Reds?"

"Just rumors, Nick."

"Yeah, I know, it's that damn German hardhead you got. I'll get Buster Calmese to straighten your ass up if you don't shape up." We all had a good laugh, and I returned to football the next day. Coach Bethea never used that phrase on me again, whether intentionally or not I'll never know. Years later, I would appreciate what I had learned from football: life and the game were so much alike.

October 26, 1949, on the afternoon of my 17th birthday, I was lying in my rack after football practice when Nick, Pete, and Sonny came into my room. Nick handed me a gift-wrapped box.

"Sonny and I didn't want to give you this, but Pete talked us into it. So here it is, Happy Birthday, Reds!"

"What can I say? Thank you, man!"

"Well, go on and open it, wild man!"

I tore the wrapping paper off the box, and inside was the pair of leather-sole blue suede shoes that I'd seen in Sam's Haberdashery window and had said to Nick how cool I thought they looked.

"See if these size-twelves fit you," said Sonny.

I took them out of the box and put them on. They were a perfect fit. They felt so good and looked so cool that I did a little dance step to show them off.

"Reds, you got more black in your ass than half the folks at the Silver Moon Cafe. You can't help yourself when you hear that jive music," Nick said.

I just kept on dancing, and they shouted, "Go! man, Go!"

* * *

1949 was fast coming to an end, and so was my time at Porter. I'd been told that because of my algebra grades at Benedictine, I didn't have enough credits to graduate with the class of 1950. I found myself restless as the Christmas break grew nearer.

When Curley Tabares told me about his interview with the 1950 yearbook staff, I knew I wouldn't be returning to PMA.

"Reds, my superlatives will read: 'Best Private; Baseball Team. Chief Delights: Olga. Senior Ambitions: To manage the Havana Airport. Senior Will: To leave my M1-Rifle to any poor devil who is unlucky to have to carry it!'" He paused. "Reds, spend Christmas with me and my family in Havana."

"Curley, I'll take a rain check on that, but I would like to visit you one day."

"Reds, I'll leave you with this thought for Christmas from Mark Twain's *Letters from Earth*:

> Man is the only patriot. He sets himself apart in his own country, under his own flag, and sneers at the other nations, and keeps multitudinous uniformed assassins on hand at heavy expense to grab slices of other people's countries, and keep them from grabbing slices of his. And in the intervals between campaigns he washes the blood off his hands and works the Universal Brotherhood of man with his mouth.

Don't forget those words, *amigo*."

"Curley, you and Seiler have a memory like an elephant."

During Christmas break, Mother was in the hospital recovering from a mastectomy. The surgeon told us how lucky she was that the fibroid tumors had no cancerous cells.

"The only thing that butcherin' bastard knows is to cut, cut, cut. He didn't have to remove her breasts." Dad said.

"Chief, why would a doctor do somethin' like that?

"They smell money, boy. Plus, when she decides it's time for a trip to a hospital, ain't nobody can change her mind. There's always a 'quick draw' surgeon around who has no qualms about cutting on anyone who's willing."

"So, why'd you let her do it?" I asked.

"You know her as well as I do, you can't tell her a thing about a doctor, she thinks they are all, all-knowing gods."

He was right about one thing: I did know my mother better than he — she only wanted his love and attention.

I admit that he and I thought alike about some doctors. My mother was the one who had found the quack that misshaped my eye. Every time I looked in a mirror, I was reminded of him. After my operation, a nurse friend of my dad's told him that it was common knowledge among nurses and doctors that the surgeon who operated on me was usually high on drugs when he entered an operating room.

I thought this would be the right time to ask the Chief to sign the papers for me to join the Marines. When I did he got all upset and let me know he would never sign for me to join any kind of military organization.

"Boy, you're going back to Porter! There's no if's, and's, or but's about it. You can make up your mind that you're not joining the Marines."

He didn't know that I had already decided not to go back to Porter. I knew what his answer was going to be, but I asked anyway.

"Why, do I have to go back to Charleston?"

"Because, I said so!"

"I thought you might say that," I said, grinning.

"Then why'd you ask?"

"I was hoping we might talk about it."

"Ain't nothing to talk about."

"Chief, I'll be eighteen soon, then I can do what I want."

"Well, as long as you live under my roof, you gonna do what I tell ya. Do you understand that?"

"Yes, sir! About as much as my mother does."

I knew we Helmeys were different from other families. We never talked about anything deeper than the weather. On very few occasion did we sit down and share a meal or anything else together. It seemed there was always some kind of conflict going on between my parents. They never agreed on anything, especially when it came to me. We never talked about problems. It just seemed natural to stick our heads in the sand.

That January, 1950, the Chief put me on the midnight Silver Meteor to Charleston. When it pulled into the station, I started not to get off the train, but I didn't have enough balls or money to keep on riding. However, I was determined to show the Chief that "Because I said so!" wasn't going to work this time. I went back to Savannah that morning on the thumb express.

My mother was still in the hospital recovering from her mastectomy. For some unknown reason my dad allowed me to drop out of Porter and agreed I could stay in Savannah as long as I went to school and worked at his service station in the afternoons. I enrolled at Commercial High School, where many of my old friends attended, including Bubber Feus. After four years of military school, it was nice having females around and not all those hard-ass guys.

My 18th birthday was nine months away, and I knew positively that he wasn't going to sign for me to enlist in the Marines. I would have to wait and make the best of it.

It had never dawned on me that Savannah had a kind of social pecking order. I'd heard people say, "Savannah isn't in Georgia: it's in the 'State of Chatham.' Politically and socially, powerful men control Savannah." I was raised believing the Jews owned it, the Irish ran it, and the crackers just worked in it. However, the group that puzzled me most were the Blue Bloods, the so-called "clique." I'd heard about a register that listed all the names. Who were they, where did they come from, and how did they receive their *ancienne noblesse*?

A close cousin who had been coached in the fine art of social climbing by his mother and was dating a debutante, helped shed some light on it, "They come from money, mostly old Savannah money," he said. Then he went on to explain that most of the upper crust of the city were descendants of the English ruling class, who came from England in the 18th century with Oglethorpe on the 'Debtor's Ship.'

"These people will frig anybody, but only marry within their social circle. Their daughters become debutantes and their sons become pissin' partners with other high society folks. They don't let anybody on their list or even know where it's kept, unless you've got plenty of money."

"Ain't that a bitch — where's the list kept?"

"One of three places, but they move it all the time. It's either at the Oglethorpe Club, vaults at the Savannah Bank, or in one of those high churches down on Bull Street."

"Man! how'd you get on the list?"

"Knowing the right people. You've gotta run with folks that can do ya some good; I don't mess with any poor-ass crackers who can't help me," he said.

"Cuz, that sounds like some serious 'boot lickin' to me."

"Bobby, that's your trouble! You're a rebel."

"I guess you're right, Cuz."

"Another thing, you've got to please your family."

"I know, your mama's got to be proud of you," I said.

"Yeah, and that's important," he said, grinning.

Part Three

A CALL TO ARMS

A farewell to youth

So strong you thump O terrible drums,
so loud you bugles blow.

Walt Whitman

A Call to Arms

The streets were lined with green-clad revelers awaiting the big parade that sunny St. Patrick's day.

As I crossed Liberty Street going north on Abercorn, I heard someone yell, "Reds!" I looked around and saw a young Marine with a rifle coming toward me. As he got closer, I recognized Eldred "The Neb" Neville. He attended some of my classes at Commercial.

"Neb, whatcha doin' in that uniform?"

"I'm in the Reserve."

"You look sharp, man."

He grinned from ear to ear, "Reds, we gonna be marchin' right behind the United States Marine Corps Band from Parris Island."

"Ah, do it, Neb! I'll be watchin' for you to strut ya stuff."

I found a good spot for viewing the parade at the main fire station on Oglethorpe Avenue.

As the Marine Drum Major strutted passed, the band was playing the "Semper Fidelis March." The spirited music stirred my soul and gave me goose bumps. When Dog Company marched by, there was something different about their demeanor. Although I knew many of them, I saw where the boys had grown to men. For some who wore the uniform that day, it would be their last St. Patrick's Parade.

During the summer of 1950 at Tybee Island's Solms Hotel, the soda shop was the "in" place for hanging out, girl-watching and shag music. At the Greek's hot dog stand across the alley, you could get a beer to go if you looked old enough. His vision varied from day to day, as did his prices.

Luigi Trapani and I were in a booth listening to Sonny Seiler recite one of his nasty-ass poems. He'd just started "Miss Arabella Rosewater" when 'Dumbo' Barber walked in and unplugged the juke box. Dumbo announced our President Harry Truman had just mobilized the Reserves and that Dog Company was to report to its armory immediately.

"All you swingin' dicks that joined the Corps to get boondockers, green britches and piss-cutters, fall in! You gonna be wearin' that shit all the way to North Korea."

Somebody plugged the juke-box back in and the "Tennessee Waltz" continued to play. Sonny coolly went on with his risque discourse. Dumbo and Luigi walked towards the Greek's, talking and counting their money.

Dumbo was right: 90,000 Communist North Koreans had invaded South Korea. President Truman and General MacArthur agreed we should fight, and in 1950 that was good enough for most Americans.

Savannah hosted a big parade and send-off for Dog Company the day they left for San Diego. I put Dumbo Barber's sea-bag on the train while the band from Parris Island played the Marines Hymn. When the train was pulling out from the station, I seriously thought about staying aboard, but I knew my time would soon come.

President Harry Truman called it a police action, but it sure didn't look that way to me and my buddy, Billy 'Bones' Connor. If it were, the police were in serious trouble.

We watched Movietone News at the Savannah Theatre that November afternoon and saw the latest films of U.S. troops landing at Inchon, Korea. According to the combat correspondent with the troops, "They are under intense fire from the North Koreans and are taking heavy casualties."

"It looked like the Normandy invasion," Bones said.

"Yeah, I know it'd be hard to convince those poor fuckers on the beach it was just a police action," I said.

"Reds, let's go to Gildea's after the movie."

Gildea's was the principal watering hole for the Irish in Savannah. Its front bar was a gathering place for the more politically informed Irishman and a few clued-in crackers. You could get advice on any subjects from hemorrhoids to Halley's Comet at the drop of a hat, especially if you bought the round. The back room had private booths that were used for romantic rendezvous and, occasionally, the underage drinkers were allowed in it, if they could get past the black waiter, Shorty. His rule was, tip heavy and talk lightly. It was considered an honor for a cracker to be allowed in Gildea's, and a rite of passage when you measured up to Shorty's hawk eye and itching palm.

After we had a few beers, things seemed a lot easier to deal with. Since we were both eighteen, the only patriotic thing to do was join the Marines as soon as the recruiter's office opened Monday morning.

"Reds, we don't have to wait until Monday."

"I didn't know the recruiter's office was open on Sunday."

"The Marines aren't, but the Flying Tigers are."

"Flying Tigers — who in the hell are they?"

"Reds, it's a top secret outfit that's going on active duty in January."

"Bones, that ain't a Marine unit."

"Man, fuck the Marines! Look what the C.O. of Dog Company did when folks complained about their underage sons forging the enlistment papers to join."

"What'd he do?"

"He put a fuck'n yellow ring around their names when he had to discharge'em. Ducky, Neb, Cat, and a bunch of guys whose parents bitched are joining the Tigers."

"Hey, I know those guys ain't chicken shit, and they couldn't help what their parents did, but that ain't right, man."

Bones went on to explain that this radar unit was an early

warning system that could be used on the front lines, close to the infantry. When I asked him how he knew all this shit about the Tigers, he said, "Reds, my brother Chris is a cook for the Tigers and he knows all about that secret stuff."

We didn't go home that night. Instead, we closed Gildea's and rode around drinking beer until the Flying Tigers opened their office that morning.

117TH AIRCRAFT CONTROL AND WARNING SQUADRON, GEORGIA, AIR NATIONAL GUARD, read the sign over the door that Sunday morning at Travis Field. Bones wasn't kidding, the Flying Tigers did exist.

We entered through the door marked, "Enlistments." The large room was crowded with people, some in uniform, and others like Bones and me in rumpled clothes with red eyes.

"Where's your brother, Bones?" I asked.

"Reds, he's probably feeding the tigers."

"Man, I ain't too sure I'm doin' the right thing," I said.

About that time, a sergeant asked if he could help us.

"Yes sir," Bones replied.

Next he asked how old we were.

"Eighteen, sir," we both answered. I don't remember Bones or me asking him anything about joining up. I guess he just assumed that was why we were there.

"Now all you have to do is sign these papers and go take a physical," he said.

On the way to Hunter Field to take the physical, I suggested maybe we should wait until Monday and go enlist in the United States Marine Corps.

"Reds, you've been watching too much of that John Wayne bullshit. They train Marines like the Japs did those Kamikaze pilots. They'll build your body and shrink your head."

"Who told you all that crap, Bones?"

"Reds, I don't need anybody to tell me about those fanatical bastards; besides, I can be patriotic without committing suicide.

Do you really believe those fuckin' Marine generals give a good shit about one more dead ass? All they want is another medal on their fuckin' chest. They don't care about the little man. It's all about ego and glory to them pricks."

"I think you're wrong, Bones, but I've gone this far."

There were about fifty of us on the bus going to Hunter Field to take the physical that Sunday afternoon. A corporal in charge of the detail at the hospital was busy giving out instructions on how and what to do.

"Remove your clothing and hang them on the hooks provided on the wall. Are there any questions?" he shouted.

"Corporal, can we leave our drawers on?" someone asked.

"No, get buck naked," the corporal shouted. "Then fall in according to your size, I mean higher numbers up front."

"Bones, you can get in front of the line," I said.

"Reds, the man's tongue slipped. All these long peckers got him nervous, and if he ain't queer, he sure missed a good chance."

"When I sober up this is gonna be a bad dream," I said.

Soon we were standing in line moving toward the door marked Examination Room. After entering the room we were handed a cup and told to pee in it. Bones was having a hard time pissing, so I filled his cup for him. We were asked a few questions about our general health, then the doctor took charge.

"What happened to your eye?" the doctor asked.

"I ran into a rose bush when I was child and injured it."

"How's your vision in that eye?"

"Good."

"Do you drink?"

"Just a little beer."

"Bend over and spread your cheeks ... look to the left and cough, now to the right and cough ... take in a deep breath and hold it ... open your mouth and say ahhh. Were you drinking last night?"

"Just a few beers, sir."

"Damn! It must have been hi-octane, son. Read the eye

chart. Okay. You can get dressed, then report back to the corporal for instructions," the doctor ordered.

"Corporal, how do we know if we passed the physical?"

"Just get dressed and get on the bus. I'll read out the list on the trip back to Travis Field."

"Man, I ain't never had a doctor look up my ass, look down my throat, mash my balls, and listen to my heart that fast in my life. Now I know why they call'em 'Flying Tigers,'" Bones said."

The whole process was over in less than an hour, and nobody failed the physical.

The swearing-in ceremony that day was pretty sobering because the beer had worn off, and the reality of what I had done was beginning to sink in. I wanted to be a Marine, I didn't want to join the Air Force. But with a few beers, I'd allowed somebody to pull my string again.

When I broke the news to my parents, they didn't seem to be upset about it; in fact, they acted relieved. I told them that I would be leaving in January for training.

"What kind'a trainin' are they gonna be givin' ya, boy?" my dad asked.

"I'm not sure, Chief, but the recruiting sergeant said they needed some 60310's — I think that's got somethin' to do with the motor pool or mechanics."

"That's good. When you get out, you can make some real money."

"Maybe you're right, Chief."

"I don't want him to be a damned mechanic, Mac." my mother said.

"What's wrong with a mechanic?" the Chief asked, as he shrugged his shoulders.

"Because, Bobby can do better."

"When the time comes he can make that decision." he replied sharply.

"That's right," I said trying to head off an argument.

"No, Mac! Bobby is not a Helmey!" she snapped, "you can't dictate to him, like you do me!"

I could always tell when my Mother was on medication. Her eyes would be as big as saucers and she'd tell the damnedest tales, like the one she told Gongie, that I'd joined the Flying Tigers and was being stationed in China. I knew she was over the edge, but I understood the root of her frustrations.

When the Tigers were issued uniforms, I knew we were in the irregulars — they were old World War II olive-drab issue. The regular Air Force was wearing the new blue uniform.

"Reds, I know where we can get 'Flying Tiger' patches to dress these rags up. They've been in moth balls so long they smell like Maggie's drawers," Bones said.

That afternoon Bones and I stopped in an Army-Navy store on Broughton Street. The Jewish gentleman who ran the place asked, "What can I do for you fine young boys?"

"We need Air Force shoulder patches," Bones said.

"I've got 'em all."

"How 'bout the Flying Tigers?"

"I got it. Are you boys in the Tigers?"

"Yes sir. We're on our way to Korea."

"If I could turn back the clock, I'd go with you. I was in the field artillery during the big war; we kicked the Kaiser's can all the way back to Berlin," he grinned.

"How much we owe you, sir?" I asked.

"Nothing, I'm proud of you boys."

We both shook his hand and thanked him for his kindness. As we walked out of the store, he said, "Keep 'em flyin', boys, and God bless America."

It was the same old antiquated railroad station that had seen many young men off to distant wars. The music of the Savannah High Blue Jacket Band echoed through the rusty iron and steel shed. The terminal was crowded with people gathered to see their relatives and friends off to another conflict.

A local politician gave a short fiery speech about the need to stop world Communism. He quoted U.S. Senator Joseph McCarthy's line about a list of "card-carrying Communists" in the State Department, and that something had to be done to stop the cancer. It all added to the excitement of the patriotic bon voyage send-off.

Major Creighton L. Rhodes read Special Orders Number One, "By direction of the President and Secretary of Defense..." I kissed my mother and grandparents, then shook the Chief's hand. While hugging good ole Bubber's neck, he slipped a half-pint of V.O. into my duffle bag.

The band played the "Tennessee Waltz," and the 117th fell in for roll call.

"Sir, the squadron is present and accounted for," said the First Sergeant.

"Have the troops board the train," the Major stated.

"Yes sir."

As the Tigers set out for Tennessee, the band began playing, "Off we go into the wild blue yonder."

The train was pulling out of the station when Sergeant Saddlewhite spotted the 'Flying Tiger' patch I had sewn on my uniform jacket. I thought he was going to ask where I'd gotten it, since no one else was wearing one, not even Bones.

"Helmey, who authorized you to wear that patch?"

"I thought it was appropriate since we're Flying Tigers.

"Who in the fuck told you that you're flying anything."

"Don't get your piss hot, Sarge. I heard it at Gildea's."

"Helmey, take it off right now and don't wise off anymore, or you'll think a tiger has your ass."

"Okay, Sarge, I don't want any problems. It was just a mistake."

Despite getting chewed out by the Sarge, I felt good about

things. Maybe Bones was right about our going to Korea. My thoughts raced back to December 7, 1941, at Central Junction when Billy and Tot Michael had been so excited about joining up. I wanted to be as proud to serve my country as my uncles were. My imagination, fueled by the liquor, had my adrenaline pumping, and there was no way I could sleep that night. I wondered about combat. How would I react when I heard that first shot fired in anger?

The train stopped early the next morning in Atlanta to switch engines, and we were ordered not to leave the train.

"Reds, you got any more liquor?" Bones asked.

"No, have you?"

"No, but there's a package shop across the street in front of the station. I'll buy if you'll go."

I asked the red cap for directions. He pointed toward the main exit doors leading to the street. When I walked into the place, I saw several officers from my unit. They didn't say a word to me, and I didn't say anything to them. But I knew I was getting off to a shaky start in the Tigers.

The snow-covered hills of middle Tennessee were a beautiful sight for this Georgia boy who had never seen snow except in the movies. The train stopped in the small town of Smyrna, where trucks were waiting to take us to Sewart Air Force Base. The thirty-minute ride in open trucks was bone-chilling and downright sobering. As we passed a wooden aircraft hanger, the sign over the giant door read: 314th TROOP CARRIER COMMAND. It reminded me of a scene from a World War II movie, as two C-119 "Flying Box Cars" were taxiing for take-off. They must be the aircraft that would be transporting us to Korea when the time came, I thought.

The trucks finally stopped at the farthest point on the base. The old wooden barracks hadn't been used since the big war, but they didn't look too bad because they had smoke coming out of their stacks, a sure sign of heat. That January in Tennessee was colder than a well digger's ass.

I was eager for the training to begin because I knew when it was over, we would be going to Korea.

"All 60310's report to the motor pool immediately," the loud speaker blared.

When Bones and I entered the motor pool, the Sargeant asked if we had G.I. licenses. Not only did Bones not have a license, he didn't know how to drive. We both answered, "No."

"Connor, you and Helmey report to Corporal Hutchinson for instruction and class on leak inspection."

The Corporal sent us to the supply room to get two creepers. Bones asked me what the hell a creeper was. Since my Dad owned a garage, I was ahead of the game.

"It's a thing you lay on and roll under trucks or cars."

"Oh yeah, I've always wanted a lay-down job," Bones said.

The Corporal had left by the time we returned with the creepers, so we just lay down on them, rolled under a truck and waited for him to return. I don't know how much time passed because we both fell asleep. The next thing I knew, I was being pulled out by the leg, and the Corporal was telling me to report to the motor pool sergeant.

"Helmey, I've been looking at your Military Personnel Records Jacket, and I see that you've had extensive R.O.T.C. training. Is that true?"

"Well, Sarge, I don't know about extensive, but I can do right face, left face, and march a little."

"Bullshit, Helmey, you know what I'm talking about. You know as well as I do how the military works."

He said he was going to give me the opportunity to volunteer for the unit's Security Police section. I told him that I'd always heard you never volunteered for anything in the military. "Bones can't drive. So he won't be any problem to me washing trucks. Together the two of you are trouble, and I'm not asking you, I'm telling you. If you know what's good for you, you'll volunteer for the job."

"Since you put it that way, Sarge, I understand. I guess I've always wanted to be a security policeman."

"Oh yeah, Helmey, they use live ammo. So be careful."

"This is the U.S. rifle, caliber .30 MI AI carbine. It fires a cartridge of .30 caliber, but it is much less powerful than the .03-06 cartridge used in the official military rifle," the instructor said.

I was beginning to believe everything we irregulars were issued was unofficial or some remnants leftover from the war that was supposed to end all wars. Korea was just a "police action," and if that were true, the policemen were being caught with their pants down. We Tigers weren't even issued cold-weather underwear until the spring of the year. We were lucky, according to news reports from the front-lines in Korea. Some U.S. Troops didn't have any cold-weather gear at all. They just layered all the clothes they could get their hands on. Even their boots were carry-over World War II issue that did little to prevent frostbite in the sub-zero weather of North Korea.

The war in Korea took a turn for the worst. The Chinese Communists joined in the conflict and crossed the Yalu River, pushing U.N. forces back South to the 38th Parallel.

I completed the rifle range and qualified as a sharpshooter. So did everyone else who could point the weapon and pull the trigger. We were issued live ammo and told that there was a possibility of Communist sabotage; then the Articles of War were read to us.

"Sleeping or deserting your post imperils the life and safety of the entire command. If anyone is caught sleeping while on guard duty, he could be shot." The sergeant reading it sounded serious.

I was convinced he meant exactly what he had said. However, I didn't understand whether or not you would be awakened before you were shot or executed as you slept.

"Men, you've got to keep your ears and eyes open if you want to stay alive." I knew the Sarge was having flashbacks from

World War II. I made the mistake of asking him how many North Koreans had been spotted in this area of Middle Tennessee.

"Helmey, I'm glad you asked that question because I'm going to give your smart ass the opportunity to watch for them."

That February the weather in Tennessee was a record breaker. According to some reports it was colder than some parts of North Korea. The ground was frozen hard and covered with snow. The wind blowing across the hilltop felt like it was coming straight from the North Pole. When the Sarge dropped me off at a recently-added isolated guard post for my four to eight p.m. watch, he had this shit-eating grin on his face and said, "Helmey, let me know if you spot any North Koreans."

"If I do, what am I supposed to do, Sarge?"

"Shoot to kill!" he said as he drove away in his jeep, laughing.

My post was located at the farthest point of the base adjacent to an aircraft taxiway. I had my rifle slung over my shoulder and my hands in my pockets, as I was doing a skip dance to keep my feet from freezing.

A C-119 came taxiing up the strip with its engines running up, waiting for a green light from the tower to take off. A jeep came racing down the taxiway behind the aircraft, then pulled to the side of it and a paratrooper in class A uniform jumped out with his duffle bag in one hand and his cover in the other. The starboard rear side door of the aircraft opened and a crew member signaled for him to board. The plane's engines were still running as he ran toward the aircraft. When he tried to go between the propeller and the fuselage, instead of going around the wing to the rear, the props completely decapitated him. It happened so fast. The pilot cut the engines. The paratrooper's motionless body lay on the concrete still clutching his bag and cap.

After my guard watch that night, Bones wanted me to go with him to the NCO Club.

"Bones, you know I'm not an NCO."

"Reds, I'll get you in, don't sweat it, brother."

"Yeah, like you got me in the Tigers."

"Reds baby, you're too uptight. After that paratrooper thing you need a little R and R. These old Tennessee chicks dig us young Georgia boys, and the place is full of them."

As we searched for a table in the crowded club that evening, the band was playing slow country music and the lights were dim. We found a table at the rear of the dance floor next to an exit sign. There were a lot of women there, but the regular Air Force NCO's thought they were their private stock. Most of the regulars were old farts who had stayed in after World War II. It wasn't hard to tell it pissed them off for us 'National Guard call-ups' to be invading their sacred hunting grounds.

Bones had left the table, when this very attractive woman asked if I would like to dance. At first it shocked me, I'd never had a women ask me to dance before. The look in her eyes reminded me of the trip with Uncle Sherman's secretary.

"Yes, Ma'am," I said.

"Please, don't call me that."

After dancing a slow 'belly rubbing' dance, we were walking off the floor, when the band started playing a jitter-bug.

"Would you like to dance this one?" she asked.

"Sure, Pretty-Thing, let's do it," I said, grinning.

At that point, my partner went into a jitter-bug step and I went into something between a fire-ant frenzy and a whirling dervish dance. I was doing flips and steps that I had never done or even attempted to do in my life. People were clapping and shouting, "Go, man, go!" Somewhere between her ego and my vertigo she pointed me back to the table.

"What was the name of that dance you just did?" she asked.

"The Daufuskie Stomp," I said.

I invited her to have a drink with Bones and me. She said she was with someone else and didn't think it was a good idea right then, but she would see me before the night was over.

"Break a heart, Reds — that woman's got the hots for you," Bones said. We were having a good time dancing when a sergeant in uniform came over to us. He told us that he didn't allow any punk acrobatic dancing in his club.

"How you figure this club belongs to you, Sarge?"

"I'm the NCOIC of the club!" he said, sharply.

"Sarge, first of all I haven't caused any problems, and I'm not a punk. Your problem is, you don't like the attention these women are givin' us young guys — that pisses you and your old redneck cronies off," I snapped.

He started shaking all over, then he swung and hit me just under my left eye. The lick didn't hurt and I could see fear in his eyes.

"If that's your best shot, you're in trouble, Sarge."

My right fist caught him dead on his nose. He fell forward, hitting the floor with his face on my white buck shoes. The band started playing "Dixie" as fights broke out. It was a riot. When the lights came on, the Air Police were coming in the front door. Bones was gone and my dance partner was waving me toward the rear exit.

She and I went out the door to where her car was parked at the rear of the club. I didn't ask any questions because I was glad to get out there before the Air Police found out that I wasn't an NCO.

"My name is Betty," she said softly as we drove away.

"I'm Bobby," I said, smiling.

"I love that name. If it's O.K. with you, we're going to Murfreesboro. You remind me of another redhead who wore white bucks and had those good moves on the dance floor."

" I always wanted to see Murfreesboro."

"Good," she smiled.

The guard flagged us through the back gate like we were officers. As a light snow was falling, the flakes danced in the headlights of her car. This was all unreal to me, but I loved the excitement and mystery of the moment. On one hand I was scared about what might happen because I hit an NCO; on the other I was excited about the possibilities the night held.

As she opened the door to her apartment, the telephone was ringing. She answered it and said, "No, you can't come over, and I'm glad somebody finally busted your jealous ass." Then she slammed the receiver down.

"Do you know who that was?" she asked.

"No, should I?"

"It's the guy you hit at the club. He's at the base hospital and thinks he's got a broken nose."

"Does he know you and I left together?"

"No. Don't worry about him," she added, smiling.

"I hope he doesn't remember my face."

"Bobby, you don't have to worry about that, you told me you were an officer."

"Betty, I might've told you anything tonight. Since it's confession time and you knew I wasn't a pilot, I'm not twenty-two years old either, I'm only eighteen and you're with a minor," I said, grinning.

"And I'll bet you've never had sex before," she added.

"Never! I'm as pure as the snow."

She pointed at a door, "I'll work on your eye after the shower. Use the robe behind the door."

The hot shower felt great. When I looked behind the door I saw Captain's bars on the Air Force uniform that hung there. I walked out naked holding the robe in my hand; she stood gazing down at my nakedness, "There's the bedroom. I'm going to take a shower. Please don't lose that big smile."

Uncle Billy had told me about a woman in the Philippines, and how she screamed and hollered during sex. I thought he was exaggerating like hell, but that night I became a believer. At first she scared me — I knew she could be heard all over Murfreesboro. "Oh! Fuck me!" she yelled over and over. I knew I had crossed the Rubicon. Sex would never be the same. She was right, I'd never had sex like that before.

It didn't take long for a ride back to the base that morning. When I walked in the barracks, Bones was sitting on the edge of his rack trying to wake up.

"Reds, what happened? I looked for you, where'd you go after the fight last night?"

"Shit! you didn't wait around. I did the same thing you did, hauled ass when the AP's came in the door."

"Man, the police were all over the area last night looking for some guy in white shoes that assaulted a regular at the NCO club."

"Those rednecks needed somebody to adjust their attitudes. Especially those old boozers who hang out in the club."

"If I were you, Reds, I'd throw those fuckin' white bucks away and get some dark glasses to hide your black eye."

"Later, Bones. Right now I'm gonna get some rack time before my watch, I'm petered out."

"Did you get any nooky last night, Reds baby?"

I couldn't go to sleep. My thoughts jumped from one thing to another ... the lifeless body of the paratrooper ... why do things like this happen ... what was the big deal with a fight in a hillbilly NCO club ... a nymphomanic nurse. If only I could sleep ...

When I awoke for my watch that afternoon, the snow was coming down heavily. Sattlewhite gave a briefing and special orders for the post where Ducky Moore and I would be assigned.

"Helmey, you and Moore are gonna be on a special ammo dump. You two had better watch your asses tonight. The 11th Airborne has stored some exotic high explosives there. The 314th will be transporting it to Korea tomorrow, is that clear?"

"Yes, sergeant, you don't have to worry about us," I said.

"What happened to your eye, Helmey?"

"A snow ball fight, Sarge."

"You two rebels get in the jeep!" said Sattlewhite.

The ammo crates didn't block the arctic wind that was blowing. Ducky suggested we get under the tarpaulin that covered the ammo crates, to have a smoke and block the icy breeze.

"If Sattlewhite spots a glow from a cigarette in this High Explosives area, he'd shit and have us shot," I said.

We agreed that there wasn't any North Korean or Communist saboteur crazy enough to come out in this kind of weather. After moving crates marked 'High Explosives,' we took a seat, and cut holes in the tarp so we could see if any vehicle was coming up the road.

"Reds, I thought you were gonna join the Marines." Ducky said.

"Man, I listened to that fuckin' Bones' bullshit about the Flying Tigers — hell, it just happened."

"Yeah I know, things just happen. I wanted to stay in the Marine Reserve myself, but dad and the Captain of Dog Company almost got into a fist fight when he accused my dad of knowing I had forged his signature." Ducky explained.

"We can still get to Korea, Ducky."

"Reds, you sound like Bones. How's that possible?"

"Ducky, we can do anything we set our minds to. Hell, the war will be over before the 117th knows their ass from a hole in the ground."

"Hold it, Reds, we can talk about this later — there's a jeep coming down the road."

Sattlewhite's jeep stopped, and he shouted out my name. When I answered, he shined a flashlight in my face, temporarily blinding me. I said, "Man, take that damn light out of my eyes."

"Helmey, don't wise off. Were you in the base NCO Club last night?"

"Sarge, you know I ain't allowed in that place."

"I didn't ask you that. I asked if you were at the NCO Club last night."

"I might have been in the neighborhood."

"Get in this jeep. You're gonna do some explaining to the Regular Air Police, and you'd better not give them any shit."

"What's all this crap about the Regulars and Reserves, anyhow? Ain't we all in this war together?"

As we walked in the barracks I saw the Regular AP's standing next to my bunk. The provost sergeant identified himself to me and asked, "Boy! Do you own a pair of white shoes?"

"It looks like you already know the answer to that. You've busted my foot locker. Did you find any?"

"Airman, don't get smart with me. Open that foot locker."

"Man! Screw you," I said.

"Take him to the stockade," he ordered.

On the way to the stockade, I thought, sure I'd been in the NCO Club, that's no big deal. But, these people are acting like I've committed a major felony. After all, I wasn't the one who started the fight — he hit me first. This wouldn't happen in civilian life. It's a game these old soldiers are playing to show us who's in charge. No officer or NCO from my squadron is coming to help me because I'm in a chickenshit National Guard Outfit and they don't have the balls to stand up to the regulars. It's all politics and I'm the one they're making an example of. This wouldn't be happening in the Marines.

The stockade was a group of several old barracks surrounded by a high chain link fence topped off with concertina wire. Armed guards continually walk the perimeter. It didn't seem like the sort of place they should take a person for a simple battery.

"Helmey, follow me," the guard said.

"Hey! Why am I goin' to jail, I haven't been tried yet!"

"Boy! get your motherfuckin' ass in gear, or I'll handcuff you," he yelled.

"That's the thing to do — before I bust your ass," I said.

The sign over the door read, 'Interrogation Room.' The AP removed the handcuffs and pointed at a chair. I sat at a small table facing a wall with a mirror. The provost sergeant came into the room and sat directly in front of me.

"Helmey, were you in the NCO club last night?"

"Yeah, in civilian clothes."

"Did you have an altercation with a sergeant in uniform?"

"Yeah! After he hit me."

"Did you know he was a sergeant in the United States Air Force, Helmey?"

"Sure, why should rank matter when I was only trying to defend myself, Sarge?"

"But, you're saying, you did know he was a tech sergeant."

"Sergeant, the word going around was, as long as you wore civilian clothing and behaved, it was O.K. Even civilians don't have any problem gettin' in the place."

"Your problem is you assaulted an NCO, and then tried to choke him to death," he said loudly.

"That's bullshit. I didn't choke anyone. The only thing I did was defend myself from a man that was pissed, because his woman was coming on to me."

The sergeant and the AP left the room momentarily. The only thing I knew was to tell the truth. It didn't take a genius to figure it out — the tech sergeant had to find someone to blame the riot on.

The Provost Sergeant came back in the room, smiling. "Helmey, I'm gonna give you a break. If you'll sign this, the charges will be dropped except the assault on an NCO. We can also bring charges against the NCO who gave you his I.D. card, and we know who he is. In all probability your Group Commander will give you a good lecture, maybe a few days of restriction and that will be all there is to it. Here's the charge sheet with four alleged charges against you; they are serious."

That sounded good. I was anxious to get the hell out of the room with the old bad-breath bastard anyway.

I signed a statement which obviously had been prepared before my arrival at the stockade. After I signed, he said, "Take the prisoner to get his gear."

The Air Policeman handcuffed me.

"What's the deal, Sarge? You said you were turning me over to my Group Command."

"Helmey, the deal is, you'll be turned over to him for the court-martial, but until that happens, your ass belongs to me and the United States Air Force."

I had just been conned by a diabolical old bastard and it was hard for me to understand. I had never been in jail in my life and I was pissed.

I was turned over to a corporal at the main entrance of the stockade containment area, I was body- searched.

"Pick up your gear and walk toward that building," he said, pointing. The flood lights cast a menacing shadow on everything around me.

The interior of the building looked like a large dog kennel with a narrow corridor running down the center. Cyclone wire divided each cell into an eight by ten enclosure.

"Stand in the yellow circle and strip!" the Corporal shouted as I struggled to control my anger.

"Bend over and spread your cheeks."

"For what?" I asked.

"I've got to check you for contraband."

"What's that?"

"Weapons and other stuff."

"Man, you've got to be apeshit to think I'd have a gun stuck up my ass — this is one ass you won't be looking up!"

"You'll be going to the black box if I don't."

"I guess I'll be going to the black box, then."

"Get dressed. After your court-martial tomorrow, I'll have plenty of time to adjust your National Guard attitude."

"Airman Helmey , do you understand the charges against you?" the Major asked.

"No sir, I don't."

"Let me refresh your memory. Is this your signature on this statement?"

"Yes sir, it's mine. But I never read the statement. I only signed it."

"Helmey, you're telling me you signed it without reading it?"

"Yes sir, that's a fact. I was told by the Provost Sergeant to sign it, and I would be handed over to my Group Commander for his action."

"Well, that's exactly what he did. Because you signed the statement, my hands are tied. You admitted being in the club and choking Sgt. Earles. This is not a court of inquiry, it's a Summary Court and my responsibility is to impose sentence on you."

"Yes sir, I understand what you've got to do, but I'd like to at least have somebody hear my side of the story."

"O.K., Airman, explain it to me," the Major said.

"I made a dumb mistake believing the Provost Sergeant. I was led to believe all charges were dropped, except the assault charge, and the Group Commander would more than likely drop that charge. Now I know I was conned."

"I'm sorry Helmey, but I've got a job to do, and that's to impose sentence on you. I hope you've learned a lesson from all this."

"Yes sir, I have."

"These are the specifications and charges against you: 'In that Pvt. Robert McRae Helmey, 117th AC & W Squadron, did at Sewart AFB, Tenn., on or about 7 March 1951, wrongfully commit assault and battery upon T Sgt. Leslie A Earles, Hq & Hq Sq, 314th Air Base group, by choking him on the throat.' Before I pass sentence, would you like to say anything, Helmey?"

"Yes sir, I would like to be sent to Korea as soon as possible."

"Helmey, I'm sorry I can't grant your request. You will be confined at hard labor for thirty days and forfeit forty dollars of pay, and be reduced to the lowest enlisted grade. The Sewart Air Force Base stockade is the designated place of your confinement. Signed by Major Berberich D. Pinckney, 154th Tac Con Gp. Remove the prisoner, Sergeant."

"Helmey, if you keep your nose clean for the next thirty days you won't have any problem," said the Provost Sergeant.

"Sergeant, you can kiss my ass, I fell for that bullshit once and you lied to me."

He started to hit me, but there were too many people around.

"Helmey, don't open your mouth or I'll teach you how this game is played. A couple of days in the black box and you'll have a different attitude."

The Provost Sergeant ordered the AP's to take me to his office.

"Reds, keep your mouth shut. If you don't, that sadistic old bastard will hurt you," the friendly AP said.

"Thanks, I appreciate that. What's all this about a black box?" I asked.

"Are you claustrophobic, Helmey?"

"I don't know."

"I think you're about to find out, Reds."

The sergeant was a big red faced man who looked like he drank too much. He sat behind a large oak desk that was covered with Japanese memorabilia and pictures of a Japanese woman.

"Helmey, sit down and listen. You don't seem to comprehend the seriousness of this situation, do you?"

"Yeah, I comprehend that I've been seriously fucked."

"A little time in the black box and you'll understand everything," he said grinning. "When you've had enough, just knock and tell the guard to open the door."

"You mean say 'uncle,' Sarge?"

"Strip and put your clothing in the bag," the guard ordered.

Outwardly, it looked like the entrance to a mop closet. The door opening was next to the Sergeant's office. That was where the similarity ended. As the guard opened it, it looked like a thick refrigerator door made from plywood.

The guard then handed me a blanket and a bucket with water. As I wrapped the blanket around my body, I bent forward and grabbed the bucket and twisted my naked body into the hole. When the door was closed it became pitch black.

It didn't take long to discover that I couldn't stand up or lie down. The only position that helped at all was a vertical fetal squat. I felt buried alive. My body played games with my head, fear and panic gripped my every thought: the black hole had swallowed me.

The only mistake the sadist who designed the torture chamber was an acoustical flaw.

"It won't be long and he'll be begging. Then the Sarge will be happy and we can get the hell out of here," the guard said.

When I heard that, it helped my resolve to show the man that I wasn't going to give him the satisfaction of saying 'uncle'.

The lights blinded me as the door opened suddenly.

"Stay down. Here's food and water."

"Thanks, gentlemen," I said, my words laced with sarcasm.

"You're a hard-headed son-of-a- bitch, Helmey."

I could feel the canteen and slices of bread. I found out what the bucket was for and the smell became overwhelming. The pain and cramps in my legs were so bad that my body got mad at my brain for not pounding on the door and begging to get out. I lost all track of time. However, I made up my mind that when the door opened, I was coming out one way or the other, dead or alive.

When it finally opened, I could not move a muscle. The same guard who had given me the advice about keeping my mouth shut was standing looking down with a smile on his face.

I couldn't stand. He reached down and helped me to my feet.

"How long were you planning on staying, Reds?"

"When that door opened and I saw your smiling face, I knew it was time," I said, putting on my underwear.

The remaining twenty-eight days were spent working at a sewage treatment plant, shoveling human waste into trucks from a drying bed. That humbles a man. The Sarge had the 'ups' on me and I knew it.

After a while, even the Provost Sergeant's attitude changed. "Helmey, did you learn anything from this experience?"

"Yes sir, stay out of the NCO Clubs, keep my mouth shut, and know when it's time to knock on a door."

"Helmey, you've grown on me, and for some strange reason I'm gonna miss you. How about staying around a little longer?"

"Sarge, I'm gonna miss you, and I've got a confession to make. I thought you were a redneck, but after getting to know you, I've changed my mind. You've taught me things that I ain't never gonna forget," I said, looking into his eyes.

"Helmey, I'm showing on your release papers that you served your sentence with good conduct."

"Thanks, Sarge."

"Oh! by the way, Hank Williams is playing at the NCO Club tonight. You wanna go with me and have a few beers?"

"Sarge, I've really learned my lesson."

"You'll make a good soldier, one of these days, Helmey."

Sergeant Sattlewhite was waiting to take me back to the squadron area in his jeep.

"How you feeling, Reds?"

"Pretty good, but I don't wanna see that place again."

"You still wanna go to Korea?"

"Yeah."

Sattlewhite's attitude had really changed. He didn't act like he had the red ass with me anymore. He told me that the Tigers had received a lot of new radar equipment.

"What's our chances of going to Korea, now?"

"Some of us will be going to Korea, others going to North Africa and a few will be having an A-bomb tested on them."

"With my luck, I'll get that last one. I'm volunteering as soon as we hit the squadron area."

"Helmey, you're gonna have that opportunity — the first sergeant wants you in his office the minute we get back."

The first question the top sergeant asked me was, "Helmey, are you ready to settle down and soldier?"

"Sarge, I was ready when we left Savannah, but I just got off on the wrong foot."

"Helmey, I've talked with the Provost and he tells me that you can follow orders when you want to. The problem with that is, the military doesn't run on whether or not you like it. It runs on following orders. Do you understand that?"

"Yes, Sergeant."

"I'm assigning you to Sergeant Peters, AP Section. Maybe you can get off on the right foot with him. You've given Sattlewhite ulcers with all your talk about the Flying Tigers."

Before I left his office, I again volunteered for Korea. Later I found out from a corporal who worked in the orderly room that there never was any paperwork initiated on my request for Korea.

Sergeant Johnny Peters was of Greek and Irish heritage, his father was Greek and his mother Irish. Both showed in his personality — he was a competitor and I knew right away that I was going to like him.

"Helmey, I'm gonna give you a break, you're off for the next twenty-four hours. Before you leave, next week there is a base-wide physical competition, and our section is gonna win. Get yourself in shape. Catch ya later, friend."

When I entered the barracks, the first face I saw was Bones. "Reds, we missed you, baby."

"Yeah, I know how much you've missed me. Not one of you cocksuckers came to see me the whole time I was in the brig."

That night there was a ten-cent beer call at the service club. The beer was flowing and so was the bullshit.

"Reds, what does that sign say?"

"You must be twenty-one years old to drink alcoholic beverages."

"Reds, think about this. This country can use your ass for cannon fodder, but you can't legally drink beer on this base."

"Yeah, a bunch of hypocrites.

"Reds, you still think we can get to Korea?"

"Yeah, Ducky. Are you interested?"

"Maybe."

The spring of 1951 brought on new and potentially unstable changes in the world. MacArthur and Truman were having as much trouble with each other as I was with the Air Force. MacArthur wanted to kick ass and cross into China. But Truman didn't want to risk a general war, so he fired MacArthur and brought him home. The general who said, "I shall return," had just given his farewell address to a joint session of Congress on April 19, 1951: "Old soldiers never die, they just fade away."

One of the places he faded away to was Sewart Air Force Base. He and his wife came to visit her family home in Murfreesboro, Tennessee. The 117th was selected as honor guards for his arrival at Sewart. Wearing our newly issued Air Force blues and white gloves, we stood at Present Arms with empty rifles and full hearts as the Bataan rolled to a stop.

As the Old Soldier stepped from the aircraft, my thoughts went back to another general whom I'd seen earlier in my youth. His words had been almost the same. "You are the future of this great nation."

I felt the goose bumps on my arms, and I was proud to be an American. After the ceremony, I went to the first sergeant about my request.

"Helmey, I haven't heard anything, but you keep up the good work, I'll get your stripe back."

"I'd really appreciate anything you do, Sarge."

"Helmey, why are you so anxious to get killed?"

"Sarge, I've never thought about it that way."

"Reds, don't you understand they're not playing some kind of a game over there?"

"Sarge, I'm not playing a game either. But I'd feel like a damn traitor if I didn't try."

"O.K. I'll do what I can. By the way, this may interest you. Captain Billy Hearn of our squadron was assigned as 'Officer In Charge' of the I.G.'s inspection of the base stockade. During his inspection of that facility, he found a room they called the black box. In World War II, the captain was shot down over Germany and spent a couple of years in a POW camp. When he saw and heard what the Provost Sergeant was using that box for, the shit hit the fan. The good captain told the sergeant that the fuckin' Germans didn't pull any shit like that on him, and if he didn't destroy the box and his ideas of how to break men, he'd open an investigation that he'd never forget."

"Thanks, Sarge, I'll check with you later."

"Ducky, I just talked with the first sergeant, and I can tell he's just handing me a line of shit about my request."

"Reds, I got a letter from my sister Rosie yesterday. Andy Farie was killed in Korea."

"Ducky, you're kiddin', it seems like only yesterday we were playing basketball with him at Daffin Park."

"Reds, I don't need anymore convincing, let's do it."

I explained that Luigi Trapani was stationed at Camp Pendleton, California. He'd help us get uniforms and whatever information on troopship departures.

"Man, you were in the Marine Reserve. A stowaway on a ship shouldn't be hard to pull off."

"Yeah, but..."

"But what?"

"Man! that sounds like Houdini shit to me. We'd have a better chance stowing away aboard an aircraft."

"Shit, we couldn't hide ourselves aboard an airplane without being discovered."

"Reds, how do we get to California?"

"Next week, I'll go home and get my Studebaker."

"Shit that raggedy-ass old car won't make it to Tennessee, much less California."

"Ducky, we can talk shit until we're blue in the face. But

until you got a better idea, I'm headin' home and gettin' that land rocket and pointing it due west."

"You get the car and I'll go. But right now, let's have another beer," he said, grinning.

Somewhere on U.S. Route 80, in Texas, I said, "Ducky, check the map and tell me how far El Paso is."

"Forty-five miles. Let's visit Juarez, Mexico."

"That sounds good."

"Reds, you do know they shoot deserters during war time, don't you?"

"Ducky, you worry too much! They shoot 'em because they run from a war. Man, we're tryin' to get to the action."

"I hope you know what you're talking about."

"Ducky, you ain't had a change of heart, have you?"

He grinned and said, "No, I was just checking you out."

We found Corporal L.J. Trapani at Tent Camp Two, Camp Pendleton, California. Almost a year had passed since I'd seen him. After a few minutes of small talk, Trapani asked, "What are you guys doing this far from Tennessee?"

"Man! We wanted to see ya before you left for Korea."

"Bullshit, Reds, I know you two fuckers didn't drive 2500 miles to see my smiling face, you're up to something."

"Can we talk, Luigi?"

"Not here, I'm off tomorrow. Where y'all staying?"

"Studebaker Hotel," I said.

"Man! you can't do that around here. The shore patrol checks papers all the time. Get a room in San Diego, and I'll be there tomorrow," he said, shaking his head.

"Tell us where to stay," I said.

"The Knickenbocker in San Diego. I'll see you at 1600 hours tomorrow."

Luigi knocked on the door at exactly 4 p.m. the next day.

"O.K. Now tell me. What are y'all doing here?"

"We wanna catch a boat to Korea and your Italian ass is gonna help us."

I could tell by the look on his face he thought we had lost our minds. The more I tried to explain our plan to him, the more he shook his head.

"That's not possible. Without proper papers or identification by a troop handler, you can't get near a ship."

"Luigi, you got a better idea?"

"Yeah! Take your asses back to Tennessee. It won't be long before we're all in combat. Tonight let's go to Tijuana and blow it out for old times sake."

"Luigi, sometimes your wisdom amazes me," I said.

On the drive down to Tijuana, Luigi said, "Here's a couple of pro-kits just in case you get laid."

"Why?" asked Ducky.

"V.D. One of the guys in my company caught the bull-head clap, and a doctor had to hit the head of his dick with a rubber hammer."

"Who hit, whose dick?" I asked.

"Why'd the doctor hit the head of his dick?" Ducky asked.

"Not his dick, dummy." Luigi answered loudly.

"Trapani, you Marines are nuts — ain't nobody hittin' my dick," Ducky said.

"You two crazy mother-fuckers need to be turned loose on the North Koreans." Luigi said, laughing.

Tijuana was a place to get drunk, get laid, and get back across the border before you caught something you couldn't get rid of.

I still wanted to convince Luigi that my plan was noble and possible. But he said something about following orders that really hung in my mind. Disgrace had never entered the picture. I'd never drunk tequila. The more I did, the more I bucked my ass. I'd danced a few times with this Mexican hooker who had more tits than I'd ever seen, when she suddenly announced, "*Rojo*, I teach jew de Zapateado."

She grabbed my arm and stomped her feet. I then went into an airborne acrobatic maneuver, jumping on the bar, then doing a one and a half onto the dance floor. My partner yelled, "You *mucho loco, Rojo.*" When I went to the head, I discovered that I had busted out the crotch of my pants, my left knee was swollen and I could hardly walk.

Ducky had also found a senorita. She was teaching him the Mexican hat dance when his tequila kicked in. After a couple of turns around the brim of her sombrero, he stopped, took out his dong and urinated on it.

On the drive back to Camp Pendleton, Luigi and I talked while Ducky slept in the back seat.

"Reds, I know your intentions were good. Believe me, I wanna go to Korea, too. You guys need to go back and turn yourselves in."

"Luigi, you're right. I'm going back and straighten my dumb ass up."

"Bobby, you ain't dumb. But when you get that fire water in you, Reds takes over."

"Luigi, I love you like a brother. Take care of yourself, and thanks for being my friend. I'll see ya when this is over, one way or the other."

The decision to return as a failure was tough. The pain and swelling in my knee told me the Korean odyssey had ended. As I limped into the Squadron Orderly Room, the First Sergeant said, "Helmey, I see you were wounded in action."

Everyone in the Squadron knew about our trip. Some were betting we'd make it; others were laughing their asses off.

The smile came off his face, and I knew it was time for me to get serious and listen as he explained what he had to do.

"Reds, you were gone for ten days. That's AWOL and there's no getting around it. It'll be your second court-martial, bad news."

"Sarge, I know you won't believe this, but I'm ready to settle down and soldier."

"Helmey, I don't know why I've got a soft spot for you. During World War II, I fought all over Europe with all kinds of crazy men. But you're the best fuck-up I've ever had the privilege to soldier with. You take it to new heights. If it were up to me, I'd give you a Purple Heart for your Tijuana campaign. All I can do to help you is send you to the hospital before you're court-martialed."

After the x-rays showed that I had a fractured tibia with damage to the patella, the doctor applied a cast and admitted me to the hospital for possible surgery at a later date.

The following day a second lieutenant came to the ward and introduced himself. "Helmey, you're being transferred to a new squadron."

"What squadron is that, sir?"

"The 129th. I'll also be handling your court-martial."

"Sir, will I be court-martialed while I'm in the hospital?"

"Yes, I'm going to read the charges against you now. 'In that Private Robert M. Helmey USAF did, on or about the 6th November, 1951, without proper authority, absent himself from this organization, to wit: 117th Aircraft Control and Warning Squadron, and did remain so absent until on or about the 15th November, 1951.' Would you like to make a statement, Helmey?"

"No, sir, I'm guilty as charged."

"Helmey, help me understand — everybody I spoke with in your squadron said you were a nice guy. Your Section Sergeant even bragged that you were one of his best men. But your conduct record doesn't reflect that. You could be discharged because of your behavior. Tell me, what does the Air Force need to do to get your attention?"

"I hope they'll give me another chance."

"Do you deserve one?"

"No, sir."

"Believe me, Helmey, this will be your last opportunity to show that you are serious."

"Yes sir, I understand."

"Your sentence is to be restricted to the 129th AC&W Squadron area for fifty-four days and forfeit forty-five dollars of pay. Do you have any questions?"

"When does the sentence start, sir?"

"It's already started, and your hospital time will be counted as time served."

"God bless you, sir," I said, grinning from ear to ear.

"Airman Moore wasn't as lucky. He was sentenced to thirty days at hard labor."

"Sir, Moore's a good man, his motives were honorable."

"Your ass, Helmey. There's nothing honorable about going AWOL, and you had better not fuck-up again."

"You don't have to worry about me — I'm a new man, sir."

"I've advised the head nurse of your restricted status. She has a reputation as a hard charger. I wouldn't get on her bad side," the Lieutenant said, smiling.

The sandy-haired, shapely nurse snapping out orders about my transferring to a private-room was no stranger to me.

"Private, I'm having you moved," she announced in a very commanding voice. "You are not to leave your room or have visitors without my permission — is that clear?"

"Yes, ma'am! I understand," I replied.

Could I be dreaming, or am I delusional from the drugs? My luck isn't supposed to be this good.

Later that evening she came in the room and asked how I had injured my leg. Her tone was entirely different.

"Captain, you wouldn't believe me if I told you."

"Try me."

"A bad landing in Mexico," I said.

"I'm gonna have you psychoanalyzed." She had that same carnal look in her eyes as that night in Murfreesboro. "Helmey,

I'll see you after I talk with the doctor. Remember not to get any funny ideas about... I can play hard ball."

She didn't have to worry about my stepping out of line. I knew the lady had the ups on me.

The doctors decided to let nature take its course with my injury. My mobility was limited to a wheelchair, and without the captain's permission, I couldn't leave my room.

"Bobby, in college I majored in abnormal psychology. But I've never studied anything in that science that would remotely resemble your strange condition. I wanna get inside your head," she said, looking deep into my eyes.

After her nightly visits, I knew it wasn't my head that she was interested in ... her efforts to analyze my mental state by asking Freudian questions only fueled the fires of our passion. Her physical therapy was unyielding.

The doctors concluded after a month that my knee had healed sufficiently and surgery wouldn't be necessary. The cast was removed and I knew that my stay in the hospital was nearing an end.

I could tell by her body language that my final therapy session was near. The last night ended with us in a seldom-used obstetrics room. The table wasn't designed for double occupancy. While she struggled to keep her legs in the stirrups, I became so aroused by her loud groaning noises, that it caused me to prematurely reach an orgasm. "Bobby! don't stop! If you do I'll have you court-martialed again." she moaned.

"I'm doin' the best I can, captain," I replied weakly. That ended the therapy and our relationship. Nature truly had had its way with me ... and so had she.

The ride from the base hospital to my new squadron didn't take very long.

"Welcome aboard the 129th, Helmey. I'll make this short and sweet. You've got until 1300 hours to be at the 314th Flight Operations Office with all your gear."

"For what, Sergeant?"

"I can't answer that. You're to report to Sergeant Ferris at Operations, and he'll have your sealed orders. It's something to do with a 'Top Secret' exercise," he said grinning.

"Sergeant Ferris, I was told to report to you."

"Yeah, Helmey. You're one of the hand-picked men who is being assigned to a special night-fightin' unit. Here's your orders, good luck, and may God bless you."

As the C-119 lifted off the ground, I was reading the orders. I was temporarily assigned to a unit at Pope Air Force Base, North Carolina, which was being deployed to an atomic test maneuver (Operation Longhorn) in Texas. Because of the aircraft's engines, it was impossible to talk without shouting. So I just lay back and enjoyed the ride.

"Welcome to the home of the Red Ball Express," read the sign over the entrance to the barracks.

It was the only all-black squadron in the United States Air Force with the exception of the Commanding Officer, who was white. Many of its men had distinguished themselves in World War II, during the Battle of the Bulge, where they had kept fuel and ammo flowing to Patton's tanks and front line troops.

I would be lying if I didn't say it was a cultural shock. It was 1952, and I had been taught that blacks couldn't run anything, much less the military. But to my surprise, they had it together and made me feel like I was actually in a military unit for the first time. I was proud to be a member of the famous 'Red Ball Express.'

My new sergeant won the Bronze Star during WWII. He had a zeal for telling stories about the Red Balls, he had even written a ballad:

> Patton was out of gas and couldn't move his men.
> Black asses started double clutching rigs,
> and got the 3rd Army rolling to Berlin, again.

"Sarge, what's all this talk about an atomic bomb test?"

"Helmey, you know as much as me. Ain't it strange that a load of blacks and crackers are head'n to Texas?"

"What'cha mean, Sarge?"

"They need some guinea pigs to test that thing on."

"Man! What kind of guinea pigs you talk'in about?"

"The kind like you'n me."

I knew he was joking, but it did seem strange that "odd balls" and "irregulars" were together.

I was assigned as the driver for the "end of convoy" jeep. Sergeant "Pop" Washington and I would be bringing up the rear of the 30th Motor Transport's exodus to Texas.

It was the first time since the Reconstruction that a white man chauffeured a Black through the deep South. After we crossed the Mississippi, Pop took off his steel helmet and gave a sigh of relief.

While driving the C.O. of the 30th to a Commander's meeting, I discovered that Operation Longhorn was only an exercise in logistics, not an atomic test as I had originally heard.

"Sir, when they gonna drop the bomb?"

"It's already been dropped on paper, Helmey."

"Well, I'll be damned, I didn't know that, sir."

"It was only simulated," he said.

"Then I guess we're simulated guinea pigs, sir."

"Helmey, simulate your cracker-ass back to the squadron area and pick me up at 1300 hours."

"Yes, sir."

There was a cease-fire in Korea. Meetings between the North Koreans and United Nations troops were being held at Panmunjom, Korea. The talk going around was that we'd be released from active duty within a few months. To celebrate the cease-fire and my success as a paper guinea pig, I thumbed over to Killeen to see Tex Ritter sing, "Rye Whiskey, Rye Whiskey."

However, my celebration was short-lived — soon after

entering the building a fight broke out, and I was hit in the head with a beer bottle.

I don't know who brought me back to South Fort Hood, but when I opened my eyes the next morning, Sergeant Washington was standing over me.

"Reds, you're going to an aid station," he said, with a concerned look.

I was hurting too bad to argue. After X-rays showed that I had a concussion and broken ribs, I spent the next ten days in a field MASH unit.

The day I was released, Sergeant Washington handed me orders back to Sewart Air Force Base and the paper Tigers.

"Pop, I'll never forget your kindness, I've learned a lot about people from you," I said, smiling. "If you ever get down to Georgia, look me up. I'd be proud to drive you around, and you won't need a steel helmet this time."

"O.K. Reds, I'll always remember you as a cracker with soul."

The "Red Ball" experience was an epiphany in my life. I realized that the color of a man's skin has nothing to do with the depths of his heart. Sergeant "Pop" Washington will always be an American hero to me.

The rumors about our being discharged in a few months turned out to be correct. On May 3, 1952, I was released from active duty in the United States Air Force.

Part Four

YOUTH

My Salad Days,
When I was green in judgment.
William Shakespeare

Youth

Cross examination, Savannah, 1969

"Now since you've been back in the United States, you went into a great amount of testimony about all of the prisons you've been in here. Do you claim that at any time, in any of those prisons, that you were mistreated?" asked Prosecutor Smith.

"In some, yes, sir."

"In other words, you've had a very hard time?"

"I feel that I have, yes, sir."

"You've been out of jail on bond since you got back to Savannah, have you not?"

"Yes sir, I've been out."

"Did you ever get out of jail in Cuba?"

"No sir, I didn't."

"Now, Mr. Helmey, when you got back to this country, you didn't think this country would take the position that you had a bad time down there and let you out of jail, did you?"

"No sir, I didn't expect it."

"You expected you were going to be punished?"

"No sir, I didn't. I didn't know exactly what was going to take place, to tell you the truth."

"You didn't think you were going to be punished when you were brought back?"

"I can't answer that and say that I thought that. I don't know what you're talking about, degree of punishment, or what?"

"I'm not talking about the degree of punishment at all. I'm talking about this trial right now."

"Yes, I knew what I had to face."

"You know, then, that you were going to be punished, that you were going to be tried."

"Yes, sir, I knew that I was going to be tried."

"And you knew that kidnapping and hijacking are a very serious offense?"

"Yes, sir, I did."

"All right, sir, you also know that it could carry the death sentence?"

"Yes, sir, I do."

"Well then, how, Mr. Helmey, can you expect to come back into this country and not be incarcerated in jail?"

"I didn't say I didn't expect it, sir, in coming back to face what I had to do."

"All right, sir, now can you in any way say that you have had every possible advantage that the law could give you?"

"I feel that I have had a very fair trial."

"All right, sir, you are in fact being tried in Savannah, which is your hometown, is that not correct, sir? And is that some good little distance from where this crime was committed?"

"Yes, sir."

"And all of that is done with the consent and help of the United States Government. Is that not so?"

"Objection, Your Honor," said Defense Attorney Clark, "the Government has objected all along to reducing the bail. They have objected to the change of venue. They have not cooperated in any way, including bringing witnesses that worked for the U.S. Government."

"All right, Mr. Clark, you've made your little speech, now sit down. All right, proceed," ordered the Judge.

"Mr. Helmey, you have been cast as a very thoughtful and loving person that would hurt nobody. Would you tell us, please, for what purpose you were going to Cuba?"

"To assassinate Fidel Castro."

"In other words, you were going down there to commit murder?"

"Yes, sir."

"Any way you cut it, it's still murder, is that so?"

"Yes, sir."

"All right, all your friends and all this military, and I don't for one minute contend that you were not a fine and wonderful soldier and had great patriotism, but in all this time, what was all that training leading to?"

"You're trained to kill."

"Oh! You were trained to kill."

"Yes, sir, that's only part of what I've been trained to do."

"And as a matter of fact, that was your whole and primary purpose in this life. Was that not so, sir?"

"To kill someone?"

"To be trained in the U.S. Special Forces for whatever that training led to?"

"Yes, sir, for whatever it led to and not just for killing. No, sir. I think we have to stand up for something and be prepared to do whatever it takes to defend this country. If we have a strong defense, then you don't have to worry about so much killing."

"But you were going to Cuba to kill Castro?"

"Yes, sir, I was."

"I have no further questions."

Judge: "Mr. Clark?"

Clark: "You can step down."

As I stepped down from the witness stand, I couldn't get my mind off the statement I'd made so many times: if you believe in something strongly enough, you'll die for it. But now I was having a struggle with that. Many times in Cuba I had faced what I thought was sure death.

The Cuban officer shoved the magazine into the pistol, racked the slide, and pressed the muzzle to my head.

He was so close I could smell the alcohol on his breath. My heart felt like it was going to beat out of my body. The worn-out old Buick stopped on a lonely stretch of beach in the dark of the night. The driver got out and crossed in front of the car. The headlights cast an eerie shadow as he loaded a magazine into an AK-47 assault rifle.

Only the officer who had the pistol against my head spoke in English: "Get out and stand in front of the automobile."

As I stood there blinded by the headlights, I knew I was going to die. How many times had I said, "If you believe." Now that phrase seemed foolish and unreasonable.

"Why are jew in Cuba, Holmey?" he shouted.

"To talk with Fidel Castro."

The very second I saw the flash of the weapons, I heard, Bam! Bam! Bam! My life flashed before my eyes, and I was paralyzed with fear. When I didn't feel anything, and then heard their laughter, I shouted, "You miserable bastards!"

Re-Adjustment Act of 1952

"The government understands that some of you men need aid in overcoming the disruption in your normal lives due to your military service. The 82nd Congress has seen fit to give you some benefits: the Veterans' Readjustment Act of 1952. Better known as the Korean GI Bill. So take advantage of it."

That's what the lieutenant said as he dismissed a group of us from active duty. The Tigers hadn't heard a shot fired in anger, and it made me feel a little guilty because we weren't sent to Korea. But the man had said take advantage of it.

Determined to take his advice and the government's $120 a month, I enrolled at the University of Georgia in Athens for the '52 fall quarter. The free tuition was more money a month than I'd make on active duty in the Air Force and seemed too good to be true. I also was excited by the prospect of receiving a commission through the Reserve Officers Training Corps at Georgia. I dropped off my discharge and DD-214 at the office of the professor of Military Science and Tactics. I was told to check back in a few days. In the meantime, Bubber Feus, Pete Bougas, and I moved into the YMCA building across from the main campus.

"What the hell is rush week, Pete?" Bubber asked.

"That's when the fraternities and sororities have open house," Pete explained.

"Are you interested, Bubber?" I asked.

"I don't know until I check it out."

"I ain't into that secret hand shaking shit," I said.

"Bubber! Before they give you the hand shake, they carve a Greek letter on the head of your dong," Pete said, grinning.

"What the hell do they do to the sorority sisters?"

"They have to spend the night at Effie's whorehouse giving hand jobs to the local firemen."

"How 'bout you guys gettin' serious so I can study — I'm here to get an education," I said.

"Yeah! Bubber, you're a bad influence on us," Pete chuckled.

"Shit, you two taught me everything I know."

We always attended Georgia's home football games together. Pete was as gifted as Nick when it came to concealing whiskey on his person. He could get a gallon into Sanford Stadium without looking suspicious or even being stopped.

Georgia was having a hard time with the University of Maryland. The Red Coat band was playing the Dog's fight song, and the three of us were caught up in the spirit of the game.

"The Dogs are in trouble!" Bubber shouted.

"If those hedges weren't there, I'd be on that field," I said.

"Don't let 'em stop you, Reds — jump over the bitches!" Pete yelled.

We were twenty rows up in the student section when I started the takeoff down the steps. However, I didn't have enough lift to clear the hedges. Amazingly, I had the velocity to burst through onto the playing field. The official said I was off sides and they ejected me from the stadium.

Monday, when I attended English class, Miss Appleby said, "Mr. Helmey, please report to the Dean of Men, immediately."

"Son, would you please explain your conduct at Saturday's football game," Dean Tate said, calmly.

"I'm not sur I can, sir."

"Go ahead and try, Mr. Helmey."

"I believe it was the intoxicating music of the Red Coat band."

"It was intoxication, all right, but it didn't come from any band. It came from a bottle. After seeing the hole you opened through the hedges and observing the buck dance you performed on the field, I'm sure Coach Butts or the band director would gladly give you an opportunity to try out for a position with them."

"Sir, I don't remember dancing."

"That doesn't surprise me — I can't excuse your conduct. Not only did you make a public spectacle of yourself, but the YMCA reported you urinated in their night watchman's hat. If it weren't for your being a Korean veteran, I'd expel you from this institution. I do realize that it takes time for some of you to readjust. However, I will not tolerate this conduct. Again. I'm placing you on social restriction until I'm personally satisfied that you can conduct yourself in a responsible manner. I also strongly recommend you apologize to the night watchman and compensate him for his hat."

"Yes, sir, I understand."

"You will not be allowed to attend any social, athletic, or other events for one year at this college. If after one year your conduct has improved, I will consider restoring your privileges. I also recommend you stop drinking alcohol and remember that you're at this institution to receive an education."

The night watchman was very understanding and accepted my apology and five dollars for his hat. He explained that he'd been a Marine during World War II and had pulled some pretty good shenanigans himself. In fact, we became friends. He told me not to worry about social restriction because there was a place on Elm Street that could provide all the social life I could stand while in Athens.

I went by the R.O.T.C. office and received more bad news. After they checked and found that I had received two courts-martial while on active duty, they wouldn't enroll me in the program. It was frustrating knowing something as trivial as a fist fight would follow me the rest of my life. Nevertheless, I managed to swallow my pride and maintain a sense of *savoir faire* — I was a pro at hiding my feelings.

During the Christmas break, I stopped at Gildea's.

"Reds, I heard Coach Wally Butts recruited you for the Bulldogs, after the hole you made in the hedges," George 'Sham' Killerin said loudly.

"Shady Sham, the Umbrella Man, it's good to see you made it home from the wars." Back in the late '40s when Sham had worked summers at Tybee Beach renting out umbrellas, somebody hung that alias on him.

We drank beer half the night.

He was going to Armstrong Junior College on the GI Bill and was on the basketball team, which amazed me because I'd never known him to have an athletic bone in his body.

"Reds, quit Georgia. You're like the rest of us — all you want is $120 a month and when that runs out, go to work."

I took Sham's advice. Bubber and I both said *adios* to Athens and Pete. We enrolled at Armstrong.

At home, nothing had changed. My mother and father still had the same old problems, no communication between them. They constantly blamed each other for their problems. He'd accuse her of keeping him broke paying hospital and doctor bills. She'd accuse him of having more feelings for a dog than for her, and screwing everything that walked. They'd both deny each other's accusations and continue on the next day like nothing had happened. They were great at hiding their feelings from friends and the world. But not from me.

I dropped out of Armstrong after basketball season.

Gildea's always seemed to be the place where my fiascoes started.

"Reds, I know where we can get a college education, make some serious money, and get a suntan at the same time."

"Bones, this sounds like more of your Flying Tiger shit."

"Maybe, but the Tigers did get you out of this cracker-ass town. Reds, if you don't ever leave Savannah, you gonna wind up at the paper mill."

"O.K., I'm listening, Billy Bones."

Bones painted me a picture of us working as bellhops on Miami Beach during the tourist season and going to the University of Miami in the off-season.

"Miss Willie said that you can make a couple of hundred a week in tips. Bang all the old rich broads you can stand. If you do it right, you might find one that'll sign a service contract."

"Bones, who the hell is Miss Willie?"

"A black guy that plays the piano at the Novelty Bar."

"So why do you call him Miss Willie?"

"Hell, he thinks he's a broad, he's got more balls than a Roman gladiator."

"Man, that's hard to believe. But I'm ready to get out of this town."

Miami Beach was everything Miss Willie had told Bones it would be. Even the fact of how the Jews owned the place and had the power. However, he forgot to tell him you had to grease a head bellhop's palm to work at any hotel where serious money was being made. And the payola was out of our reach. We hit all the smaller hotels off the beach looking for any kind of a job. No luck the first week. Our money was about to run out when we found a cheap room at Sam's Hotel in Hollywood.

"Tomorrow I'm finding me one of those rich broads Miss Willie told me about," Bones said.

I looked over the want ads in the *Miami Herald* and saw: 'Helper needed at cabana bar. Roney Plaza Hotel, Miami Beach.'

The next morning I left Bones sleeping and thumbed over to the beach. When I asked the bartender at the cabana about

about the job, he pointed his finger and said, "See Manny over in the office."

"Mr. Manny, I'm here about the job."

"Where you from, kid?" Manny was a dead ringer for a movie mobster; flashy clothes, body language, and throaty voice all added to his gangster demeanor.

"Savannah, Georgia."

"No shit, I've got a friend there — you know Gully Silver?"

"Yes, sir. I was in the Air Force with his nephew, Murray."

"It's a small fuckin' world, kid. What brought you to Miami Beach?"

"I heard you could make good money if you're willin' to work."

"I like ya attitude. Got any I.D. on you?" he asked, smiling.

"Yes, sir."

"O.K., kid, go back to the cabana and see Sammy. He'll fill you in on the job."

"I appreciate it, Mr. Manny. I won't let'cha down."

He grinned and said, "Just call me Manny, kid."

The bartender pointed Sammy out. He was seated next to the pool with a shapely, long-legged blonde. I went over and introduced myself and told him Manny had sent me.

"You must have impressed the man. He's interviewed ten guys in the last few days. You're here less than fifteen minutes and you get the job. You know somebody," commented Sammy.

"I know Gully Silver."

"How'd you know Gully?"

"From Bo Peep's place in Savannah."

"Yeah, Manny and him go way back."

Sammy looked like he had the same ethnic heritage as Manny. After he finished explaining all my duties, I knew I was the bartender's gofer. What really puzzled me was how a two-bit job seemed like such a big deal. But I passed it off as the way I'd always heard Jews did business: nothing gets past them. We walked over to the bar and he introduced me to Eddie the bartender.

Then Sammy said, "Eddie, he's yours." He looked at me and said, "Be here tomorrow morning at nine sharp."

That night when I got back to Hollywood, Bones was two sheets to the wind. He had met a woman in Fort Lauderdale who told him about a job that paid big money, if he was willing to do it.

"Doing what?" I asked.

"I don't know yet, but she's gonna pick me up in the morning and we're going to talk with the man."

"Bones, I start tomorrow at the Roney Plaza Cabana."

"Doing what?"

"Cabana Coordinator."

"Motherfucker, you were serious about findin' a job."

"What happened to hustlin' old broads?" I asked.

"Man! You gotta perform too often for them old bitches."

"I know that's right, brother," I said, laughing.

"Reds, if this broad is right about big money, we just might hang around for a while, but if it's more prevarication, we're moving to Key West where the livin' is much easier."

I was at the cabana at 8:30 a.m. waiting on Eddie when Sammy walked up. He told me his driver hadn't shown up and asked if I could drive, and I told him I could. We walked a couple of blocks, and he handed me a set of car keys.

"We're gonna pick up some people at an airport and bring them back to the beach. All you got to do is keep your mouth shut and play it cool, kid."

Sammy drove the 1953 black Fleetwood Caddie, and I drove the 1950 Roadmaster Buick. Both looked like they were on loan from a funeral home.

At the small air strip, Sammy told me to take care of the suitcases when they arrived. He explained that his friends had been to Havana for a few days.

I watched the DC-3 make a straight-in landing. My thoughts

momentarily went back to my boarding school days, to Curley Tabares and the other Cuban cadets with their fiery spirits and intense love of country, and Curley's invitation to visit Cuba.

The aircraft rolled to a stop with the engines still running. Someone opened the door and hurriedly handed out luggage before the steps were in place to off-load the passengers. Sammy and I had all the luggage in the cars before anyone stepped off the plane.

The first person to exit looked like a Jewish Johnny Weismuller, except he didn't have any loincloth. He and Sammy walked quickly toward the cars, trying to talk over the engine's chatter. I was standing at the door of the aircraft when six other characters in flashy shirts and alligator shoes exited the plane. The propeller turbulence and noise all added to the excitement of the moment.

Sammy signaled for me to come to him. "Wait here, I'll be back for you," he shouted. The cars pulled off with Tarzan driving the Buick.

The DC-3 departed as swiftly as it had arrived. I was trying to figure it all out, but I had learned from my father never to ask any questions when you already know the answer.

On the ride back to the hotel, Sammy handed me a twenty dollar bill and said, "You're O.K., kid, but that sorry fucker that didn't show put my ass in a crack, and that won't happen again ... he's history."

When I got back to the cabana, Eddie asked why I was late. I told him that I was helping Sammy. He got this puzzled look on his face and said, "You know some guy named Bones?"

"Yeah, he's a friend of mine — why?"

"Him and this butch broad were here lookin' for ya."

"Eddie, what's a butch?"

"It's a lesbo with a twist."

"Oh! a bull dyke. I thought only black broads were dykes."

"Man! The one with your buddy is lily white. She's probably got more clit than he's got dick."

"Damn!" I whistled, impressed. "She's gotta have one hell of a clit, because Bones has got a dong big enough to wear a wristwatch on."

He laughed and said, "Man! Everybody on the beach knows that broad. Word is, her family is super wealthy. They live up North and send her money if she'll stay in the state of Florida."

"He met her yesterday. She's supposed to be helping him find a job," I explained.

"Yeah, the only job that broad could find your buddy is feeding the 'closet queens' that hang out at the Echo Club. Man, she's bad news. You'd better wise him up before he's up to his ass in cocksuckers," he said, shaking his head.

"Eddie, could ya help find him a job around here?"

"Hell no! I don't want a motherfucker with a dong like that working around me," he said, grinning. "O.K., let me tell you what your duties are. She that mop and bucket over there?"

Eddie was a trip. He was a walking encyclopedia of Who's Who of hoodlums in Broward and Dade counties. He talked about Capone and the Purple Gang like they were his long-lost family members.

He looked around like he was checking to see if anybody was listening, and asked, "Hey, kid, you know what was in those suitcases you helped Sammy unload?"

"Nah, I didn't give them any thought — none of my business."

"That's cool ... the casino's in Havana."

He'd drop names like Joe Adonis, and Meyer and Jake Lansky. At the time I didn't know who the hell he was talking about. I figured he was just an over-the-hill, bullshittin' bartender trying to impress this cracker boy.

It wasn't long after that conversation with Eddie that Sammy started using me to chauffeur him around at night. I was fascinated by his life-style. His cronies were high-rollers and gangsters and sex. Sammy was from Chicago and loved to hear my Southern drawl. Every time he got high, he'd tell me, "I'm taking you to Havana soon, kid." It was easy to like him. But I knew the bottom line, and I was headed for trouble.

"Billy Bones, I've had all of Miami Beach I can stand for a while. I'm heading back to Savannah even if I have to make bags or shovel shit. I'm burned out and ready to settle down."

"Reds, we can work the cruise boats to Cuba and make money."

"Bones, it ain't the money; it's the company we keep down here. if you don't watch it, this life-style grows on you, and then you're in a world of shit. I think you've already forgotten about suntans and a college education, haven't you?"

"Not really — it's better than a PhD," he said, smiling. "Reds, if we hang in there, we're going to make the big times. These people can make things happen for us,"Bones said, motioning to the bartender for another round of drinks.

"Yeah, I know, and that scares me. I'm catching the next bus North. If you're ready, I've got enough cash for us to get our big time asses back to Georgia."

"O.K., Reds, I'll go back, but first let's catch the forty-five cent cocktails at the Five O'Clock Club."

I knew what he was trying to pull, but I wasn't changing my mind. "All right, Slick, but tomorrow we ride."

"You got it, Reds."

That night we dressed in our best rags. You couldn't tell us from the high rollers. Bones had salted away some money. To this day, I don't know how or even what he did to make it. The only thing I'm certain of is, he had a bankroll that night. Bones was always mysterious with his money.

We hit all the joints on Dade Boulevard. One of the place's claim to fame was that it was run by Al Capone's brother. Another joint looked like an airplane hanger. They were all classy places where you couldn't act up too much or they'd throw you out, especially if you looked a little too gentile.

We met a couple of fine-looking older chicks in a lounge and sat with them. They persuaded us to enter the rumba contest. To my surprise, Billy Bones could rumba like a champ. He and his partner looked like Xavier Cugat and Carmen Miranda, and they won the contest that night. When the master of ceremonies called for the winners to come forward, they stood in the spotlight and were handed a bundle of roses. Bones kissed his partner and everyone in the club cracked up laughing. After they returned to the table, Bones said, "Reds, let's go to the head."

In the light of the restroom, I could tell Bones had something on his mind.

"That motherfucker I just kissed, needs a shave."

"What'cha mean?" I asked.

"I mean, that ain't no woman — that's a man!"

"Yeah, I got a funny feelin' about the one I'm with."

"Now I know why the lights are so low in this place."

"Bones, that's exactly why I'm goin' back to Georgia. This town is too fast for us."

As we passed Hialeah going North the next day, Bones looked at me and said, "Next time, Reds baby, we're gonna play the horses."

"It ain't gonna be a next time, Billy 'Bones' Connor."

"Reds, it's in your blood and you can't help yourself."

"Watch me," I said, closing my eyes.

I tried to sleep, but my mind was occupied with thoughts of where do I go from here. I leaned back in the seat, with my hands clasped behind my head as scenes from my life drifted past. Why do I make the same mistakes over and over? Is it booze? Lord, this crack boy sure does need your help.

I was ashamed that I hadn't spent any time with my Gongie and Papa Waters, so I went to visit them.

"Bobby, you've been giving me a wide berth lately, and I wanna know why," she asked, holding my hand.

"Gongie, I don't have any excuse — you know I love you."

"Bobby, when you love someone, you want to be with them."

"You're right."

"I know why you haven't been coming to see me and Papa. You think I'm going to preach to you."

"No, ma'am, it ain't that."

"Bobby, you're just like your daddy. I love you both, but ain't nobody gonna tell either one of you what to do."

"Gongie, you tell me and I'll do it."

"O.K., for starters, you drink too much. You need to stop and get your priorities in order."

"Yes, ma'am, I know."

"Son, you've got the Waters and Helmey blood mix. None of you can drink alcohol. You all act like monkeys. The higher you climb, the more you show your ass when you drink that old bad liquor."

"I can't argue with that, Gongie."

"Since I'm preaching, I might as well tell you one more thing. Without the Lord in your life, you ain't nothing but a monkey anyway."

"Yes, ma'am."

"One last thing, son, and I'm over my preaching. Always remember this scripture from the Bible, John 3:16: 'For God so loved the world' ... and he loves you, too."

I kissed her, and reminded her that I hadn't forgotten the hymn, 'Amazing Grace.'

As I walked out the door, she said, "I love you, Bobby." I knew she was right about what she had to say. I truly loved her and was sorry I hadn't been a better grandson.

I knew it was time to get serious about a steady job. So I put in applications with Savannah Electric and Power Company as well as Southern Bell Telephone Company. I gave up on the idea of becoming a college graduate or a Marine and reconciled myself to the fact that it was time to grow up and quit chasing dreams. After all, I was twenty years old, now. My dad had always told me about how he left home at thirteen with a hungry belly and thirteen cents in his pocket.

Part Five

WE HAVE NO CHOICE

Common sense is not so common

Voltaire

We Have No Choice

A couple of weeks had passed and I hadn't heard from any of my job applications, so I figured they just weren't hiring.

I swallowed my pride and went to the Chief and asked if he could still use me. He said he needed somebody to work the service station. "I'll pay you thirty bucks a week."

"Chief, is that for five days?" I said, grinning.

"No, sir — that's for six days."

"O.K. Chief, I knew I could never out-figure you. When can I start?"

"Right now."

"Thank you, boss-man."

During my Commerical High School days, I had dated a young attractive girl named Angelyn. She had written me several times while I was on active duty and at the University of Georgia. I had always enjoyed her company and she seemed to enjoy mine.

Nick Bougas was dating Angelyn's best friend, Joyce Caterina. We'd all go to the Dixie Land Drive-in, watch free movies, drink beer we had smuggled in, and do a little smooching.

Our bull sessions seemed to always get around to matrimony. The moral philosophy passed on to the young women of the fifties by their parents and society was, catch a young man with a job and marry him as quickly as possible; or, every good girl must be married shortly after high school, have at least three children and live happily ever after. They really thought they had no other choice in the matter.

Soon circumstances dictated that neither one of us had much of a choice in the matter.

"Bobby, we've got to talk."

"About what, Angelyn?"

"My mother knows we've been having sex. Bobby, we've got to get married," she said, sobbing softly.

Saying NO was the hardest word in the English language and the one that had caused me the most problems. It happened so fast it was hard to figure it out. We both wanted to do what was right. I honestly can't say I was in love because I didn't know what love was. I can't speak for Angelyn, but at seventeen, her mother apparently called that shot. We never discussed our feelings about the present or future with each other.

The marriage ceremony in Ridgeland, South Carolina, was conducted by the magistrate and was as fast as our pre-nuptials. My old friend, Ducky Moore, was the best man. After the civil ceremony he said, "I wish you both the best, but, Angelyn, don't let him take you to Tijuana for a honeymoon."

"He ain't takin' me anywhere, Ducky."

That statement proved to be deadly accurate because the next twenty-seven years were spent within hollering distance of her mother's house. As far as a honeymoon, we had just enough money for one night at the DeSoto Beach Hotel and that was located only twenty miles from her parents' home.

Getting serious about a steady job wasn't an option anymore, it was a matter of arithmetic. Rent, food, and the fact that Angelyn was pregnant dictated it. I knew there was no way we could make it on what my father could afford to pay. I'd always said that I would never work at a paper mill. But I was learning that every time I said I wouldn't do a certain thing, that's exactly what I had to do. There were two things that scared me about paper mills — the odor, and the thought of spending the rest of your life in the same place doing the same thing. I don't know if it was fate or predestination, but the morning I decided to go to Union Camp, I stopped by Southern Bell's office to check on my application.

"Mr. Helmey, we've been trying to get in touch with you. Could you talk with Mr. DeGaris today?"

"Yes, Ma'am, I sure could."

My interview with Mr. Fred DeGaris didn't take as long as it took to get married in Ridgeland.

"Mr. Helmey, can you report to our work center on Gwinnett Street, Monday morning at 8:00 a.m.?"

"Yes, sir, I'll be there early," I said, smiling.

It was one of those times you don't forget. I was so excited I could hardly wait to get home and tell Angelyn the good news.

"Bobby, Savannah Electric called and they want you to report to work Monday," Angelyn said, smiling.

"Girl! I've just accepted a position with Ma Bell. Damn, when it rains it pours," I said excitedly.

"Yeah! Red and Ruth (her parents) are gonna be glad to hear the news — I can't wait to tell them."

"How about you, honey?" I asked.

"You know I am, we got a young'n on the way."

Our first child, a beautiful little girl, Saundra Kim, was born January 16, 1954. Since our marriage on April 23, 1953, my world seemed to have done an about-face. I was married to a good girl, had a job and a healthy child. What else could a young man ask for? Yet I couldn't shake the feeling.

Everytime I drank, I thought about the military career I'd screwed up. I knew I could forget that dream, but it still obsessed me. I always felt a little selfish after it was all over. I knew that deep down in Angelyn's heart, her dreams were upside down, too. But, what the hell? Life ain't fair anyway, I thought. Let the hair go with the hide, was always the Helmey antidote for everything.

A lot of the guys at the Telephone Company were ex-Marines. I would hear their war stories. They would always end the bull sessions with, "If this country ain't careful, the Communists won't have to fire a shot — these long-haired

'Beatniks' are gonna give the damn thing away."

Jimmy Prince, one of my new friends at the Telephone Company, asked me about joining the Marine Reserves.

"Jim, I screwed up so bad in the Air Force, I don't think they'd let me join the Salvation Army."

"Reds, let me worry about that."

"Yeah, but I've had a couple of courts-martial."

"Just go with me Friday night and check it out."

Jimmy was right. I don't know what he said to the recruiting sergeant, but he made me feel like the U.S. Marine Reserves really needed me. The paperwork, physical, and swearing-in ceremony were all done that night before I left the Wheaton Street Training Center.

"Welcome aboard, Helmey," said, Major Vernon W. Risher.

"Thank you — I'm proud to be aboard, sir."

Nick and Joyce had married. Nick worked with his father at the Silver Moon Bar and Grill. My job as a telephone repairman gave me the flexibility to travel around Savannah. If I was on the west side of town, I loved nothing better than having lunch with Nick and his dad at the Silver Moon. They had the best sausage sandwiches in the world. I also loved to hear Mr. Nick tell about life in the old country and how lucky we were to live in America.

"America! America, it's a great cuntree, but it won't last unless de young folks change ... like a big tree without da roots. Everytime the wind blow hard, she gonna fall over. Everybody needa da roots. Young people don't got no pride." He said the family was the most important thing in life.

Later in life, those days would whisper from the past, reminding me that Mr. Nick was a wise man and a good father.

In the summer of '55 I trained with the 5th Rifle Company, U.S.M.C.R., at Camp LeJeune, North Carolina. The Marines were everything I expected and more. I loved the *esprit de corps*, the camaraderie — the feeling that you were a member of a brotherhood.

I returned to Savannah with that same dream of a military career. Now that I was married, had a child, and was only a Pfc in the reserves, my rank and number of dependents didn't meet the enlistment criteria for the regular Marine Corps. My only chance was to make sergeant in the reserves and then request active duty. I was still determined to try, even though I'd promised myself to give up the dream. I also knew that it would be next to impossible to convince Angelyn to leave Savannah and her mother. But I couldn't give up on the possibility.

"These be some serious times," said an elderly colored lady as I changed the number on her telephone. It seemed like an accurate observation because science and technology had reached the point where man could destroy the planet.

The telephone company had recently converted to a system where two additional digits were added to the dialing, which now included the prefix, Adams. I had been dispatched on a complaint to the lady's home. She insisted on my replacing the new telephone set with her old one. She was convinced this new-fangled telephone was part of that atomic technology.

"Lord, this world is in a mess now because of these *AD*am bombs. Please sir, put my old telephone set back in, and take this devilish thing out. The Lord will bless ya if you do," she said, her voice cracking slighty.

There was a public hysteria about the bomb. With doomsday prophecies running wild, people seemed unsure of the future in '56.

At the reserves we had to watch training films on how the Communists were infiltrating every aspect of American society, the film industry, labor unions, government and even the PTA, according to Senator Joseph McCarthy's inquisition.

People were building bomb shelters in their backyards and looking for Commies under every rock. It was truly serious times we lived in.

"Bull shit! You're a Green Beret."

I'd heard some pretty terrifying accounts of torture by the Cuban G2 Security Police. They had the power of life or death over the people of Cuba. They could search and arrest anybody at will. In many cases, the persons arrested were never heard of again. Now I was seated at a desk facing an officer of that feared police.

"Do you know where you are?"

"Yes, in Cuba," I replied.

"Why are you here, Holmey?" he asked, lighting a small black cigar.

"To speak with Fidel Castro."

"That's impossible," he laughed.

"Why?" I asked.

This answer obviously upset him. He stood up quickly with a look of outrage on his face. Removing his Tokarev TT-33 pistol from its holster, he slammed it on the desk. "I'm not here to answer your questions. This is Cuba. Unlike your country, we have no pimp politicians controlling our authority. For the last time, what is your connection with the CIA and why are you here?

"I don't know anything about the CIA. I only wish to talk with Fidel."

"Bullshit, this card identifies you as a member of the 11th Special Forces, a Green Beret and a trained CIA whore."

"I'll clear all this up if you let me speak with Fidel Castro."

"The bastards who killed Che Guevara and sent his severed hands to Fidel are the same breed of dog as you, Holmey," he said, fidgeting nervously with his pistol.

He then walked out of the room leaving the weapon on the desk in front of me. I knew he had done it deliberately, and that it was probably unloaded, but I would never know because I had no intention of touching it to find out. He was gone for what seemed like hours. I was sleepy and almost dropped off, but my mind was full of the things I'd learned about Castro.

At first I believed in the man. I thought he was a real hero of the oppressed people of Cuba. Batista was a puppet of the Mafia and anybody else who would grease his palm.

But on May 1, 1961, Castro showed his true colors in a speech that helped change my mind about him.

"I am a Marxist-Leninist. I have been a Communist all my life," he announced to the world.

Skreech, skreech, skreech, was a sound that would become forebodingly familiar to me over the next few months. Every Cuban soldier's boots made a sickening squeak.

"*Arriba, arriba,* Holmey!"

As I stood to my feet the officer pointed me to the door where the same soldiers who had brought me from the airport were waiting.

Hugh "Red" Dent, my father-in law, was a wise man, a prodigy of the school of hard knocks. "You're living in the best of times, Bobby."

He told me about the struggles of his youth, no jobs, no money, and damn little food to be found during the '20s and '30s. He had hitched rides on freight trains from coast to coast looking for any kind of work. At sixteen he stowed away on a passenger ship sailing from Savannah to New York. After being discovered at sea, he was forced by the ship's captain to work in the galley to pay his passage. When the ship arrived in New York, he was locked aboard and compelled to work his way back to Savannah to make restitution. Red was right — we did live in better times when you compared the '50s with all I'd heard about the Great Depression.

He was a realist in the truest sense of the word and was eager to give sound advice. He lent me the down payment for our first house, which was only three blocks from theirs. Angelyn made her daily pilgrimage to visit her mother. I was a little jealous at first; there was a lot I didn't know about family life in those early years. But it felt good to be part of a family which was able to sit down and discuss things without always ending up in an argument.

Angelyn and I had agreed that Kim would be our only child. We blew that agreement and a few others. Our second child, Kerry McRae, was born on May 10, 1956. Kelly Hugh, our third child, was born March, 23, 1959.

In the Marine Reserves, I was promoted to Sergeant E-5 Permanent, and the possibility of active duty came back to haunt me.

About that time a mercenary named Fidel Castro had taken over in Cuba. I was watching the television as Castro's troops and tanks entered Havana like conquering heroes. Huge crowds sang and embraced them, others held up placards inscribed, "*Gracias, Fidel!*" With his rifle slung over his shoulder, he mounted the palace steps and walked up to a microphone to address the people of Cuba. Then I recognized my old quizzer schoolmate, Curly Tabares, standing in the crowd near Castro with a weapon over his shoulder. I remembered the last words he said to me: "Man is the only patriot, and he sets himself apart ... don't forget that, my friend."

There really wasn't a lot of extra time for Angelyn and me to work on our relationship. It was the same old routine. Taking care of three children and the house filled her days. My job and the reserves seemed to leave little time for much else. Many of the young couples we knew were in the same boat.

Despite the unmentionable reason we were married, Angelyn and I were perceived by our families and many of our friends as a perfectly-matched couple.

American Legion Post 135 was not only the birthplace of "The Mighty 8th Air Force" but it was home of the much-touted Lemon Dances of the '50s and '60s. On Saturday nights, the Russ Peacock Orchestra transformed the dance floor into a panacea for those who loved to engage in amorous flirtations, and a safety valve for bored couples.

Before each Lemon Dance, an announcement was made by the band. The Post Commander or his designee would randomly pass out lemons to a few of the couples, which permitted them to cut in on whomever they pleased. The person who received the lemon could do the same, swap it for another dance partner.

When the dance ended, those left holding a lemon had to pay a fine. It was like hunting is to the hounds.

Some stalked their prey like half-starved cats. Others searched as if they were on a quest for the forbidden fruit. A few cared less who their partners were as long as they didn't get caught with the lemon and have to pay the fiddler when the music stopped and the lights suddenly came on.

Usually, Nick danced with Angelyn, and I tripped the light fantastic with Joyce.

After dancing and rubbing elbows for hours, the guys would wind up at one end of the table and the gals at the other. We guys assumed that the girls were comparing notes on the virtues of married life or other high-principled things that nice Southern girls should busy themselves with. However, we really never knew what they were discussing because they did so much whispering and giggling. Our conversations centered on sex, softball, and subjective politics.

"Hey! I read an Associated Press story about a hit squad trying to kill Castro. The Cubans believed the would-be assassins were from the Dominican Republic and were hired by our CIA. Reds, I thought Fidel Castro was your hero," Pete said sarcastically.

"Well, he looked good at first — time will tell," I said.

"Yeah, he's startin' to take over American companies and properties," Charlie added. "Next it'll be the hotels and casinos."

"You can kiss his ass good-bye," Nick added. "The Mafia ain't gonna let that happen."

Pete slurred, "Reds, you'd better get out of that Reserve before Eisenhower has your ass charging up San Juan Hill."

"Yeah, did y'all read the story in the *New York Times* by a guy named Matthews who says Castro is a freedom fighter, and he ain't no Communist," Nick remarked.

"Man! Who reads that fuckin' Yankee propaganda sheet?" Charlie replied.

"I do! You bunch of dumb crackers, that's real news."

"Greek, the only thing that's real in this friggin' world is mother's milk and the seductive Lemon Dance," I said.

"Reds! You've become a philosophical motherfucker since you read that *Huckleberry Finn* book," Nick said grinning.

"You guys get serious. Look at the ass on that blonde tiptoeing across the dance floor." Charlie said, chuckling.

"Charlie, cool it man. Sara is watchin'."

"Yeah, so is Angelyn."

The American Legion was a bastion of what America was all about in those days — our country, right or wrong.

The 19th Hole Bar & Package shop wasn't your average watering hole. It was like Gildea's, except it had more listeners than talkers. It was beyond a shadow of doubt the best gossip grapevine on my side of town. You could voice your political preference without fear or prejudice, especially when you bought a round of drinks. In those days, grass was mowed, Coke was a drink, and pot was something you cooked in.

Usually, after drills on Saturday afternoon, a group of us from the 5th Rifle Company would meet at the 19th Hole to unwind. It seemed our conversations always centered on some crisis in the world that held the possibility of our being called to serve our country.

Cuban Communism became a campaign issue in the 1960 Presidential race. Nixon and Kennedy tried to outdo each other on the issue. Castro had now formed a ruthless, Moscow-supported military regime that jailed and murdered dissidents, ending any vestige of legal process, and put Cuba on a totally socialist footing. America was now Cuba's archenemy. Betrayed by Castro, many of the ones who had helped Castro to power found their way to exile in Miami where they were taken into the welcoming embrace of the CIA.

"Pardon me, Marines. I'd like to buy jew a round of drinks," said the man with a Spanish accent.

"Have a seat, friend," the gunnery sergeant answered.

After a few rounds of drinks, the man told us about himself, a Cuban ship's captain who had delivered sugar to the Savannah refinery for many years, but had recently fled Cuba because of the Communists.

He told us he had grown up in Oriente Province, near Fidel Castro's father's farm. "Angel Castro is a murderer, a swindler, and helped the Nazis during the World War. Maybe the apple falls close to the tree," he said excitedly.

When he spoke, I saw that same fiery spirit I'd seen years earlier in my Cuban friends at Porter Military Academy. He informed us that there was a group of mercenaries being trained in Florida by the CIA for an invasion of Cuba.

One of the regular Marines assigned to our Company as an instructor was seated with us. He confirmed that the captain knew what he was talking about. His last duty station had been on the Island of Vieques in the Caribbean. "I know that something hush-hush is going on down there, but it's supposed to be Top Secret," he said, jokingly.

"Shit, we'll never be called up for a Cuba war. It wouldn't take a squad of Girl Scouts to take that fuckin' island back," said the gunny, as he wobbled out the door.

Finally, only the captain and I were left at the table, and the bar was about to close. I offered him a ride. He accepted and I took him to the Cuban *Charge d'Affaires* office which was only a short drive from the bar. At the time it seemed odd because I had just read an article in the press about the closing of the Savannah office. The United States Government had seized Cuba's money in local banks in retaliation for Cuba's nationalizing of American-owned companies and property in that country.

Before he got out of the truck, I asked if he could tell me how I could talk to someone about the possibility of joining the guerrilla operations against Castro.

"Only de Cuban exiles are being trained now — but maybe some special mercenaries are being hired by the CIA. Jew would hab to go to Miami and talk wid de people," he said, writing something on a card. "Be bery careful in Miami. There are many pro-Castro people dere," he said, handing me the card.

"How do you know, which is which?" I asked.

"Jew don't! Maybe dis card will help jew find the right people," he said, grinning.

"Captain, did you ever run into a man named Curley Tabres in Cuba?"

He paused a moment, then shook his head and said, "No."

"How can I get in touch with you?" I asked, as he opened the truck door.

"Jew can't. *Buenos noches*," he said, walking away.

The next day when I told Nick about the conversation I'd had with the captain, he asked me all kinds of questions. The thing that surprised me most was his interest in going to Miami and checking it out. I had always known that he was a romantic.

"Let me hold that card," Nick said. "All this thing says is, C. Lopez, Miami Detective Agency, Flagler and 7th streets. Man! There ain't even a telephone number."

"That's all he gave me, Nick."

"Is he still in Savannah?"

"No, I don't think so. Before I came over, I went to where I'd dropped him off and talked with a Mrs. Mendes. She acted like I was crazy as hell and said she didn't know any such man."

A big smile twisted across Nick's round face, "Well, she was right about one thing ..."

"Nick! You just don't have a heart, my friend."

"I wonder how much the CIA pays its mercenaries?"

"Nick, the only way we can find out is from the horse and he's in Miami."

"Reds, I ain't gettin' my rear shot off for no romantic, soldier-of-fortune bullshit. No money, no go," Nick added. "Joyce is gonna be out of town for a few days. If I can work somethin' out with my Dad, we will go."

"O.K., I've got a long weekend coming up. Let's do it."

"Man! What's gonna happen if we cut a deal?" Nick asked.

"Shit, if that happens our brides would be happy, we'd be able to send them some serious bread," I said.

We drove south on U.S. 17 toward Miami.

"I don't know what I'm doing with you two crazy motherfuckers," commented Gary Wise, another wild friend we'd recruited.

"Gary, this ought to be a vacation for you — don't this beat the hell out of bricklaying?" Nick asked.

"I'll answer that question after I see what the job pays."

We had my old Ford station wagon loaded down with military equipment: survival gear, semi-automatic rifles with high-powered scopes, hand guns and enough ammunition to start a war. I had driven most of the night and was pretty tired. So I pulled over at a truck stop for breakfast and a short rest.

"Hey! Wake-up, it's time to feed the alligators."

"Man, fuck the gators," Gary said as he sat up.

"Where we at, Reds?" Nick asked.

"Near Fort Lauderdale," I answered.

"I'm hungry, I need grits and eggs," Gary said, yawning.

"Reds, tell this cracker they don't eat grits down here," quipped Nick, as he picked up a Miami newspaper.

"Yeah, Corn Bread! I know this is the farthest you've ever been from home. But act like you got some class and eat hash browned potatoes in this neck of the woods," I said.

"Fuck Yankees and potatoes this early in the morning."

Nick interrupted. "Nixon's speaking at the American Legion Convention in Miami today according to this newspaper."

"Yeah! He'll be our next president," Gary blurted.

"Bullshit!"

"Nick, Kennedy's an Irish Catholic. He's got about as much chance of bein' elected president as Adam Clayton Powell has of joinin' the Knights of the Klu Klux Klan."

"Corn Bread, Kennedy's a real American hero; he saved the crew of his P.T. boat after a Jap destroyer rammed them. The man's got balls, and that's what this country needs."

"How you know all that bullshit, Nick?"

"Unlike your cracker ass, I read the newspaper everyday."

"Hey, let's eat breakfast and forget politics," I said.

"Nick, I ain't no damn Republican, but ..." As we drove off, Nick and Gary were still knocking heads over who would be elected our next president.

"Nick, check that paper and see if you can find a Miami Detective Agency with a Lopez in the ads."

After arriving in the Little Havana district of Miami, we telephoned every Lopez and detective agency in the area directory, but to no avail.

Eventually, we parked near Flagler and 7th Streets, hoping to find the recruiting cover for the Cuban freedom fighters and mercenaries mentioned by the boat captain.

I walked to a service station which appeared to be a hub of activity at that intersection. When I asked this well-dressed mulatto standing outside the station if he could tell me where the Lopez Detective agency was, he yelled something to another high yellow a short distance away. That person started shouting obscenities in Spanish. I knew it was time to leave. Before I could get back to the wagon, I had to use a snub-nosed .38 to convince the two men who had followed me to back off.

When I finally got back to the wagon, Nick and Gary had opened a bottle of Jack Daniels and were feeling no pain. After I told them what had happened, they wanted to go find the two. But I suggested that we should just go on down to Key West and find a ride to Cuba.

Nick said, "Man, fuck these strange motherfuckers. I thought they needed some help getting rid of Castro. We'd been better off goin' to Washington and seein' the Director in person."

"Man! Gimme a shot of that Black Jack," I said.

On the trip back to Savannah we stopped over at Daytona Beach and vented our frustrations with some Florida State girls.

* * *

Nick's prediction of Kennedy's being elected proved to be accurate. His short story characterizing Kennedy as a real American hero inspired me to vote for the man. It was my second time picking a presidential winner. My first was Ike in '53. I had no problem believing Eisenhower was right for the job. He had been a general of the Army and that was good enough for me. Nixon would have gotten my vote solely because he didn't take any crap from Nikita Khrushchev on his visit to Russia when he was Vice President.

After hearing John Kennedy's inaugural address, a new spirit was awakened within me.

> Let the word go forth from this time and place, to
> friend and foe alike ... that the torch has been passed
> to a new generation of Americans born this century.

What he said that day in January, 1961, sounded as strong as green onions. He ended with a phrase that would become famous and would touch my heart like the old hymn, 'Amazing Grace.'

> And so, my fellow Americans, ask not what your
> country can do for you, ask what you can do for
> your country.

The secret invasion plot that the Cuban sugar boat captain had told me about proved to be one of the worse-kept secrets in American history. A handful of journalists had uncovered most of the plans and had interviewed Cuban exiles during their training in the Florida Everglades and Guatemala. Consequently, the media unwittingly tipped off Castro and the world.

On April 17, 1961, some 1,400 Cubans, poorly trained and underequipped, were set down on the beach at the Bay of Pigs. The death toll was 114 Cuban invaders and many more defenders killed in the fighting; 1,189 others from "La Brigada" were captured and held prisoner until they were ransomed from Cuba by Robert Kennedy for food and medical supplies. Four American fliers, members of the Alabama Air National Guard working for the CIA, died in the invasion, but the American government never acknowledged their existence or their connection to the not-so-secret operation orchestrated by the CIA.

The war jitters erupted from events happening all over the world: Soviet Russia exploded a "monster bomb" in the atmosphere over Siberia. In Berlin, the Communists were building a wall dividing Germany. Southeast Asia was engulfed in conflict; both Laos and South Vietnam were in a state of civil war. President Kennedy sent a military adviser to Saigon to determine the extent of American military and economic aid necessary to defend that country. At home he called 100,000 reservists to active duty.

In my personal life, it seemed those same feelings of uncertainty and wariness that prevailed in the world also spilled over into my marriage. I had come to believe that a man's role in the marriage knot was to provide the material needs of his family. I turned my pay check over to my wife, didn't lay down a bunch of rules, and I never beat her or the children. What else could I do? I'd always heard that you couldn't satisfy a woman, no matter how hard you tried.

A woman's place was to raise the children, do the cooking, keep the house, be submissive in the bedroom, and be thankful for the opportunity. It seemed I could never satisfy Angelyn based on these learned beliefs of mine, and that bothered me greatly. But I had seen enough of the Helmey psychology in action to understand that a woman ain't supposed to run a man's life. I didn't know what I didn't know. Marriage was an enigma to me.

Angelyn strongly suspected that I was running around on her. She accused me of all kinds of things and said she wasn't going to put up with my crap anymore.

One particular night, I was late getting home after a league softball game, and she was waiting up for me with fire in her eyes.

After I took off my pants to get in bed, much to my surprise she discovered that I had my drawers on backwards. I couldn't explain it fast enough for her satisfaction.

"Bobby, you smell like a wild whore and it looks like lipstick on your drawers!" she yelled out, waking the kids.

That same night Joyce accused Nick of an affair with some mysterious woman who had been looking for a house to rent in their neighborhood. Nick's story was that the lady had mistakenly written down the wrong address and was lost. Nick saw her predicament and asked if she would like to come in and use their telephone. When Joyce arrived home, she found Nick and the woman seated on the couch having a drink.

Joyce said, "They had sheepish looks on their faces. The woman was dressed like a hussy and had a white silk scarf wrapped around her arm, shrouding a missing left hand."

Nick said, "I guess that's why the fuckin' woman had the wrong address. She couldn't write good with a missing hand. Besides, I felt sorry for the bitch."

Angelyn and Joyce seemed to support one another in their resolve to catch us monkeying around.

The next day after work, Angelyn and the children weren't home when I arrived. Nick came over about dark and we started talking about all that was going on with our wives and their crazy accusations of our unfaithfulness. We had a few beers and laughed about the whole thing, not knowing that Joyce and Angelyn had crawled under the house on their bellies and were listening from beneath the floor to our conversation.

Angelyn later said I was joking and laughing about running around on her. Her ears either lied to her or the strain of being under the house caused her to have an acoustic distortion of some sort. I never said anything like that. But Nick and I were talking about some of the wild times we had before we were married, the kinds of things a woman would never understand. Joyce went to Nick's father and he recommended that she talk with an attorney. She took his advice, and she and Angelyn went to see H. Sol. Clark, attorney at law.

Skidaway Road was the main artery I drove every day. It was my pathway to work; the street on which the U.S. Marine Reserve Armory was located and home of the 19th Hole. I could drive it blindfolded. The first thing I heard as I walked in the back door of the Hole was, "Reds, did Fish (Angelyn's nickname) kick you out of the house?"

"Yeah, I'm on my way to a three o'clock appointment with Brannan, Clark & Hester. You bunch of reprobates know if someone breaks wind a mile away from here, don't you?" I said, laughing.

"Man, these old farts gossip worse than women," Harry the bartender shouted.

"The problem with you boys today is that ya let women rule your life — I'm the head of my house."

"Bullshit, Smokey, the only thing you're head of is your short pecker and big mouth," Harry said.

I was a little uptight because I had to meet with an attorney. I'd always heard that divorce lawyers were unethical characters and some even exchanged sex for legal fees. So, I was pumped up I when walked into Mr. Clark's office. But, after talking with him for a while, I realized how wrong I'd been in judging all lawyers as scoundrels. His concern and frankness impressed me. He gave the kind of counsel you'd expect to get from your pastor, or in his case a rabbi, because he was Jewish.

"Mr. Helmey, your wife says she wants her freedom."

It was then I realized that Angelyn had come to grips with some of her frustrations over our detached marriage.

"Reds, what did Mr. Clark tell you?" asked Nick.

"He said Angelyn wants out. Then he told me that marriage was like a savings account — if you didn't deposit, you couldn't withdraw."

"I wonder what the fuck he meant by that?" asked Nick.

"Man, I don't know, that's one of those Jewish proverbs. So, what'd he tell you?"

"He said that Joyce loves me and only wants me to straighten up. Now, ain't that a bitch? How much straighter could I be?" Nick snapped. "Reds, Angelyn's mama ain't gonna let her divorce you — Ruth knew what she was doin' when she picked you."

"I'm serious, Nick. It's hard to believe that Angelyn and I have been playin' a game for eight years."

"Reds, life is a fucking game anyway you cut it. If you want my advice, get the hell out of Savannah."

"I've tried; remember two years ago when I transferred to Atlanta with the phone company? That didn't last three months. Angelyn's like a homing pigeon — when the sun goes down, she's heading for the barn."

"Hey, what can I say?" Nick remarked. "Straighten her ass up. Me and Joyce might leave Savannah ourselves."

"I guess you're right, Greek."

"Reds baby, you know I'm always right," he said, smiling.

"Yeah, and that scares me," I said.

"Ain't nothin' scares you except your mother-in-law."

I knew our marriage had had more than its share of ups and downs but I never suspected that Angelyn was ready to throw in the towel. Her "freedom" statement to Mr. Clark totally overwhelmed me — I felt rage and rejection at the same time.

Something an old black man once told me suddenly came to mind. "There's only two kinds of women in the world. One is named Leaner, and the other is named Lifter. A Leaner will always push ya down and destroy you. A Lifter will hold you up, in the bad times and good times.

Angelyn seemed to have a little of both.

I thought, if she believed our marriage had been a cakewalk for me, she was sadly mistaken, and I wanted my freedom too. I'd done what was right. I'd worked hard to provide a home for her and the kids; while she was free to ride around and go to her mother's daily, I was humping telephone poles.

I was torn between pride and common sense. I didn't want to go home and face her with what I had known for eight years. We should have never married. I also knew our problems were no more her fault than mine, yet we were both guilty of the same mistake — wanting to please someone else. Now there were three children who needed a father and mother.

I can't remember all that was said that day, but we decided against divorce. The reason was the children. At least, that's how we justified it to ourselves and others.

Nick accepted a job in Washington, D.C. with the Marriott Corporation's Hot Shoppes. He and Joyce agreed that their problems were related to his occupation and possibly the Savannah lifestyle. It was strange how some things were perceived — the 'ole sod' got more than its share of the blame in those days.

It was hard to believe that my best friends were leaving. The weekend before they left, all the old gang got together at the American Legion for a farewell party: 'I can't stop lovin' you ... I've made up my mind ... to live in mis..ery.'

As Joyce and I danced to that song, I was glad there were no windows in my head. It was hard to hide my heart. I had never told a soul how I felt about her, not even her. Nick was my best friend and that pretty well settled that. I knew she only looked on me as a friend. But, it still hurt like hell. I truly loved the girl. This would probably be our last Lemon Dance, and she'd never know how I felt about her.

The week after they left, I went to see the First Sergeant of the Fifth Rifle Company.

"Sergeant, I want to go regular Marine Corps."

"Helmey, it's the same story. You don't meet the criteria. But I can get you in a regular Marine Corps school and that will help you make staff, and then there's a better possibility."

"What kind of a school are you talking about, Sarge?"

"Here's a list of available schools. You pick one."

"Sergeant, my problem is the telephone company only gives me two weeks a year for reserve training."

"Reds, I can't help you with that. Let me know what you can work out, and we'll go from there."

The Chief had recently purchased his partner's share of their lumber and building supply company and now was the sole owner. I had previously talked with him about working for him if the opportunity ever presented itself and he could use me.

"Bobby, are you sure you wanna quit the telephone company and work for me?" my dad asked.

"Yes, sir."

The Chief and I talked for at least thirty minutes or more, setting an all-time conversation record between the two of us. That day we agreed I'd work for him at the same salary the telephone company was paying. He also would allow me the time off to attend reserve training and schools, provided it would be at the government's expense.

I talked it over with Angelyn and she agreed. I felt good about that because it was the second time in our marriage we'd agreed on anything. But I did feel a little bad that I hadn't been completely honest with her or the Chief about my motives at the time. I submitted a letter of resignation to Southern Bell and went to work for Savannah Planing Mill Company.

"First Sergeant, I'm ready for that school now, and I know which one I want to attend," I said.

"Which one, Helmey?"

"Escape, Evasion and Survival at the Cold Weather Training Center at Bridgeport, California."

"Helmey, you picked a ball buster. They separate the men from the boys at Pickle Meadows. Are you sure that's the one you want?"

"Yes Sergeant, that's the one."

"O.K. Reds, I'll put in your request today," he said.

As the aircraft lifted off the ground and disappeared in the clouds, I sat reading the *Savannah Morning News* headlines of March 16, 1962 : "Airliner Crashes In Ocean; An airliner with 107 aboard, including 93 U.S. soldiers, is lost en route from Guam to South Vietnam; it is believed to have crashed in the ocean...."

An Air Force Captain seated next to me asked, "Where you headed, Sergeant?"

I laid the newspaper down and said, "Escape and Evasion School at Pickle Meadows, California, sir."

"I'll be damned. So am I, but I'm going to Fallon, Nevada."

"Sir, would you happen to know where South Vietnam is?"

"I'm not really sure — I think somewhere in Southeast Asia."

Part Six

'THE RIDERLESS HORSE'

In the helmet of the Soldier
nestles a dove of peace
Unknown

"The Riderless Horse"

Marine Corps Cold Weather Training Center,
Bridgeport, California.
Escape and Evasion School, March, 1962.

"Welcome to Pickle Meadows, I'm Colonel Martin, the Commanding Officer of the Training Center. Good to have you aboard. The Commandant of the Corps has seen fit to train you in the art of escape, evasion, and survival. Probably those of you who are married have already learned some of the techniques," he said with a sly grin. "Korea was a hard lesson for POW's. Many young Americans died needlessly because they didn't know how to survive behind the barbed wire of POW camps.

"The Code of Conduct says, 'I am bound to give only my name, rank, serial number, and date of birth.' The enemy can take everything you have, including your life. The only thing he can't take is your self-respect, you have to give him that. People and Marines can be divided into three groups: those who make things happen, those who watch things happen, and those who wonder what the fuck happened. When this class is over and if you're still around, you'll know what group you're in. Anybody that wants out can quit at anytime. Remember, conduct yourselves as Marines and act accordingly and you won't have a damned thing to fear from anybody. Semper Fi, and now, Gunnery Sergeant Martinez, your NCOIC."

There was the crunching of feet on the crisp snow as the column of Marines, weaponless for once, moved along the frozen trail surrounded by mountains and hills.

The blaring of bugles and automatic weapons' fire came as

a bolt from the blue. It was as bizarre as anything I'd ever experienced. A banzai charge of assault troops wearing Chinese quilted uniforms and sneakers came down the snow-covered slopes encircling the column. My first reaction was to haul ass, but there was no place to hide. To my left was a mountain stream and in all other directions these Mongolian hordes. My first thought was that it was just another war game. But the way they pounced on us, the realism was startling.

One of the Mongol aggressors knocked me to the ground with his rifle butt and two others shoved my face in the snow. At first, I figured they'd stepped over the line, or gone completely apeshit.

"Strip, Marine!" he yelled out like a lunatic.

"You bastards are crazy," I groaned out.

I could see other Marines being roughed up. Some were herded into small groups and marched off by our make-believe captors.

After forcing me to strip naked, the three marched me to the frozen stream. At the icy water's edge, I decided to play their game with all that was in me. I stood there shivering from the cold. I was pissed at these bad actors' attempt at making fun of my shriveled-up gonads and realizing that's exactly how they wanted me to react.

"All capitalists have little dicks and dirty asses. Get in the water and clean yourself, comrade."

"It'll take all three of you Charlie Chan-lookin' cocksuckers to put me in that ice water," I said.

I'm sure had it been a real life situation, they would have shot me and thrown my naked body in the creek. I gave them a good scuffle, but in the end they managed to throw me in. The shock when I hit the water was a bitch. I stood there in the waist deep water, teeth chattering, speechless.

"O.K. Comrade, get out of the water before you freeze to death."

"Fuc...fuc..fuck you. If you wan...t me, come get me," I sputtered.

As traumatized as I was, I didn't budge.

"You hardheaded bastard, come out of that water or we're coming in to get you," one of them shouted, and that's exactly what they had to do. After they dragged me ashore and returned my clothing, one of them gave me the evil eye and said, "Where the fuck are you from, wildman?"

"Helmey, Robert M., Sergeant, 1547729, 10-26-32."

As the Cuban soldier slammed my cell door, I felt as if I were being buried alive. The deafening clang resonated through my body. I explored the cell, but there wasn't much exploring to be done. It was the size of a small bathroom. I could lie down in the middle of the floor and touch every wall with my hands and feet. There were no windows, only vents near the ten foot-high ceiling.

A dim light came from two bulbs, one in the center of the ceiling, the other set behind a metal grate in the wall over the door. The switch outside was controlled by the guards.

There were names, dates and other words scratched in the masonry walls. Some things were scrawled in human feces and blood.

A missing toilet now consisted of a hole in the floor, topped by a board. Above the hole was a water spigot that was also controlled from outside the cell. The smells coming from the hole hit like a 2x4, attacked every sense. Solid, putrid, it was the stench of human excrement, urine, and rotting refuse.

At first, nothing unnerved me more than the horrifying screams that echoed in the night. I was in a prison within a prison in this Cuban solitaire.

The walk to the POW camp took about an hour. My clothes were dry, but my captors shivered in their wet uniforms.

It was the beginning of a long night.

"Comrade 49, you could save yourself this misery if you'd just tell us what unit you belong to."

"Helmey, Sergeant, 1547729, 10-26-32."

"Take him to the snake-pit!" shouted the interrogator.

I was so tired from the cold and constant interrogations, I could hardly think. It was hard to separate reality from fiction. My body was telling me this was real, but my brain was saying it was only a game.

Then I was shown a box containing an big ugly snake. Both my body and mind agreed that the serpent was real. "This is one of the most deadly species of reptile known to man. A North American Snow Viper. Better known as, The Icicle Snake." I didn't like the idea of what they might do with it.

Then they took me over to another box that looked like a wooden coffin with a hole in the center of the lid.

"Get in the box, Comrade 49," commanded the guard.

A short scuffle ensued, and I was forced into the box.

"Comrade, unless you tell," a voice said from the outside. "We're putting the snake in with you."

My first thought was to tell them anything they wanted to hear, but then I realized they'd still put that fucking snake in the box and laugh at me. "Screw you," I said.

"O.K. Comrade, we're putting the snake in the hole, and you'll feel him on your belly as he crawls in."

I could feel it touching my stomach. I closed my eyes so tight I couldn't see anything. I could only feel the weight of the snake as he crawled down.

One of my guards shouted, "Comrade, the reason this snake is so deadly is because of its chilling effect as it crawls up your ass and into your belly and freezes you to death. There was belly-busting laughter from outside.

When they opened the box, an ugly rubber snake lay on my stomach. Even if they'd used the real reptile, it wouldn't have mattered because my ass was drawn so tight nothing could have penetrated it, not even a snow snake.

The remainder of the POW portion of the school was spent in Communist interrogations and indoctrination methods. More candidates dropped out of the course during that phase of training than any other.

We were also schooled in the techniques of escape and evasion, the fundamentals of survival, and ended with an 89-hour survival and evasion field exercise.

After it was over, I was proud that I'd never given any more than my name, rank, serial number, and date of birth to my brother Marines, even though, at the time, I believed some of them had stepped over the line. Who's to say where the line is when it comes to preparing soldiers to face battle?

I was the only Reservist in the class and graduated in the upper third. It was an experience that would later help me to survive a real life drama.

The bus ride from Pickle Meadows to Reno was a welcome break. My flight back to Savannah wasn't scheduled to leave until the following day. The sign arching over the street said, "Reno, the biggest little city in the world."

I was so worn out that before I got off the bus, I vowed I'd check into a hotel and sleep until it was time to catch the plane home. When I walked into the Mapes Hotel and stopped at the bar, all that changed. It was either the alcohol or the atmosphere, or maybe both, that revived me. After checking in, I went to my room, took a hot shower, shaved and went back to the lounge in my uniform.

As I walked in, I recognized a face, but I couldn't for the life of me put a name with it. He was seated in a booth with two of the finest young women I'd seen in a long time.

"Excuse me, but are you from Savannah, Georgia?" I asked the gentleman.

"No, I'm not, Marine," he said in a condescending tone.

I thought he probably figured I was trying to move in on his women or maybe I was just a wise-ass jar-head. "Sorry. I didn't mean to bother you, sir. Your face just looked familiar," I said. I walked over to the bar and ordered a drink. When the bartender returned with my V.O. and water, he said, "Marine, your drink is on Mr. Sammy."

"Who's Mr. Sammy?" I asked.

"The gentlemen seated over there with the ladies."

I turned and nodded a "thank you" to him. He smiled and motioned for me to come to his table. As I walked towards the table it dawned on me who he was. My old Mafioso friend from Miami.

"Miami Sammy! How in the world ya' doing?" I said.

He was smiling from ear to ear when he stood up and gave me a bear hug.

"When I saw your big smile and gimp eye, I knew it was you. It's been over ten years, ladies, since this kid used to drive me around Miami."

"Remember your promise, Sammy?" I asked.

"Hey, what can I say, kid? You flew the coop before we could make it to Havana," Sammy said.

He'd aged a little, but he still looked like he was in good shape. His personality and body language reminded me of Nick; they could have been brothers.

"Reds, you look like John Wayne in that uniform. You've come a long way since Miami. How'd you wind up in the Marines?"

"I'm not regular, Mr. Sammy, I've been to a special school near here and I'm on my way home. Man, I'm married, got three kids and struggling to keep it all together."

"Sit down, kid," he said.

He introduced me to the ladies and told them they'd better watch me. "He's been away from home for awhile. You know he's horny as a friggin' rabbit." They smiled and excused themselves and headed for the ladies' room.

"You still got it, Sammy," I said.

"Yeah," Sammy nodded his head. "As long as I got this..." He pulled out a roll of C notes big enough to choke a horse.

I asked him what he was doing this far from Florida. He said he was helping some friends put a deal together in Vegas and was here for a short visit before going over to Tahoe.

"Sammy, how bad did Castro screw things up for you?"

Lighting a cigar, Sammy said, "So, I'm a patient man, he'll be taken care of soon. Don't you think it's our patriotic duty, Reds?"

"Whose, yours or mine?" I asked, smiling.

He never answered that question, instead he just smiled and said, "How 'bout going over to Tahoe with me, Reds?"

"I wish I could, but I've gotta get back to my family."

"That's good kid, family is what it's all about. How many kids did you say you have?" he asked.

"Three, one girl and two boys," I answered.

"That's great, be a good papa."

"I'm trying, Sammy, but it's hard."

"You'll make it, if you keep that pecker in your pants," Sammy said chuckling at his own wit.

One of the women returned to the table and reminded Sammy that they needed to get to Tahoe before his friends left.

The surprising reunion ended with Sammy slipping me a hundred-dollar bill and telling me to buy something for the *bambinos*. He wrote down my address and telephone number and said he'd be in touch. Looking back as he walked away with the attractive young blonde, he said, "I still know how to pick 'em, Reds." My eyes followed her tight-skirted wiggle through the lounge and out the door. I knew he had his work cut out for him.

The other woman who had been at the table came over and sat next to me at the bar. She was classy, had a nice figure, big boobs and long blonde hair that hung down over her shoulders.

She had also had too much to drink.

"Excuse me Marine, I'm Angie. I didn't catch your name when Sammy introduced us. The only thing I remember was that you're a friggin' horny rabbit." We both laughed.

"I'm Bobby. How long have you known Sammy?" I asked her.

"Not long. Jolee met him at Tahoe a few weeks ago."

"It's a small world. I haven't seen the guy in ten years, and he hands me a C note and tells me to buy my kids something."

"Yeah, Jolee says he's a millionaire, and if he likes you he can be your Santa Claus. He's getting us jobs in New Orleans, making some real money."

"Doing what?" I asked curiously.

She hesitated. "Bobby, how long are you going to be in Reno?"

"I'm leaving tomorrow, why?"

"Are you into sex?" she said in a business-like manner.

"What'cha mean by that, Angie?"

"I'd like to fuck you — if you have time," she said in a sexy low voice.

"Damn, girl, you don't mess around do you?"

"I can't afford to," she said.

"And I can't afford you," I whispered.

"Did I say anything about a charge, Bobby?" She paused, looking into my eyes. "Everyone has a price; even when you're married, you pay dearly for it," she quipped.

"You're right — never thought about it from that angle."

She was drinking double vodkas like there was no tomorrow.

"Angie, I'd like to take you to dinner..."

"That would be nice," She said with a surprised look.

While we were eating, I watched her drink herself into oblivion. She poured her heart out about how she believed that she was "nothing but a piece of meat to men." She sobbed about not seeing her family in years. I finally got enough coffee into her to guide her back to the Mapes. After getting her to my room, I undressed her and put her in bed. Then I fell in the other bed and died until my seven o'clock wake up call the next morning.

When I stepped out of the shower, she was standing there naked.

"Sorry about last night. You're a gentleman — thanks for listening to me cry in my beer."

"Girl, if you don't get some clothes on, I won't guarantee that I'll be as understanding as I was last night."

"Right now I'm not looking for understanding or underwear, it's something else I want," she said.

The flight back to Savannah passed quickly, but the memories of Pickle Meadows and Reno would last. Especially those of the snow snake, and the fascinating lady who refused to put her drawers back on in the spring of '62.

I was making the most of my job at my father's lumber company. The Chief's type-A personality didn't come as a surprise, but discovering that he was a gambler at heart did.

According to most old timers in the industry, the mill was a dinosaur that should have been extinct years earlier. The old steam engine, band saw and lumber machines were outdated and dilapidated.

I found out later that he'd put his life's savings on the line to buy his unambitious partner out of the business. His partner had initially inherited it from his father-in-law and had milked its assets long before the Chief bought in.

"This mill is a gold mine if you work it right," was the Chief's favorite expression. He was a jack-of-all-trades and a mechanical genius. During World War II, when things were rationed and new equipment was next to impossible to find, he earned the reputation of a man who could keep old equipment and young things running like a clock.

The feelings that I'd harbored since childhood, about how he felt about the military, had softened, even though I knew deep down he felt like "playin' soldier" was just a bunch of crap. He never discussed the Reserves or anything else pertaining to the military. I couldn't figure out why he loved marching with the Mystic Order of the Shrine and wouldn't walk a block for his country. His justification was that he did it for the crippled children.

Throughout the spring of 1962, the Cold War paranoia persisted. The *News* and *Press* carried stories about extensive U.S. and allied exercises in the Caribbean designed as a possible invasion plan for Cuba.

In June the Fifth Rifle Company was air lifted by Marine C-130 aircraft to Vieques Island, just East of Puerto Rico. The scuttlebutt going around the island was that the green light for the invasion of Cuba was just days away. The operation was even named after the little snake-eating animals that infested the island. After training with live ammunition and practicing amphibious mock raids on Cuba, I was beginning to believe that it was more than just a rumor. But it turned out that Kennedy had other options to consider. If it ever existed, Operation Mongoose was scrubbed.

The only combat the Fightin' Fifth experienced in the Caribbean was a few fist fights with French sailors, rum hangovers and several cases of clap from Isabella Segunda.

Oh yeah! The gunnery sergeant almost drowned when he passed out at the Hotel El San Juan's pool bar.

I wasn't as anxious for active duty in the Marines as I'd been in the past. For the first time in my life, I was really happy in my job. The challenge of being yard foreman and having to work men was so much like the military that I loved it.

Angelyn and I seemed to be getting along much better. It was mainly because of our improved financial situation. Regardless of the reason, I wanted it to work.

The Chief gave me a nice lot on Talahi Island, and I wanted to build on it. At first Angelyn was reluctant to sell the house her father had helped us purchase. Finally, she agreed and we sold it for enough profit to pay him back with interest and also swing a mortgage for our new home. As the crow flies, it was only eight miles from our new home to her mama's. She was happy and so was I.

In August of that same year, I received a telephone call from Miami Sammy.

"Hey, I'm sorry we didn't get to talk in Reno, kid."

"Yeah, it was good seein' ya after all these years."

"How's your family?" he asked.

"Fine. They appreciated your gift."

"How'd you like to make some extra bread?" he asked.

"Doin' what, Sammy?"

"The Cubans pay big dough for submachine guns — BAR's, grease guns, Thompsons. Shit, 50 calibers bring a couple of grand."

"What's that got to do with me?"

"I thought you might know somebody in the military could ... you know, maybe surplus or something — cash and carry, you know what I mean, kid."

"Sammy, that's a little heavy for me."

He laughed. "Shit, we can make a million off this. They need guns to kick Castro out, and if we don't, they'll get'em somewhere. It's almost patriotic."

"What happened to all the CIA help?"

"After that screw-up at the Bay of Pigs, most of these Miami Cubans don't trust 'em. You blame them?"

"Sammy, I don't know if I can do you any good. How can I get back in touch with you?" I asked.

"I'll call in a few days. Do what you can, kid."

His call was tempting, but the thought of anything illegal had never crossed my mind. It seemed sacrilegious to think of making money on anybody willing to fight Communism. However, the intrigue and thought of bringing Castro down was tempting. I had recently read *Red Star Over Cuba*, a book by Nathaniel Weyl. "As early as 1949," says Weyl, "Fidel Castro was not merely an implacable enemy of the United States, but a trusted Soviet agent as well." After reading it, I felt that I had a better understanding of Castro and the Communist assault on the Western hemisphere.

On Monday October 22, 1962, at 7:00 p.m. Washington time, President John F. Kennedy spoke to the nation:

> Good evening, my fellow citizens. This government, as promised, has maintained the closest surveillance of the Soviet military buildup on the island of Cuba. Within the past week, unmistakable evidence has established the fact that a series of offensive missile sites is now in preparation on that imprisoned island. The purpose of these bases can be none other than to provide a nuclear strike capability against the Western Hemisphere ... We have no wish to war with the Soviet Union for we are a peaceful people who desire to live in peace with all other peoples ... Our goal is not victory of might, but the vindication of right ... God willing, that goal will be achieved.

Kennedy was right — Khrushchev had put nuclear missiles in Cuba. For a few days in late October, 1962, it seemed the world was on the brink of Armageddon. Kennedy gave Khrushchev an ultimatum: remove the missiles or risk the certainty of war. Khrushchev backed down, and Kennedy had his finest hour.

By Thanksgiving, the Cuban Missile Crisis seemed to be over, but the winds of change were blowing from all directions. Civil rights and Vietnam were about to divide the American house and Western society.

A young black man who worked at the mill asked, "Mr. Bobby, what'cha think about that nigger Meredith going to college in Mississippi?"

"He's got more balls than me. What do you think, Arthur?"

"Somebody is gonna kill him. They ain't gonna let a black man go to a white man's college in Mississippi."

"Arthur, that could happen. But I'm sure he's thought about the consequences. A man's gotta do what he's gotta do."

"So, what'cha think personally ... has he got the right to go to a college in Mississippi?"

"Sure, he's got the right — the Constitution says he does. The color of a man's skin shouldn't make any difference but it does to some people. I hope it changes in our lifetime."

"I doubt it ... but a lot of people gonna die before that day ever come," he remarked.

"Ain't much we can do about it, is there, Arthur?"

"I guess ya right, Mr. Bobby," he said, smiling.

Arthur was right: a few days after his gloomy prophecy, demonstrators surged across the Oxford campus for two days, clashing with 3,400 federal troops and United States marshals. Two people were killed and 350 injured.

Some months later, I listened as Martin Luther King, Jr. spoke on television from Washington, D.C. "I have a dream that one day, on the red hills of Georgia, the sons of former slaves and the sons of former slave owners will be able to sit together at the table of brotherhood..."

That speech helped me to see my own two-facedness that I'd worn like a halo. I'd heard it preached many times that, "All men are created equal in God's eyes." And I believed that theology, but I acted as if people of color were under a different arrangement with God. Hypocrisy and prejudice has no father.

News reports throughout 1962 stated that United States Army Special Forces were instructing South Vietnamese soldiers in guerrilla warfare, demolition techniques, the collection of intelligence, and psychological warfare.

In October, Gen. Maxwell Taylor was sent by Kennedy to study the problems. He reported an urgent need for American combat troops, helicopters and equipment to be sent to Vietnam.

* * *

Nick and Joyce made it home for the Christmas holidays in 1962.

It was obvious that Nick had something bothering him that New Year's Eve at the Legion's Lemon Dance.

"Reds! you still in that fuckin' Marine Reserve?" he asked sarcastically.

"You know I am, brother. It would be crazy for me to get out — I've got over ten years invested."

"That bullshit keeps you fired-up and on the ready box all the time. Hey! Life's too short for that crap."

"Look here, man! I don't know what the problem is, but I didn't come here to hassle — life's too short for that."

"You two ought to be ashamed of yourselves!" Joyce said.

"She's right, Nick, you're my best friend."

"Hey, I'm sorry. I got a lot on my mind and I don't wanna see anything happen to you," he replied.

After Angelyn and Joyce had gone to the ladies room, Nick said, "Bobby, I miss all the shit we use to pull. You think we could turn back the clock to our Porter days?"

"I wish we could, brother."

"You got it man! Pass that bottle. It's another year." When the Russ Peacock orchestra played, "Should auld acquaintance be forgot and ...," we all hugged and kissed and toasted to a "happier and more peaceful 1963!" Whatever was bothering Nick that night remained a mystery. However, one thing I am certain of: it wasn't my health that had him acting a little strange that night.

The three C-119 aircraft carrying the 5th Rifle Company landed at McAlister, Oklahoma. It seemed unusual that no other Marine units would be joining us for our annual field training that year. The facility was a naval ammunitions depot located in the most remote, red-bug, tick-infested area of the state.

The gunnery sergeant said, "Some fuckin' politician in Washington must own the beer concession in this neck of the woods. If this is a infantry training facility, I'm a Chinese aviator."

The scuttlebutt was that because the 5th had won the Commandant's Trophy for the best reserve unit east of the Mississippi, they'd given the Inspector/Instructor C.O. a choice of where the unit could train in '63. The word was, he was anxious to visit an old friend who lived in the area. That must have been close to the truth, because the gunnery sergeant and I hitched a ride with him to Dallas for a weekend liberty. It would have been the least remembered two weeks of my entire reserve career — except for Dallas, Texas.

When the C.O. dropped us off in the downtown section of Dallas, he said, "Helmey, keep the gunny out of the strip joints. We don't want him falling in love in Texas, like he did in Isabella Segunda."

"Skipper, ain't a chance — his head's the only thing that'll get hard any more."

After checking into the hotel and showering, I realized that I was eaten up with red bugs. I threw on my tropical worsted uniform and set out to find a drug store. But before I could locate one, I was forced to stop for a drink. I was having an itching fit, and needed relief fast. The worsted fabric in my trousers and the bugs on my scrotum were at war.

While in the bar, this character wearing a beat up old ten-gallon cowboy hat started a conversation. "I served with Puller on the Canal, son. Lem'me buy ya a drink."

"I'd appreciate that — double Jack Daniel's."

After he'd bought the drink, he commenced telling what he perceived was a deathblow to the Corps, "When dat hard headed son of a bitch from Missouri allowed women, niggers and dogs aboard, it's steady gone down hill," he said as he inhaled a Camel cigarette.

"You mean old Harry S," I said, laughing.

"That's the bastard. Ain't nothin' sacred anymore."

After downing the double, I reciprocated and continued the

search for a drug store. After finding it, I purchased a large bottle of calamine lotion and stepped into the next alley way and coated my cods with the pink zinc oxide. Then I started looking for strip joints. When I passed a movie theater with its marquee advertising double feature films such as, "It's a Mad Mad Mad Mad World" and "Gone With The Wind," I knew Dallas was a serious town.

The only strip club I sojourned in that night was the Carousel Club. The manager seemed to have an affinity for Marines. He kept sending over free drinks. When I walked over to thank him, he patted me on the back, shook my hand and introduced himself as Jack Ruby.

Usually the gunnery sergeant's lustful exploits made every year memorable. This year was no exception; he got tangled up with a lady whose husband was a rodeo bull rider.

The woman's husband came home unexpectedly while the gunny was riding his heifer. Fortunately, the sergeant's camouflage and concealment expertise paid off when he had to jump naked from a second-story window. He managed to find enough clothing hanging from the neighbor's clothes line to cover his body and make it back to friendlier lines.

Three months later, November 22, Friday afternoon. A friend and I were traveling south on U.S. 17, heading for a weekend of deer hunting.

"We interrupt the regularly-scheduled program to bring you this bulletin from Dallas, Texas: President Kennedy has just been shot while in a motorcade ... Stay tuned for further developments."

As we pulled off 17 onto Union-Camp property where we had permission to hunt, a game warden was parked under a large live oak tree, napping. When we pulled next to him, he sat up and started rubbing his eyes. "Excuse me, Cap'n, have you heard about the President being shot?" I asked.

"Naw, but it don't surprise me," he yawned. "You boys are kiddin' — ain't cha?"

"No, sir, it's all over the radio."

He leaned forward and switched on his police radio at full volume. "... shot in the head, and his wife, Jackie ..." was the only thing audible as he sped away without saying another word.

Paul and I listened as the news from Dallas worsened. The President had died. The Governor of Texas had also been shot. Dallas police had chased two gunman up "a knoll" in the vicinity of the shooting. Then later a single assassin had been apprehended and identified as one Lee Harvey Oswald, an ex-Marine, a pro-Castro activist who once lived in the Soviet Union.

We agreed that the murder sounded like an armed coup d'etat. We did very little hunting. Mainly we listened to the radio, drank I.W. Harper, and discussed the sad chain of events. We both argeed that Kennedy had been a damn good President and hoped they found the bastards responsible for his death.

"You know, I remember hearin' Kennedy would be killed if he was ever elected President," Paul said.

"Yeah, I heard that same crap — because he was Catholic, he'd be killed. I don't believe that had anything to do with his death, Paul."

"Probably not, but you can bet your ass the KGB, Castro, or the Klan had something to do with it."

"Hey, if the Feds know so much about the guy they've just arrested, you know damn well it won't be long before the truth comes out," I said, as I picked up my rifle.

"What'd they say his name was, Reds?"

"I think they said, Harry Lee Carswald, an ex-Marine who has lived in Cuba or Russia, or did they say both? Hell, I can't remember — we've listened to that damn radio for ten straight hours. I'm hittin' the sack and worrying about it tomorrow."

"Yeah Reds, I guess this'll be a day to remember," Paul said putting the top on I.W. Harper.

* * *

The next morning as a light drizzle fell, we decided to stay dry and forget the deer hunting. As we sat in the cab of the truck eating pork skins and drinking whiskey, Paul told me he wouldn't be re-enlisting in the Marine Reserves.

"Paul, you shittin' me, why you doin' that?" I asked.

"Reds, have you ever heard of the Green Berets?"

"Hell yeah! The Irish women's auxiliary — now that's a sharp outfit."

"Your ass, you know they're Army Special Forces."

"Yeah, I've heard of the crazy bastards," I said, smiling.

"Reds, why do you stay in the Reserves?"

"I really don't know. Nick said it's my German blood. Maybe I played soldiers too much when I was a kid."

"They're organizing a Special Forces unit in Savannah," Paul said.

"So, you're thinkin' about enlisting?" I ask.

"Yeah, I always wanted to jump out of an airplane, but I don't know if I've got the balls, so I've joined a sky-divin' club to find out before I enlist."

"Damn, you've lost your mind; it ain't the jumpin' that worries me, it's eatin' those fuckin' snakes."

"Well, if I qualify for Special Forces, I've got a good shot at a commission in the Reserves. You know that ain't possible in the Marine Reserves."

"Paul, I know it's the liquor, but I'd like to try that sky divin' myself."

"Good! I'll line you up with the 'Swamp Jumpers' in a couple of weeks."

"Who the hell are the 'Swamp Jumpers'?" I asked.

"A parachute club down at Fort Stewart."

After dropping Paul Hammock off at his home that Sunday afternoon, I met Angelyn and the kids at her mother's. When I drove up, Angelyn opened the front door and shouted, "Hurry, Bobby, somebody has just shot the man that killed Kennedy."

My mother-in-law started giving me a blow-by-blow

description. "Oswald was being transferred from one jail to another. Then this commotion broke out right in the Dallas jail. I heard a pop! pop! and people started screaming. Oswald fell, and I saw a fat man wearing a suit and hat. They wrestled the man to the ground. It looked to me like Oswald was shot in the stomach. Then everyone started screaming, including the television announcer. Ain't it terrible how crazy people are nowadays, Bobby?" Then Ruth took a deep breath.

As we continued to watch, the announcer said Oswald was badly hurt and had been rushed by ambulance to Parkland Hospital, the same one that the President had been taken to days earlier.

"Did you kill a deer, Daddy?" asked Kerry, my seven year-old son, coming into the room.

"No, son. Next time you can go and help me find one."

He looked at his mother. "Mama, can I go next time?"

A few days later I sat watching television as the caisson with the President's flag-draped casket moved down Pennsylvania Avenue. It was followed by a prancing, riderless horse while the unforgettable sound of muffled drums beat out a funeral cadence, and the image of little John- John's salute was forever embedded in my spirit.

At the graveside, Cardinal Cushing prayed, "Oh God, through Whose mercy the souls of the faithful find rest, be pleased to bless this grave and the body we bury herein, that of our beloved Jack Kennedy, the thirty-fifth President of the United States ... I am the resurrection and the life. He who believeth in me, although he be dead, shall live, Amen."

I walked outside to hide my emotions. Why had the death of a man whom I'd never met cause such feelings of loss? Jack Ruby, who had killed Lee Harvey Oswald in the Dallas Police Station, was the same man I'd met and drunk with in the Carousel Club three months earlier.

* * *

It didn't take but a couple of weeks for Paul Hammock to get me lined up with the Swamp Jumpers.

"Reds, if you can train a couple of nights this week, we can make our first jumps on the weekend."

I knew my mouth had overloaded my ass, but, again, I didn't know how to say no. "O.K. Paul, when and where?"

"You student parachutists will initially make five static line jumps before you free fall. Remember, face into the wind on landings and stay away from trees, ditches, and power lines," instructed Ed Rector, the Jump Master.

The Cessna 182 lifted from the runway as I sat near the opening where the right door once hung. The roar of the engine and the sound of wind was deafening. My eyes were fixed on the Jump Master, and the only thoughts were his final words of encouragement as we boarded the aircraft. "If the main parachute doesn't open, and the reserve chute fails, lean over and kiss your ass good-bye, partner."

He gave the "get ready" signal, and pointed to the opening. I struggled against the force of the wind until finally I stood with my feet planted on the aircraft's wheel and my hands firmly gripping the wing strut. As he signaled "Go!", the pilot released the brake and I plummeted from the aircraft. Suddenly, the main chute opened and I hung under the 28-foot canopy watching the earth slowly come up. I was so overwhelmed with the bird's eye view that I completely forgot the drop zone until it was too late. I was headed for a group of tall pine trees about 300 yards from the target.

Paul, who had jumped on the first lift, was standing below the giant pine that I swung from. He shouted, "Hey! you don't get credit for the jump 'til you've touched the ground, Birdman."

Fortunately, the only injury was to my ego. After the adrenaline from my first jump reached normal levels, I made a second jump that day. I remembered to steer the chute toward the drop zone and landed dead center. I was immediately smitten by the airborne bug.

On the ride home that day, Paul gave me a brochure of the Army's Special Forces. He reminded me that John Kennedy was thought of as the patron saint of the Green Berets.

"Paul, I know it's a strike outfit, but it's still part of the doggie Army. If the Corps had a paramilitary unit near, I wouldn't hesitate to transfer."

"Before I was discharged from the 5th Rifle, I requested a transfer to a Marine Recon unit in Mobile, Alabama. But some colonel up at district headquarters turned me down. He said it was too far for me to travel."

"I never knew that. Fuck 'em, Paul, you're the one travelin'. It wouldn't be any skin off his ass. He'd have to give me a better excuse than that. I'm still pissed at being turned down for active duty so many times. It's all politics — you gotta know the right man. Maybe this civil rights thing will spill over in the military and some of these fuckin' little Caesars will have to eat their own shit," I said.

"Reds, you know there's no politics in the Marines. Man! You can get your piss hot in a New York minute, can't cha, Buddy?" Then he broke out in laughter.

Paul qualified and was enlisted in Company B, 13th Special Forces Group. He then went to Fort Benning, Georgia, for the airborne phase of his Green Beret training. I stayed in the Marine Reserves, and continued to jump at Fort Stewart when I had the time and the money.

On my first clear and pull jump, I spent too much time in free fall and never gained a stable body position. When I finally checked my altimeter and realized the ground wasn't but a few seconds away, I pulled the rip cord. It seemed like an eternity waiting for the opening shock of the parachute. I didn't have many druthers; either turn the chute and land in a busy street or risk hitting a power line and electrocution. I chose the street. The last thing I remembered before my head hit the asphalt surface was the sound, "Crr-ack!"

When I came to, there were soldiers standing over me, "Don't move buddy, the ambulance is on the way."

As I was being lifted on the stretcher, I glanced down at my feet. My left boot seemed to be in the proper position, but the right boot dangled limply in the opposite direction, and I felt a sharp pain as it moved.

The Doctor who prepared me for surgery said, "Son, if your right leg had been as hard as your head, you and I wouldn't be having this meetin'."

After screwing and pinning my tibia and ankle joint back together, his prognosis was, "it should heal in time, but I'd advise you not to jump from any more airplanes, unless you wanna walk with a limp — or worst, be crippled the rest of your life."

The remarks of the Jump Master in my parachutist log read: Free Fall and Out of Control. That seemed reasonably accurate.

There was scuttlebutt that the 5th Rifle Company was about to be shelved. When I asked the Inspector-Instructor C.O. if there was any truth to the rumors, he said, "Helmey, I personally can't answer that, but if it should happen, you'll be given the opportunity to transfer to either Jacksonville or Charleston."

"Skipper, Jacksonville's unit is amphibious, Charleston's is Beachmaster. Sir, I'm infantry."

"You're whatever the Corps says you are. Besides every Marine is infantry, Sergeant."

"Yes, sir, I understand that, but I don't plan to travel to Jacksonville or Charleston."

"Helmey, I don't like your attitude. With that broken leg, you're not worth a damn to the Corps anyway," he snapped.

"Sir, you can transfer me to the inactive Reserve anytime you see fit."

"Consider it done, Helmey."

After leaving the Captain's office that afternoon, I stopped at the 19th Hole and had a beer with one of the I&I Sergeants.

"Reds, I heard you and the old man had words."

"Yeah, he got his knickers in a knot," I remarked.

"Man! The minute you walked out of his office, he called Sixth Marine District and transferred you to inactive reserve."

"Yeah, he let me know I wasn't worth a fuck to him with a broken leg."

"He's pissed because he thinks you've been talking to the Army Reserve; like Hammock, you'll be the next to leave."

"Man! Fuck that condescending, arrogant Yankee bastard. I haven't talked to anyone about joinin' the Army Reserve."

"Well, the Fifth is gonna be shit-canned anyway."

On the 67th day of my solitary confinement, I heard automatic weapons, explosions, and the sounds of anti-aircraft fire. It sounded as if Havana were being bombed.

On my 68th day, I was so sick that I couldn't answer when a guard barked "*Nombre! nombre!*" for a routine cell check. He angrily flung open the door and found me lying in a puddle of vomit. "*Arriba, arriba*," he shouted. I could barely move. He yelled something in Spanish and another guard came into the cell with a bucket. As I struggled to get to my feet, he doused me with a white milky liquid that burned my flesh and stung my eyes.

They dragged me into the passageway and dropped me onto a stretcher. I was then taken to a room where a cross-eyed man used a straight razor and cold soapy water to shave me. The last thing I remembered was a syringe in his hand and the needle being pushed into my arm.

When I awoke, I lay naked in a hospital bed covered only by a sheet. A young olive-skinned, brunette woman stood over me wearing Cuban Army fatigues and a stethoscope.

"How do jew feel, Roberto?" she asked.

I was hesitant to answer at first. I didn't know where I was, but I was satisfied just to be out of that dungeon and looking at a friendly face.

"Weak, and real hungry. What's your name, ma'am?

"Maria," she answered, smiling.

"Could you tell me where I am? I asked.

"Doctor Rivera say jew hab a cerebral concussion before jew come to Cu'ba."

"Yes, I had several head injuries."

She pointed to the foot of the bed. "Roberto, jo soap, towel, and bathrobe, now chow'er?"

"Wha'cha mean — chow'er?" I asked.

She laughed and did an impromptu impersonation of a woman taking a very sensual shower. Then she pointed to a door at the end of the empty ward. "Tomorrow jew x-ray, but now chow'er, den jew hab soup."

As she turned and walked away, I had my first sexual fantasy since arriving in Cuba — that was the finest ass I'd ever seen wearing a pair of olive-green combat fatigues.

A Cuban soldier watched our every move through the barred door. He sat under a large portrait of Che Guevara with an assault rifle resting in his lap and a pensive look on his face. After she left the room, the soldier motioned for me to come to the door. He then showed me a 7.62mm cartridge with the letters of my last name scratched on the bullet's point.

That night I listened as a radio played Latin music from the guard's station. Not until I heard Bob Hope's recording of 'Thanks for the memories' did I realize that it was tuned to a Miami station. I drifted off with memories of my wife and children as a gentle rain fell outside the barred window.

The next morning I was escorted by Maria and two armed soldiers to a hospital building nearby and x-rayed. There would be more tests to come.

A month after having the cast removed from my leg, I was interviewed by Major Lindsey P. Henderson, the Commander of the Army's Subsector in Savannah.

"Helmey, Special Forces ain't for everybody. I'll tell you the kind of men we're looking for — men who wanna try something new and challenging. Innovators with imagination. Men who can work with minimum supervision, self-confident, yet team players. You got any of those talents?"

"I'd like to think I do, Major."

"Helmey, I'd advise you to be tested before you request a

release from the Marine Reserves. There's always that possibility that you might not qualify for Special Forces."

"I'd like to be tested as soon as possible."

Two weeks later, I received a copy of a letter written by Major Henderson to the Director of Sixth Marine District:

Staff Sergeant Robert M. Helmey has been interviewed and tested for a TE vacancy in Company B, 13th Special Forces Group (abn), 1st Special Forces and has been found to be fully qualified, and if favorable consideration is given this request, he will be enrolled in the Army Pre-Commission Course. Completion of this course, added to his special qualifications which are already a matter of record, will lead to appointment in a commissioned status in the United States Army Reserves.

Signed, Lindsey P. Henderson, Jr. Major, AIS Commanding.

The Marines released me on the 14th of May, 1965, and I enlisted in the United States Army Reserves the following day.

Curtis E. Harper had also been a member of the 5th Rifle Company. He, too, had qualified for Special Forces and the Pre-Commission Course. We were both scheduled for Jump School at Benning and Jungle Training in Panama at the same time.

Everyday after our regular civilian jobs, we would meet at his house and work out. When we started jogging, every time my right foot impacted the pavement I felt a sharp pain and thought back to the doctor's warning, "Don't jump, unless..."

"Reds, you think that ankle's gonna be strong enough to make it through Fort Benning?" Curt asked, glancing down at my uneven stride.

"I think so, it's just stiff and sore. It'll be O.K. if I don't give in to the bitch."

"I know that's right, Tiger!" he said as he stepped up the pace.

After a few weeks of jogging, the pain and stiffness did disappear. But, psychologically, I had a tendency to favor it.

Angelyn was five months pregnant that hot muggy morning in July when Curtis and I pulled out for Jump School.

"Bobby, if you gotta break something, make it your dick this time, big boy," she said perniciously.

As the C-119 "Flying Boxcar" lined up on Fryar drop zone at an altitude of 1,000 feet, the jumpmaster shouted, "Stand in the door." The light flashed green; then he yelled, "Go!"

I was out of the door. I glanced up to check my chute, then down to check the drop zone, then collide with earth.

When I regained consciousness, I was on a gurney in the base hospital. A beady eyed character in a white jacket and stethoscope was leaning over me. "You earned those wings the hard way, Sergeant Gordon," he said, gazing at me.

The next day during our trip back to Savannah, Curtis, who had jumped in the same stick, told me what had happened at the DZ. "I heard the Drop Zone Safety Officer tell the medical corpsmen as they put you in the meat-wagon, 'When I got to him he was unconscious, his head hit the deck so hard it busted the webbing in his helmet. The head trauma must have brought on some kind of amnesia. He doesn't know who he is; he thinks he's Flash Gordon'." After that, he pinned your blood wings on and had you transported to the base hospital, Tiger."

"Curt, it was the weirdest feelin' I've ever had. My memory was gone. But I do recall telling someone I was Flash Gordon from Fayetteville," I said as I rubbed my head.

"Yeah, you didn't even recognize me."

"I'm telling you, Curt, it was like I was standin' over myself, watching all this shit going on in a dream."

"What'd the doctor tell you?"

"I ain't sure I talked to a doctor. If I did, the motherfucker must have been a gynecologist, after explainin' a lot of shit about a 'cerebral kotex,' he released me and told me if I had any complications I should report to the Hunter Field Hospital in Savannah," I said.

"You're a lucky bastard. If it weren't for your helmet, you'd be goin' home in a body bag," Curt remarked as he drove.

"You're probably right," I answered.

"Reds, when's the President gonna mobilize the Reserves?"

"He ain't, but he could call-up some Reservists who have critical MOS's (Military Occupational Specialty). I'll tell you what might happen — it'll be a hell of a lot easier to get on active duty now since Congress has passed the Gulf of Tonkin Resolution. Why, you thinkin' about volunteering?"

"Yeah, but what's this Tonkin thing got to do with it?"

"Shit, you know it's all about power and politics, my man. The Resolution is like grandma's nightgown — it covers everything. Johnson needs more combat troops in Vietnam. At home he's up to his ass in alligators. The doves and liberals wanna give this fuckin' country to the Communists. He should ship those antiwar, draft card-burnin' bastards to Cuba where they could talk their love shit and cut cane for Castro 'til their asses drop off. I'm tellin' you if somethin' ain't done soon, you can kiss this country good-bye," I said, reaching into the cooler for another couple of beers.

"Yeah," Curt nodded his head in agreement. "He also needs to do somethin' about this women's liberation crap. They've gone ape-shit wearin' miniskirts up to their asses. The bitches have even started burnin' and throwin' away their bras. What's this fuckin' country comin' to?" Curt asked, reaching for his beer.

"That ain't all bad, good buddy — unless it's your women that's doin' the throwin' and showin'.'"

"Reds, I don't know whether I'm talkin' to you or Flash Gordon. But damn if one of you ain't a fuckin' philosopher. All three of us need to volunteer for Vietnam."

"We'll drink to that. AIRBORNE ALL THE WAY!"

I wasn't able to make jungle training that August because the Chief had to take my mother to the National Institute of Health for open heart surgery. In November our fourth child was born, Freda Kristi. I now had five dependents, which automatically disqualified me for active duty. Once again I was faced with disappointment over a military career.

A few days before Christmas, I was in the Crow Bar on Wilmington Island and ran into an old Benedictine School friend whom I hadn't seen in years. "Arsenault, where the hell you been, man?" I asked, hugging his neck.

"Round the world and back again," he remarked with a surprised look on his face.

"You must be in the Merchant Marine?"

"Naw, I'm flyin' with Air America, Reds."

"You mean the CIA's airline that flies the unmarked aircraft to those secret wars and exotic places?"

"Oh, we've got plenty of identification. But we paint over it with cosmolene so the cocksuckers will hesitate a little before shootin' at us. What'cha been doin', Big Boy?" he asked.

"The family thing — married with four kids and workin' at a lumber mill."

"I thought you were in the Marine Corps."

"No, but I did put in eleven years in the Reserves, after comin' off active duty with the Air Force."

"Damn, you'd better hang in there. You've almost got enough time to retire."

"Oh, I'm still active, but in the Army's Special Forces."

"Damn, Reds, I remember you as a skinny-ass kid when we were at B.C. Now, like the song says, 'you're one of America's best, with silver wings upon your chest'," he said as he lifted his glass.

"Yeah, and I remember you havin' more bullshit than a Texas midget. Bartender, give this pirate whatever he's drinkin'."

We sat and shot the bull for about an hour. He told me enough about his job, I was able to read between the lines. I was convinced that he had seen a lot of covert operations and had worked with mercenary types all over the globe.

Before leaving the bar that day he gave me a couple of addresses in Washington, D.C., and Langley, Virginia. "Should you wanna apply directly to the Central Intelligence Agency, or Air America, which are both Equal Opportunity Employers. Don't use my name as a reference if you wanna be treated equally," John quipped.

"Merry Christmas, John — take care of yourself, man."

"Hope to see you around, Reds."

That chance meeting with Arsenault rekindled the possibility of another approach for service to my country.

By June, 1966, I had received my Security Clearance and graduated from the Special Forces School at Fort Bragg, N.C. This was the *piece de resistance* of my military adventure. I was now qualified to wear the beret, but because of courts-martial I'd received while in the Air Force, I could not be commissioned as an officer in the United States Army.

As the Delta 727 began its descent, the Captain announced that we'd be landing at Newark's International Airport in ten minutes.

The bus ride from the airport to Staten Island's Miller Field took less than an hour. I'd looked forward to this "job" training for a long time. It was my first opportunity to work as an Operations and Intelligence Sergeant with an "A" team. I knew this was only a war game, but also understood that Special Forces played them hard and serious. The word going around the 13th Group was that we would be field testing new equipment, and a dirty trick or two. The CIA and other intelligence agencies would also be monitoring the operation as part of their paramilitary training but in a passive role.

The team that I was assigned to was given the mission of rescuing a downed pilot from a POW camp in the Rappahannock swamps of Virginia.

During the preparation and rehearsal phase of the mission we were sequestered in a special holding area at Miller Field. Before our CSAR (Combat Search and Rescue) operation began,

I introduced a unique piece of equipment to the team.

"Gentlemen, this is the Mark 1 E&E Suppository. The purpose of this device is to allow a prisoner to free himself from most restraints. The tools within this kit are: one pair of wire cutters, screwdriver, pry bar and tool handle (in combination), two pointed saw blades, two flat saw blades, one drill, one flat file, one ceramic blade, and one reamer. The actual size is four inches in length and one inch in diameter — and yes, it should be concealed rectally, as circumstances require."

"Excuse me, Sarge — but did you say rectally?" asked the team demolitions specialist.

"That's what I said, Dynamite Dan. The end result is that it all gets shoved up your ass."

"Airborne! — all the way!" echoed in the room.

I stood in the aircraft's door watching as cobalt blue flames shot from the engine's exhaust, waiting for the Jumpmaster's tap to "Go" I'd always heard that a person had to be a little nuts to jump out of a perfectly good aircraft. But jumping at night into a swamp with over 100 pounds of weapons, explosives, assorted supplies and equipment strapped to my body seemed to border on insanity.

During our mission at Fort A.P. Hill Military Reservation, Virginia, a group of U.S Navy Seabees who were being deployed to Vietnam requested assistance in POW (Communist interrogation methods) training from Special Forces.

Three days later, as the team waited at an LZ (landing zone) for a chopper lift to Andrews Air Force Base, Lieutenant Mitchell said, "Helmey, you really impressed the Seabees Commanding Officer. He wanted me to personally commend you for your graphic demonstration of Communist interrogations methods. You knew several of his men were at the Bay of Pigs with Brigade 2506 (the CIA-trained Cuban Exile group)?"

"No, sir, not until after I'd done my thing. Then one of their ensigns told me about it. He explained that President Kennedy had given some of the survivors an opportunity to join the U.S. Military, after Castro traded them for medical supplies. How'd I get picked for the detail, Jim?"

"Reds, it must be your flamboyant personality. You've evidently bedazzled somebody in the S-2 Section or somewhere with your horseshit and gunsmoke discourse on 'The POW and Code of Conduct'."

"Hey! No disrespect to the good Lieutenant, but that's no bullshit; I'm dead serious about how I feel. I believe anything you give the enemy, beyond name, rank, serial number, and date of birth, is collaborating with the bastards."

"Sergeant, I hope you never find yourself in a place where those principles are tested. When you said 'if you believe in something strong enough, you'll die for it,' that sounded like pretty radical shit, my man."

After arriving at Andrews Air Force Base the team was debriefed and assigned sleeping quarters for the overnight stay in Washington. At the base NCO Club that afternoon, Paul Hammock and I watched as a television reporter described how a man had killed twelve people and wounded thirty-three from a tower at the University of Texas. "The student, a former Marine marksman, carried with him a footlocker filled with firearms, ammunition, food and water to the top of the twenty-seven story tower. Finally an off-duty patrolman managed to sneak up behind and kill him," he announced.

Shaking his head in disbelief, Paul said, "Did he say an ex-Marine?"

"That's what the man said," I replied.

"Son-of-bitch, it wasn't long ago that a ex-jarhead killed Kennedy. You think it's something in the drinking water down there, Reds?"

"Damned if I know, but I'll bet most folks are gonna be squirrely as hell around ex-leathernecks from Texas."

I thought I recognized the man wearing a coat and tie seated next to me. "Excuse me, sir, don't I know you?" I asked.

He smiled, "You might remember my face from A.P. Hill the day you ran the POW compound exercise for the Navy."

"Oh yeah, I remember. You must be one of those observers from the Tea & Biscuit Company?"

He grinned and said, "Helmey, I don't think I've ever heard a better interpretation of the Code of Conduct than the one you gave. I wanted to talk with you after the exercise was over, but you and the ensign disappeared."

"I appreciate that. I wouldn't have been so damn gung-ho had I'd known some of those men had survived Castro's dungeons."

"You don't owe anybody an apology," as he puffed intently on a cigarette.

"Thanks," I nodded. "But what did you wanna talk to me about?"

"Let's take a ride," he said.

"Man, I can't leave this base in tiger stripe fatigues."

"You don't have to worry about your uniform or your buddy."

When I turned, I saw Paul in deep conversation with the man seated next to him. "Paul, I'm gonna take a ride with my friend here, I'll see you back at the barracks."

After being flagged through a gate at Andrews Air Force Base, he identified himself as an employee of the CIA.

"You mind showin' me some identification, friend?"

I saw the words Central Intelligence Agency on the card.

After riding for a while and his talking about everything but the business at hand, my curiosity got the better of me and I asked, "Partner, what's this all about?"

He pulled his car over and parked across from a bar somewhere in D.C., then looked at me smiling, "We're both two sides of the same coin, Helmey — Special Forces and the CIA. At times our government can't do shit on the up and up. Sometimes dirty work has to be done and it calls for people with out-of-the-ordinary mettle. When you said to those Seabees, you must be willing to defend and protect the principles of God and country with your life if necessary, I believed you."

"What's the bottom line here, my friend?"

"Let's have a drink. We'll talk about it later."

"No, let's talk now."

"O.K., Helmey. We might be able to use a man with your kind of passion and skills. If the opportunity should arise, would you be interested?"

I had to laugh, "What cha' talking about? Frankly, this ain't how I thought you people did business."

"We're always looking for motivated people with special talent." As he laid his cigarette in the ashtray and looked me in the eyes, he said. "Helmey, you ever had any assassination training?"

"If you're CIA, you know what training I've had ... my personal habits ... probably even my sexual proclivities. Man, oh man, I've heard the agency uses cabdrivers, hookers and housewives, now I believe it. Let's go have that drink," I said.

A jukebox blared out Nancy Sinatra's 'Boots' as we walked into the small crowded bar. It smelled of stale beer and perfume. After being there for a few minutes, I knew it was a rendezvous for horny government employees. The women outnumbered the men.

We sat in a rear booth and ordered drinks and continued our conversation. "Is it possible to get me on active duty?" I asked.

"We don't need you on active duty ... maybe later."

"If I agree — what happens next?"

"I'll be back in touch. But regardless, remember this, don't discuss anything we've talked about with your family, your S.F. Buddies, your priest or even another CIA officer. I will be your only contact. I'll identify myself as *Merlin*. Is that clear?"

"Yeah, I understand. This may sound crazy, but do you know how to get in touch with me, Marvin?" I said.

"Helmey — Merlin, not Marvin, and you don't have to worry about that, I've got your number."

"Yeah! I'll bet you have. How about the blond with the big tits who keeps lookin' at you — you got hers?"

"Sure do, would you like to be introduced?" he asked.

On the flight back to McGuire Air Force Base, Paul and I compared notes on what had taken place the previous afternoon at the NCO Club.

"Reds, that was some strange stuff that went on yesterday."

"Wha'cha mean?"

"After you and that queer left, the guy I was havin' a conversation with asked if I'd like to ride over to Maryland and eat some seafood."

"What makes you think the guy I left with was a fag?"

"Huh, if he wasn't, he missed a damn good chance. I watched him as y'all left the club. The way the guy walked you could definitely tell he had some serious bitch in him."

I had to unbuckle my safety-belt, I was laughing so hard. "You mean you can tell a cocksucker by the way he walks?"

Paul nodded. "Man! the whole Andrews thing was strange — you leaving with 'Nature Boy' and me with some dude I'd never seen before."

"So what happened to you?" I asked.

"Nothing, really. We rode over to Maryland and had a few beers. So! Where'd you and 'Liberace' go?"

I burst out laughing. "Arlington, to Kennedy's grave. Then into D.C. and had a few highballs at this weird waterin' hole."

"Man! you look like warmed-over death. Must have been some serious liquor in those highballs."

"Paul, don't laugh, but somebody anesthetized me. I've got to get some rest before Staten Island," I said, closing my eyes.

After landing at McGuire, Paul shook me. "Reds, let's go over to the Big Apple tonight and check out those 'dime a dance' halls."

"O.K, I feel a little better now. I've always wanted to see the Statue of Liberty. And I've got to get a few things for my wife and kids before I go home."

As we stood on the deck of a Staten Island Ferry watching the Statue of Liberty pass, my thoughts went back to one of my Cuban friends' favorite discourses:

> Give me your tired, your poor ... your huddled masses ...
> send these, the homeless, tempest-tossed, to me, I lift my
> lamp beside the golden door!

"Didn't the French give us that?" Paul asked.

"That's what I was told. Hammered copper sheets, built in France, disassembled and brought to this country on a ship. I guess the greenish color comes from the copper rust."

"Probably, but it's still one hell of an awesome sight. It seems almost spiritual," Paul said softly.

"Yeah, it gives ya goose bumps, don't it buddy?"

"Yep, it sure does, Reds," Paul said, shaking his head slowly.

Part Seven

PREDESTINATION

That God has foreordained everything
Rene Descartes

Predestination

On the flight back to Savannah, I couldn't get that crazy meeting with the CIA emissary off my mind. Why would they be interested in me? What kind of talent was he talking about? Why had he asked about assassination training? Was this guy for real? Maybe he was just a maverick who'd had too much to drink and was playing some kind of game with me.

The strangest part of the whole baffling experience was, I didn't remember anything after going up a flight of stairs to a room where a woman who spoke with a Spanish accent addressed me as *El Rojo*. Not much was clear after that. It was like my accident at jump school, except this time in color, and Flash Gordon wasn't around to watch over me. I felt as though I had been drugged; psychedelic lights, faces suddenly looked grotesque; vertigo, choking, and then I felt as if I were out of my body.

Later that night, when my head began to clear, I was sitting in a taxi. The blond with the large breasts who I'd seen earlier was leaning in the window, wearing my beret and giving directions to the driver. "No charge, tiger — the lady paid for your ride," the driver said when the cab stopped. Before I could clear the cobwebs out and ask where I was, I realized I was back at Andrews, directly in front of the barracks that Paul and I had left some ten hours earlier.

The bizarre part of the entire episode was — why was my memory so foggy about happenings in that room over the D.C. bar? Merlin didn't have to worry about me telling anybody about our meeting. Who the fuck would believe it anyway?

As the flight landed at Travis Field, Paul leaned over and said, "Reds, you were so deep in thought I didn't wanna bother you. But I had to let you know I've taken a job in Prattville, Alabama, with Union-Camp. So, this'll probably be our last tour together. I'm gonna miss your smiling face, ole buddy," he said reaching over to shake my hand.

"Man, it looks like all us gung-ho 'weekend warriors' are movin' on. First it was Jim Prince going regular Marine, now he's in 'Nam. Curt Harper will be goin' as soon as he gets his gold bars."

"Reds, we're gettin' too old and brittle for this shit."

"I know what'cha mean. I wish we had a bottle of I.W. Harper, so we could blow it out one more time. But since we don't, here's an Irish blessing for you: 'May the road rise to meet you, may the wind be at your back,' Paul."

"Same to you, brother."

"Oh! by the way, that guy I left the NCO club with did have a funny little wobble in his walk. I think he might have been hiding one of those E&E Suppositories up his gu-zoot."

We waited at the Island's Expressway bridge for a shrimpboat to pass. On the bow of the boat was painted *Johnny Reb*.

Kelly, my seven-year-old son, asked, "Daddy, is that Johnny Reb's boat?"

"Son, that's just the name of the boat. See the flag on the mast pole," I pointed at the trawler. "That's a Confederate battle flag. The captain is probably a rebel."

I should have known what his next question would be. "What's a rebel, Daddy?"

Before I could answer him, Kerry, my oldest son, said, "Kelly, that's a man who wears a sheet over his head. You know! A Ku Klux Klan man." He looked at me with a big grin and said, "Ain't it, Daddy?"

"Who told you that, son?"

"Uncle Spanky."

I laughed and tried to explained that Johnny Reb was a nickname given to Confederate soldiers during the Civil War. For just a moment it awakened memories of my own childhood and how all-knowing I thought my Uncle Billy was.

When the bridge closed, Kelly looked at his brother and said, "Kerry! Uncle Spanky don't know everything. I heard Aunt Liz say he don't know his ass from a hole in the ground."

In early March of 1967, some seven months after my Washington encounter with the CIA officer, I received a call from a man who identified himself as a member of an anti-Castro group. He said my name had been given as a trusted and motivated individual with special talents. He asked if I would be interested in a possible operation against Castro. I explained that it was the second time I'd heard the word talent and I was just as confused then as I am now. But I might be if someone with the right credentials, and a good explanation of what they considered my talents to be, were willing to talk with me on my turf.

Two months later, I received a large manila envelope with a Miami, Florida, postmark and no return address. The only thing it contained was a note and an old *Miami News* newsprint of Castro and Khrushchev hugging on a Harlem street during a visit to the United Nations some years earlier. Fidel's picture was crossed out with a red marker, and written across the top of the paper were the words "Alpha 66."

The note read:

Fidel is exporting revolution to American campuses. In all, some 4,000 young American Leftists have traveled to Cuba to show their "solidarity with the Cuban revolution." About half have gone as part of the student "Venceremos Brigades." And we know at least 1,500 have been schooled in the techniques of urban guerrilla warfare and terrorism — terrorism in this country can be traced back to one source: Cuba.

I was promoted to Sergeant First Class and scheduled to train at the U.S. Military Academy at West Point in October. I continued in the Reserves with a renewed enthusiasm.

I had always believed something my Primitive Baptist grandmother had told me years earlier was working in my life. "Bobby, everything is predestined by God, and what will be, will be."

Shortly after receiving that envelope, I began studying everything I could find on Fidel Castro, Cuba, and the Communists.

Fidel's childhood and youth were particularly interesting. He, too, used a bicycle in his youth to get recognized as a fearless daredevil; he bet that he could ride his bicycle at top speed into a stone pillar, which he did and was unconscious for days. The bicycle episode supposedly caused him brain damage that some suspected brought on his logorrhea, a psychopathological condition that causes excessive and often incoherent talkativeness. There were occasions when he became so unintelligible during one of his three-to-five hour harangues that he had to be pulled away from the microphone by aides. When this happened, he would submit in what seemed to be a dazed state. People who knew him well report that he sometimes had momentary fainting spells suggestive of petit mal epilepsy. I continued my research.

I hadn't seen Bobby 'Dumbo' Barber in a couple of years, although I'd occasionally get postcards from some pretty exotic places. The last one was from Cabo San Lucas, Mexico. The only thing written on it was, "Aboard Standard Oil yacht. What's happening? See you soon, 'Sinbad' the Barber."

The day he drove up at the mill in an old beat-up Chevy van with this young attractive hippie chick was a pleasant surprise. I had always loved to hear his travel tales and adventure stories, especially those about Korea and the "Frozen Chosen" Marines.

Dumbo had been with the First Marine Division at the Chosin Reservoir, along with many other reservists of Savannah's Dog Company. But Dumbo was one of a kind — he had his own philosophy on life and never seemed to be lost for words, women, or political opinions.

"Boolas," he always had a new name for me, "this is Bonnie Marx. She's queen of the mambo, and one-third of the world's most famous haberdasher — Hart, Schaffner and Marx."

"Nice meetin' you, Bonnie," I said, hugging her neck.

"Reds, I've heard some wild stories about you. I figured you'd look like Huckleberry Finn and speak like Captain Rhett Butler," she said, smiling. "Bobby, he's nothin' like you described."

"Give him a little time, girl."

"Bonnie, when Dumbo tells you somethin', you can take it to the bank, but you'd better divide by two before you make the deposit."

"Boolas, you still goin' to those Lemon Dances and rubbin' bellies wid the horny old broads?"

"Naw, not since Nick and Joyce moved out of town."

"Where they livin' now?"

"Washington, D.C."

Bonnie interrupted, "All the way up from Miami, Bobby has talked about this seafood restaurant on the river at Thunderbolt. He said an Italian character named Carlos uses a special sausage to season his boiled shrimp and crab dish that'll knock your socks off. You two can talk all the old times you want, but first take me there before I have a conniption fit!" She pulled on Dumbo's arm.

"Boolas, I've got to take this kosher girl to Desposito's before she embarrasses herself — go with us."

"I'll meet y'all there. Bonnie, don't wait on me to eat. I've gotta grade-mark a bundle of 2x4's first, then check with Angelyn."

Two hours later when I arrived, Dumbo and Bonnie were sitting in a booth drinking Jack Daniels with Carlos Desposito.

"Reds, baby, we got a head start on you. I'm here to tell ya, this Sicilian's sausage is the best I've eaten, and believe me, I've eaten a few," Bonnie said as she hugged a beaming Carlos.

"Hey, I know the man's secret. When nobody's watching, he dips that big Italian sausage in and stirs the pot."

Carlos burst out in laughter, then looked at Dumbo. "This is the only man in the world crazier than you. But the Reds is special, he's always got a good word and a smile on his face. Sit and have a drink, *paisan*."

I especially remember that night at Desposito's because of a conversation Dumbo and I had after Carlos closed and Bonnie fell asleep in the rear of the van. As we sat facing the Intercoastal Waterway I asked, "Dumbo, you ever felt like something was happenin' and you had no control over it?"

"Yeah, a few times. One night at the Chosin Reservoir when a million 'opium smoking' Chinese came charging up a hill blowing bugles, I was fixin' to die. Is that what you're talkin' about?"

"Not exactly. I mean predestination, you know, supernatural stuff. It's become an obsession."

"Man, shit! Predestination! Supernatural! What in the hell are you trying to say?" Dumbo ask.

"I've been having this recurring dream. In it, I'm flying down the Intercoastal Waterway in an aluminum tube that looks like an ICBM missile. I pass Key West, then I'm over Cuba, and Fidel Castro is standing on a beach staring up, smiling at me."

"Reds, I wouldn't tell anyone else. You've been eatin' too much gassy food late at night or you're watchin' too much television. One of them is screwing your head up." He paused. "Let me ask you something, you ever heard of the *illuminati*?"

"Yeah, but who in the hell are they?" I asked.

"Reds, it's a clique of high IQ'ed, aristocratic motherfuckers with the keys to the world's monetary systems. They actually believe they've been chosen by the gods. They perpetuate their deity by keeping the world in fear. Now the enemy is Castro, Vietnam and Socialism. All they do is yell 'Commie' and every red-blooded American is willing to lay down his life — and for what? So the military-industrialist barons can make millions while the 'illuminated elite' make billions, and they continue to control us ignorant unenlightened peasants," Dumbo said authoritatively.

I realized that Jack Daniels was doing most of Dumbo's talking.

For the next hour, I sat and listened as he philosophized on everything from The Protestant Reformation to the sex life of a Wall Street hooker. He ended by reciting a verse of poetry that he'd found on a dead Marine in Korea.

> Sing of Tripoli and Tarawa, young Marines.
> Be proud of your sacred leatherneck greens.
> The bloody path where death ran free,
> for ancestral soldiers of the sea,
> a road that's paved with bravery,
> crosses that are history —
> The Long Road Back from Hagaru.

"Reds, the next time I put on a uniform, the Chinese will be coming up the Mississippi in a gun-boat. I've seen and heard enough of these rich condescending cocksuckers lately to know that you and I ain't nothin' but cannon fodder," he said, angrily.

"I appreciate you unraveling the 'illuminati' mystery for me. But I think you're a little prejudiced since losing that job on the Standard Oil yacht. You shouldn't have banged that wealthy old man's young wife," I said laughing.

"Don't laugh, motherfucker! You'd have done the same thing if that beautiful, long-legged bitch had hit on you from Maracaibo to Cabo San Lucas."

A few days before he and Bonnie left Savannah, they stopped by the house to pick up some mountain sleeping bags and other gear that I'd promised them.

"Boolas, I appreciate the survival gear. You never know when you might need it nowadays. Come on down to Miami

Beach. Forget all that patriotic crap — Fidel and Che are the best things that's ever happened to that island. And if you do ride the rocket, take a load of Cubans back with you. They have no intentions of ever leaving South Florida," he said, shaking my hand.

"Bonnie, take care of the wild-man. He's the last of a breed. God threw away the pattern when He made him."

"I'll do my best, Reds. It was nice meeting you, Angelyn. You and the kids come on down and visit when you can," Bonnie replied.

As they drove out of the yard, Angelyn looked at me. "Bobby, you've really collected some weird friends over the years."

"Yeah, but Dumbo has paid the price to be a little weird."

Angelyn looked at me, grinning, "So what's your excuse, big boy?"

On the "CBS Evening News," the North Vietnamese were displaying three captured U.S. pilots in Hanoi. In another segment, heavyweight boxing champion Cassius Clay was running his mouth about why he'd refused to be inducted into the Army. Kim and I watched intently.

"They ought'a shoot him and Rap Brown. Then drop their non-violent asses on those Communist bastards in Hanoi."

"Who you talking about, Daddy?" she asked.

"The Louisville Lip, Muhammad Ali."

It angered me so, I had to leave the room to keep my daughter from seeing the rage. I couldn't stand the idea that this country was so goddamned screwed up with people trying to tear it apart. I'd always respected Clay and couldn't believe he'd hesitate to serve. Even Elvis Presley hadn't wavered at the opportunity.

I remembered Dumbo's after-dinner speech on the illuminati as the hypothesis of the world's dilemma. Although I didn't fully agree, I respected the fact that he had served bravely in Korea and was entitled to be a bit bohemian in his life-style and politics.

In June of that year, the Defense Department announced its reorganization plan for the Army's Reserve and National Guard Forces. The 13th Special Forces Group was reorganized as the 11th S.F. Group, and the word was we could be called up individually, when and if our MOS was needed.

Before the Group left for annual field training at West Point, China announced that it had successfully exploded a hydrogen bomb; General Westmoreland asked Defense Secretary McNamara for more troops in Vietnam; and U.S.Army troops moved on a riot-torn Detroit, Michigan.

On the 103rd day of my solitary confinement I was blindfolded and taken to another section of the prison where I was told to shower. I was given back the clothing that I had worn when I arrived in Cuba.

"Helmey, you travel today," said the officer. He handed me several documents and told me to sign them. When I hesitated, he said they were papers required by international law. He warned me that if I didn't sign, I would not be allowed to leave Cuba. I signed immediately. He handed me a Cuban passport and fifty dollars in U.S. currency.

I was then taken to a waiting automobile where Tom Jones was belting out "Delilah" on its radio. As the vintage Oldsmobile with its five other passengers sped along the Malecon (the plaza-like promenade overlooking Havana's waterfront), the Officer pointed out the U.S.S. Maine Monument.

"The Yankee sympathizers who sunk that battleship started the Spanish-American War and gave your country the excuse to liberate us Dispossessed Peasants," he quipped.

An English-speaking black man in the rear of the automobile suddenly freaked out. "Where you takin' me, where you takin' me?" The two Cubans seated next to him grabbed the man, subduing him.

After arriving at the Port of Havana, I was taken to a room where the Cuban officer who had done most of my interrogations sat smiling. "Helmey, I like you very much.

But you still remain a mystery to us. Why did you come to Cuba?"

"I wish I could answer that, but the truth is I don't know," I smiled, shaking my head.

He shrugged his shoulders. "Helmey, if you're not CIA, why would you wanna return to the United States and face prison or a possible death sentence?"

"Just between you and me, if I were CIA, what'cha think my mission was — checkin' out ya friggin' dungeons?"

He started laughing, "That's why I like you so much, Helmey. You're a funny fellow." He opened the door to the pier.

The name on the bow of the vessel was the *Commandant Camilo Cienfuegos*.

The easygoing officer pointed to a man at the top of the gangway. "The Captain awaits you, *El Rojo*. Be very careful, my airplane bandit friend. Bon voyage!"

The harbor was crowded with Russian and other Communist block ships as the pilot navigated the freighter through a narrow channel leading to the Straits of Florida. I watched as we passed El Morro Castle on the starboard and Castle De La Punta to port. The ocean was smooth and tranquil. The lights of Havana disappeared in the night; yet the voyage had just begun.

Early the next morning we arrived at the Port of Matanzas, Cuba. I still didn't know the ship's final destination. As I stood on the bridge watching the loading of raw sugar, the black man who had been in the car the previous afternoon was standing next to me.

"Weren't you in the G2 prison in Havana?" he asked.

"Yes, and I remember hearin' your voice many times."

"And I remember yours — you're American, aren't you?"

I told him that I was. He introduced himself as Omar from New York City. He began nervously telling me how he had fled the U.S. with his wife and infant child because of racial persecution. He said he was a member of the Black Panthers and had come to Cuba expecting a better life. But now he was being kicked out because he and a few brothers had tried to teach black culture to some of the Afro-Cubans, and Castro had branded them counter-revolutionaries.

"Man, there's more racial discrimination in Cuba than there is in Selma, Alabama. My black brothers and sisters have been though hell down here, and I want the Black

Panther Party in the United States to know the unrevolutionary way we're being treated by Castro."

"Omar, you wouldn't happen to know where this sugar ship is headed, would ya?" I asked.

"Spain or Russia." Omar went silent for a moment, staring down at an old four-door Buick that had stopped on the pier. Four people got out. Two were Cuban military, and the other two were blacks who were wearing Mao Tse Tung caps. The red star on their hats reflected the sun's rays like neon as they started up the gangway.

"Did I hear you say Spain or Russia?"

Omar quickly walked away without saying another word.

I continued to watch as the ship was being loaded with sugar and other cargo. The hatch covers on the stern of the ship had been removed and the area below decks was visible.

As longshoremen were lowering a large wooden crate down into the hole, I could read a shipping address that was written in large bold letters: Zora's House of Antiques, Prince Edward Hi-way, Windsor, Ontario, Canada.

The ship's passengers, crew, and cargo were an interesting mix.

The 11th Special Forces was assigned to Camp Natural Bridge while at West Point for demolition training. Something about the Military Academy seemed almost sacred. The name alone conjured up spirits of men who had inspired courage and patriotism in me. However, it also awakened memories of the times I had screwed up earlier in my military quest — and how the lack of self-discipline had cost me.

The earth shook and a deafening noise followed.

"Reds, that was a ten on the Richter Scale. How much damn C4 (plastic explosive) did ya use?" Casey said, as he stood brushing debris off his uniform.

"All I had — forty pounds. I didn't wanna take that shit back. You know how much paperwork is involved in returnin' high explosives to ordnance people."

"I also know how much trouble we gonna have tryin' to explain the 'big bang theory' to a West Point Public Affairs Officer and the Chief New York state seismologist."

"Hey! Didn't Lieutenant Mitchell want us to give the students 'live fire' realism?" I said, grinning.

When Casey Johnson and I completed our class that afternoon on "Field Expedient Devices for Triggering Explosives," our names were taken off the 11th Special Forces Demolitions Committee roster and assigned to "Silent Weapons" training for the remainder of our stay at the United States Military Academy.

Months had passed and I hadn't heard anything from my shifty-stepping CIA contact or the anti-Castro group. I began chewing over whether I should go to the 11th Group's S-2 (Intelligence) officer or directly to the CIA and get to the bottom of what was going on. But after spending some time with the unit's Special Forces advisor, Sergeant Norton, I decided against it.

On a trip to Fort Benning to pick up parachutes for an upcoming airborne exercise, Sergeant Norton and I belted down a few beers and got to know each other a little better. He'd just pulled a tour of duty in Vietnam with the 5th Special Forces Group and had requested to go again. Although he didn't appear to be the kind of guy who enjoyed gory war stories, he definitely got a kick regaling me with "Sneaky Pete" operations.

When he told about a CIA cross-border operation into Cambodia and the assassination of a North Vietnamese double agent and something else about a "blood oath" — which I never did quite understand — he had this childish, mischievous look in his eyes.

"Chuck, how much you know about the CIA?"

"Enough! They're in our chain of command, but mostly for intelligence. I do know this about them, they only tell you what you 'need-to-know,' and they'll bug-out on ya if the shit hits the fan. Why'd you ask?"

"I'm just curious. Evidently, the CIA uses Special Forces for their dirty work when it comes to clandestine operations?"

"You got a problem with that?" he asked sarcastically.

"Hey, relax, I wasn't born yesterday," I snapped back.

Norton grinned. "There's a good reason. Look what just happened in Bolivia. I know damn well that was a joint operation."

"What did happen in Bolivia?"

"Che Guevara's death. Who do you think trained and advised the Bolivian Rangers that captured him? The 8th Special Forces from Panama, and you can bet the CIA gave the final word on his execution. It's a crying shame Castro wasn't around to get his. 'Top secret' ain't no big thing. All it really means is to keep your mouth shut if you should know anything that might be detrimental to your health or this nation's security. It's all about trust and survival, if you get my drift," Norton said with that same look in his eyes.

I stared at him for a moment. "Then what do you mean — the CIA will leave you holding the bag?"

"Because of the politics and propaganda involved. And it's just the nature of the beast. It's almost impossible to trace anything back to them. If you should have any dealings with them, get amnesia. Reds, you ain't never seen any combat, have you?"

"No, not the kind you get decorated for," I shrugged.

As we drove into Washington, D.C., that beautiful spring afternoon, the great buildings of government stood as a reminder of that city's history and created hallowed images in my mind. I knew I was a romantic, but the feelings I experienced at times like this seemed to overwhelm me as much as a Sousa march.

Angelyn and I had looked forward to this trip for a long time. Joyce and Nick were special to us and it had been almost a year since we'd seen them.

Angelyn looked up from the map and said, "Get back on Connecticut Avenue — it'll take us to Chevy Chase. Bobby, sometimes I don't know how you find your way home in the dark."

As the snarled traffic moved at a snail's pace along the chaotic street, I watched a group of young blacks at a nearby service station pump gasoline onto the ground and ignite it. When the giant fireball erupted, I saw one of them blown into the air and a parked automobile explode into flames near the pump. Other blacks ran, shouting obscenities, throwing rocks, bottles, and anything else they could find at passing cars that were occupied by whites.

What had only taken minutes seemed like an eternity as I drove, dodging cars and debris, trying to escape the mayhem and madness that was rampant in that section of the city.

After getting out of harm's way and finding Joyce and Nick's apartment, we pulled into the parking lot. "Angelyn! Open the glove-box and hand me the pistol," I said.

"Why? I don't think you need it now."

"I ain't so sure of that. We don't know what the hell has happened. This place is like the Belgian Congo and we've got Georgia license plates. If that ain't a good enough reason, I'm gonna shoot that crazy Greek for leavin' Savannah."

It was April 4, 1968, and the Reverend Martin Luther King, Jr., had just been assassinated in Memphis, Tennessee, a few hours earlier. Washington was now a place of violent rioting and looting.

The four of us sat watching television as U.S. Army paratroopers placed sandbags and machine guns on the steps of the United States Capitol Building.

"Man, it's hard to believe this is happenin' in America," I said, pointing at the screen, "Not long ago, John F. Kennedy's body was carried down those same East steps. Now the place is a bloody battlefield. This nation is fallin' apart right before our eyes."

"Reds, don't get yourself so worked up," Nick said, shaking his head. "This country ain't falling apart, it's just adjusting its character. I'd bet my Greek ass the same people that got

Kennedy, got King." Nick grinned, obviously pleased with his assessment of things.

"Nick, your statement about this country adjustin' its character went over my head. But I'd be willin' to bet my cracker ass Castro was behind the Kennedy assassination."

"Wrong! The Mafia, working for the CIA, got Kennedy. And you watch, when the dust settles in Memphis, it'll be the same old story, a lone gunman."

"Man! You sound just like 'Dumbo' Barber, except you ain't accusing the military-industrialists or the 'illuminati'."

Nick nodded. "Hey, Dumbo ain't no dummy — we are talkin' about the same people."

I laughed a short, cynical laugh. "So you think all these ambiguous bastards get together to plan assassinations and shit like that?"

"Reds Baby, you ever heard of the United Fruit Company?"

"Yeah, those are the folks that have been manipulatin' politics in the Caribbean and Central America for decades — that is, until Castro pulled their bananas."

"You got it! They've also put dictators like Batista and Trujillo in power. Their lobbyists have been greasin' palms of Washington lawmakers for years. Now, tell me you can't believe those kind of shady bastards wouldn't be capable of assassinations."

"Maybe, but ain't that the name of the game?" I remarked.

"I wouldn't argue that, but guess who owns the company?"

"I have no idea, Nick."

"The Dulles brothers. Allen was the director of the CIA from '53 until '61, and the other brother, John Foster, was Secretary of State under Eisenhower."

"Nick, you must be using Chinese arithmetic to figure all that out. John Foster Dulles has been dead for ten years," I laughed, shaking my head in disbelief.

"Laugh, you redheaded rebel. Tell me it ain't possible?"

Angelyn interrupted, "Joyce, how do you like Washington?"

"We love it, don't we honey?" she said looking at Nick.

He nodded in agreement, "Hey, what can I say? I can't get in trouble up here — Reds ain't around to lead me astray."

"Bullshit, Greek, you know you're the instigator."

Nick smiled smugly. "Not me! You're the one that almost got us shot in Miami tryin' to join that boner at the Bay of Pigs. Then you wanted me to sky dive in a gator-infested swamp. Man, if I'd listened to you we'd both be in the French Foreign Legion."

"It's a shame, when you two get together you butt heads like two bull goats. That's one reason I'm glad we left Savannah. The only things I miss about that town is y'all, my parents and those crazy Lemon Dances," Joyce said, smiling at me.

"Joyce, Reds and I are going across the street and have a beer. You need anything from the store?" Nick asked.

"No, but please don't be gone long — Ignus and Georgia should be here any minute," Joyce said with a concerned look on her face.

"They're living in D.C.?" I asked.

"Yeah, we don't call him 'Ignus' anymore. Now it's Chef Panos Karatassos — he's the Michelangelo of ice sculptors. The kid graduated from one of those serious 'gourmet chef' schools in France."

"Man! I can remember when he couldn't warm up a can of soup."

"Let's go have that beer, Flash," Nick said, walking towards the door.

"Remember, there is a riot goin' on," Joyce echoed.

"Don't worry, baby, I've got a .38 in my pocket and 'Hatchet Man' Helmey at my side." He laughed and winked at Angelyn, then looked at his ten year-old son. "Nicky, take care of the girls for daddy."

As we walked toward the tavern, we could see a fiery-glow illuminating the night in the distant sky over Washington.

"Nick, you think this country is gonna survive?"

I had hoped Nick would be able to help me locate the bar where the CIA officer had taken me. However, Washington was now a city under siege. When I told him the story of that night, I was careful not to mention the cloak-and-dagger aspect.

"Nick, the place must be somewhere in the central area of the city. When the cab pulled away, I glanced out the rear window. In the distance, bathed in lights, I saw a building that looked like the U.S. Capitol."

"Before you tell me any more, why the fuck didn't you call me, when you got in town? Nick snapped.

"Man! I didn't know until the chopper landed that I was even in Washington. We were told not to leave Andrews because aircraft would be picking us up early the next morning for the trip back to Staten Island. Brother, I was gonna call, but I got tied up with this government man and the rest is history."

"Hey! Knowin' you, I can understand," he hesitated, "but, why the hell are you so interested in the place after all this time?"

"Nick, there's more to this than a few hours of memory loss. A lot of things have happened since I went up those stairs."

He smiled and shook his head. "I'm not gonna ask you to explain that statement. I've got a couple of Fed friends that could check the place out. After things settle down, I'll do what I can. Describe the blonde broad again, Reds."

"Five-nine, a hundred and thirty pounds, fine body, probably wears a hair piece because her complexion is too dark to be a natural blond; speaks with a slight Spanish accent and had the finest set of tits you've ever laid eyes on."

"Brother, we better get back before things heat up and Ignus's ice carving melts." Nick lifted his glass and grinned.

As we walked away from the tavern, Nick put his arms around me, "Bobby, Joyce was right, I do miss Savannah and getting together and dancing the night away. Those Lemon Dances were as good as it gets."

"Greek, you're right. Those were the days, my friend, we thought they'd never end..."

By the time Angelyn and I left Washington the following afternoon, 130 cities across the United States were in flames. Rioters pillaged and burned as antiwar activists set matches to flags and draft cards. America seemed to be coming apart at the seams. President Johnson was literally a prisoner of war; he was largely confined to the safety of the White House and of military installations. In a speech he told a nation that had elected him by a landslide that he would not be running for another term.

As we returned home that night crossing the Eugene Talmadge Memorial Bridge, we saw another fiery glow lighting the distant sky. News, the next morning, told the story. Yachum & Yachum, Uncle Sammy's Boys, a landmark clothing emporium in a predominately black section of town, was destroyed by fire during racial demonstrations.

On April 11th, U.S. Secretary of Defense Clifford called up 24,500 more military reservists. Still, my talents weren't needed.

June 5th, Senator Robert F. Kennedy was fatally wounded in Los Angeles, California. A Jordanian Arab was arrested for the crime.

In early July, I received a call from Nick, telling me that he had discussed our conversation with his friends the day after I left Washington. "It's strange," he said, "I haven't heard from them. They were regulars for coffee. Maybe they got mixed-up with brown sugar and got an amnesia fix, too." He laughed as he hung up.

The U-6A Beaver leveled off at an altitude of 2,500 feet and started the approach leg to the St. Lo DZ. The Jumpmaster signaled for us to sit in the door. Thirty seconds later he tapped us out.

Due to marginal wind gusts at the time of our safety briefing, Steve Zadach and I volunteered to jump as 'wind dummies' so that the Drop Zone Safety Officer could check conditions prior to the unit's drop.

As I hung suspended under the T-10 canopy, the August sun blazed down savagely. Temperatures neared 100 degrees, the humidity was over 80 percent, which gave a heat index of over 115 degrees. These conditions caused the most bizarre anomaly I had experienced since being smitten by the airborne bug. Vicious thermals created severe updrafts and gusting ground winds teamed together to give me one of the most memorable rides of my life.

As I was being dragged through an area of the DZ that hadn't been cleared of stumps and undergrowth, I struggled with the Capewell Releases trying to collapse my main parachute canopy. But the force of the updrafts carried me back into the air like a dandelion pod being driven by a tempest, violently slamming me back to earth, again and again. As fear gripped me, I realized I was being dragged to my death.

Nature's call placed Sergeant Roy L. Jackson in that area of the drop zone. The fact that he was swift enough to run down the erratically moving parachute and collapse it with his trousers around his knees, made it an almost superhuman maneuver. The second miracle was that I received only a mild concussion, several cracked ribs, and the heels of my Cochran jump boots were torn off.

The other 'dummy' survived with minor scratches and abrasions. Fortunately his helmet didn't come off, and he was able to free himself before having his behind dragged all over Fort Stewart. The unit drop was aborted due to unfavorable weather conditions.

That early September morning, as I passed the last buoy that marked the Savannah River channel, my intentions were to check out the newly-installed marine engine and return to the dock. But the beauty and tranquility of the sea lured me and the thirty-foot trawler, *Cracker Boy*, on like a seductress. The

Atlantic was as calm as a mountain lake. The boat's compass pointed due east towards the endless horizon as I opened another beer and looked back to see land disappear. The engine's noise faded as my mind drifted.

I thought, I've been in love with Joyce all these years, and the only time I've ever held her, is when we've danced. I know it's not right. I'm married with four children and she's my best friend's wife ... what the hell do I know about love anyway? When Angelyn and I were married, love wasn't a choice. It was the right thing to do. Man! I've heard that phony statement all my life. What a deceptive remark — who's right, mine or yours? God! Who does what's right? The people who are destroying this country, are they doing what's right? If Jimmy and Curt come home in body bags, will they be doing what's right? Damn, I'm miserable as a bastard, trying to do what's right...

A hard jolt brought me to my feet and back from the thoughts that had carried me almost to the Gulf Stream. The ocean that had been so peaceful earlier was now turbulent and menacing. Blusterous black clouds covered the entire sky, as wind and sea came together. A cold spray flew over the bow and soaked me before I could slip into my foul weather gear. I turned the small craft 180 degrees and headed for calmer waters.

I didn't have much time to daydream on the trip back in that day, but I did make my mind up to do what had to be done.

The more I studied Fidel Castro and his family, the more they intrigued me. I learned that Fidel's father, Angel, was married in his youth to a Cuban woman who was a school teacher. They had two children. Later, he had an affair with the cook in the household, Lina Ruz Gonzales. She bore him five children; among them were Ramon, Fidel, Raul and Emma. Since Angel Castro was Catholic, he was unable to marry Fidel's mother until the death of his first wife.

This situation obviously contributed to the atmosphere of tension and mutual hatred that reigned throughout the Castro family. The two children by the first wife resented the fact that a former servant was a mistress of the house. For Fidel, it meant carrying the stigma of being a bastard.

Angel Castro was an aloof man who seldom spoke to his children. He was in frequent conflict with Fidel's sense of social responsibility.

Drew Pearson published a story that Fidel's anti-American phobia dated back to his father's brutal treatment of immigrant Haitian workers while a supervisor with the United Fruit Company.

One day, while Fidel was a student at the University of Havana, his father criticized him for his strong political convictions. "I am in the University studying law and this same study of law makes me defend what is right, even with naked hands," Fidel replied. "I defend the rights of the oppressed poor against those who abuse the powers they wrenched from the people with deceitful promises; that is my battle.'"

After reading Fidel's response to his father, I was reminded of the motto of the Green Berets, *De Oppresso Liber* (freedom for the oppressed).

On the 5th of November, 1968, Richard M. Nixon, the man who had been President Eisenhower's Bay of Pigs action officer, was elected the 37th president of the United States.

"Now, were you working at the Savannah Planing Mill on the 11th day of December, 1968?" asked my attorney, Fred Clark.

"Yes, sir, I was."

"Were you injured there?"

"Yes, sir."

"Tell us what happened."

Looking directly at the jury, I amsered. "I'd gone to the pallet department which is in the rear of the lumber yard. As I walked parallel to a truck that was being loaded with pallets, someone threw a tie-down strap with a large metal hook over the rear of the vehicle, striking me in the head and knocking me unconscious. When I regained consciousness, several people were standing over me. I didn't recognize any of them, although they were mill employees. I was taken to the hospital and stitched up — that's all I remember."

Fred turned and faced the judge. "If it pleases your Honor, we'll discuss the medical testimony later?"

Judge Lawrence nodded.

"Now, since that time, would you consider yourself moved by certain events that transpired, that otherwise would not have affected you?"

"Yes, and I haven't been the same since that accident."

"O.K., tell us some of the events. I'm thinking in particular of the *USS Pueblo* incident."

"Well, my original reaction was that this country should immediately use force to get the ship and crew back from the North Koreans, but time rocked on and it appeared as though we were doing nothing. Then, I saw Commander Bucher on national television signing a confession that he was spying in North Korean territorial waters. I felt he had collaborated with the Koreans and had gone beyond name, rank and serial number. Even picking up a pencil and letting them photograph him for propaganda purposes went against everything I'd been trained not to do. I thought he was a coward.

"Then in late December and after my head injury, the U.S. government signed — and immediately refuted — the confession of guilt, composed by the North Koreans, and the 82 surviving crew members were released."

"Then how did you feel in regard to the commander of the Pueblo?"

"Seeing Commander Bucher on television after his release, I felt entirely different. He was so emotional he could hardly speak. I didn't blame him anymore, I felt sorry for the man, and I cried."

"Now, prior to your injury — would you have been moved to tears by such an event?"

"No sir, that isn't to say I didn't have feelings, but I could hold them in, as I've said — I wasn't myself."

"Now, did you go to military drills after the blow on the head?"

"Yes, sir."

"What were the instructions from the doctor in regards to parachute jumps?"

"I was told not to jump under any circumstances."

"And what were your intentions?"

"Originally, not to jump, but I felt someone would think I was chicken-shit — also I didn't wanna lose my jump pay."

"Did you?"

"Yes, sir, twice that week before I went to Cuba."

"Now, tell us about the event when Curtis Harper left for Vietnam."

It was after midnight. Angelyn and I had finished decorating our Christmas tree. As we sat quietly gazing at the blinking, multicolored lights that illuminated the room, the phone rang. "Who in the world could that be at this hour?" she said as she rushed to answer it.

When she came back in the room, she was laughing, "It was Judy Harper, and to quote your Gongie, she was happier than a dog with two peters. Curtis is gonna be home Friday and he's not leaving for Vietnam until the 29th of December. Boy! she was bubbling over with anticipation."

"Yeah, she won't be able to touch that thing with a powder puff 'til Curt leaves."

"Bobby, you're nasty. Is that all you've got on your mind?"

"Not really, Angelyn, but it does come to mind more than once a month — in fact, it's on my mind right now. It's been over six weeks," I said, trying to draw her close to me.

She laughingly pulled away, "Not tonight, big boy, I'm ovulating. Maybe Santa will bring you something, if you're a good little boy." Then she walked slowly toward her bedroom.

I stood in the yard office, sipping my morning coffee and pondering over all the crazy things that were happening in my life. I couldn't get Joyce off my mind, the desire to go on active duty, dreams and obsessions with Fidel Castro. Suddenly the office door opened, bringing me back to reality.

"Excuse me, are you Bobby?" the woman asked.

"Yes," I answered, not believing my eyes.

"The gentleman in the front office said that you might be able to help me," she said handing me a small piece of mahogany molding.

"Excuse me, but haven't I met you?" I asked.

"I don't think so, I'm not from Savannah," she answered.

"You look so much like a lady I once met in Washington, it's unbelievable. But you couldn't possibly be her. She speaks with a Spanish accent, and is blonde," I said as I stared down at the white cotton blouse that was opened provocatively, displaying the deep valley between her humongous tits. I had to shift my eyes away before she caught me staring down at them.

"This looks like a section of a boat's gunwale ," I said as I opened the shop door for her.

"Yes, that's right. I only need a small piece of it."

After looking, and not being able to find the molding in stock, I offered to manufacture it for her. But, I explained that I couldn't do it until January because of the holidays.

"That's fine. I'm not leaving for the Keys until January the eleventh. Please use a good grade of marine mahogany. My boat carpenter is somewhat of a perfectionist." As she leaned forward her nipples pressed against the soft fabric of her blouse like large protruding buttons.

Trying not to act flustered, I asked, "You live in the Keys?" She hesitated, almost stammering, and said, "No, my home is in Miami, but I hab a boat in Key West."

For just a moment I could have sworn I picked up a Spanish accent. This had to be the same woman. She was just not wearing a hairpiece, everything else fit — the body, the complexion and the boobs said that it was her.

When I asked for her name and telephone number, she

replied, "I'm sorry but I don't have a local address or phone number. If you like — I could pay now?"

"No, that's not necessary. But I do need your name for the shop order," I said, picking up a pencil.

"Carmen," she said, looking at me almost hypnotically. Her eyes expressed everything.

"Bobby, how were you injured?" she asked.

As I touched the bandage over my right eye, I said, "Oh this! I forgot to duck when my wife threw a bottle."

"Sounds as if you live a very interesting life," she said gently touching my arm and laughing lightly.

Clearing my throat, I said, "Carmen, I'll do my best to have it ready before the 11th, but call me in a few days?"

"Will do," she said. She turned away, then back. "You know, your face is familiar, now that I think of it." My imagination danced as she walked away.

Before I left the planing mill that afternoon to have the stitches removed from my head, Angelyn called and suggested that we have a welcome-home-going-away party for Curtis the following Saturday night. "I've already discussed it with Judy, and she said to tell you that they'd be here — even if she had to bring a box of powder puffs."

I awoke early the following Saturday morning, with a feeling of restlessness radiating through me. I walked down on my father's dock in the half-light before the dawn, plagued by thoughts and fears that I didn't quite understand. As I stood gazing into the heavens, I saw a bright shooting star arch over the face of the moon and disappear. My mind turned to the dreams that I'd been having about Cuba, Castro and death.

Five days after Christmas, I pulled in the driveway of 11 St. Catherine Road and gently pressed the horn. 1st Lieutenant Curtis Harper had asked me to take him to Travis Field, feeling it might be a little too emotional for Judy and the children at the airport. I told him that it would be an honor, and I would even wear my uniform for the occasion.

There was an icy chill in the air that morning. I left the pickup truck's engine running while I waited for Curt to have a last-minute farewell with his family.

Sitting in the Savannah airport lounge, we made a covenant to write each other regularly. I gave him my solemn word to make sure Jody (a figure of military legend who steals other soldiers' women) didn't have any opportunity to jam-bugger him while he was off defending his country.

"It ain't Jody I'm worried about; just keep an eye on old Leo," he said grinning.

"Well Curtis E, you're finally on your way, and I'm still sittin' on the friggin' ready-box, feeling like an old whore who never turned a trick, and couldn't even give it away."

Curt nodded his head as if he knew something I didn't, then almost prophetically said, "Reds, your day is coming soon."

"Tell me something, brother — what makes us tick?"

"I can't really answer that question, but I know this. There's mysteries in life we'll never understand. Some things are predestined in certain people's lives, that's why I'm on my way to Vietnam. Somebody up there is calling the shots and I've got a gut feeling He knows what He's doing."

"Lieutenant, you're either a Primitive Baptist or you've been talking to my grandma. Predestination covers a multitude of sins. Oh! Before I forget it, here's a little goin' away present," I said, handing him a small package.

While he was unwrapping the gift, the PA system announced his flight. "Thanks for everything, Reds, this'll come in handy," he said, putting the small Bible into his uniform pocket.

I picked up his carry-on luggage and we walked to the gate. Hugging him, I stepped back and saluted, saying, "Love you, Curt. Take care of yourself. And remember — no tattoos."

He walked a short distance, then stopped, turned, and gave

me a thumbs-up. Watching him board the aircraft I thought, "My God, if I didn't know it was the truth, I'd have a hard time believing it. A kid who's a pipe-fitter at Union Camp has the balls to go through Parris Island, serve six months on active duty in the Marine Corps. After that, he joins the Army Reserves and becomes Airborne; Special Forces and Ranger qualified. Then toughs out 28 weeks at Fort Benning, becoming an officer and a gentleman, and through it all, he manages to attend enough night classes at Armstrong State College to receive a Bachelor's Degree in Business Administration. Then he volunteers for Vietnam, because he thinks it's the right thing to do. Ho Chi Minh, Fidel Castro, and all you Communist bastards better take note because one more of America's best is on the way. Airborne!"

Later that same day, I got a call from Sergeant Norton asking me if I could go with him again to pick up parachutes at Fort Benning. "Only if you buy the beer and expound on that 'blood oath' story," I said. He laughingly consented and I agreed to meet him at the armory at 0630 hours, Friday, January 3, 1969.

Before the 4:30 whistle blew that day, Robbie Bright, the woodworker whom I had given the job of making the gunwale molding, came and handed me a small metal object.

"You know what dis is, Mister Bobby?" he asked.

"I think so, it's the business end of a bullet. Where'd it come from, Robbie?" I asked.

"From dat piece of boat molding ya gimme to match."

"I'll be damned — I saw those holes in the wood. Somebody must have been using that yacht for target practice. Strange thing about it is, this looks like a 7.62 mm short, the kind used in the Russian AK assault rifles," I said, putting it in my pocket.

Robbie shook his head and said, "Mister Bobby, did you learn 'bout dim bullets in the Green Hornets?"

"In the what, Robbie?" I chuckled.

"What'cha call that little green beanie you was sportin' 'round here dis mornin' — ya knows, the one you plays soldier in sometimes?" he asked.

"A green beret," I said, thinking of the truth in the wise old black man's perception.

When I saw Bill McGuire coming toward the planing mill's yard office, I went to meet him.

"Bobby, you got time after work to talk with me?"

"I'll make the time," I replied, nodding my head.

Bill was Irish as Hogan's goat and could be just as hardheaded, especially if you handed him any guff. He was raised in the "Old Fort" section of Savannah, a place where a man was measured by the dexterity of his fist and the depths of his heart. Even though I was his boss and he was 20 years my senior, he treated me like family.

Tony Yatro's place was only a few blocks from the mill and across the street from Bill's apartment. Tony, the Greek-American proprietor, was also the unofficial mayor of Liberty Street. Yatro's clientele included people from all walks of life. Politicians, policemen, priests, and plumbers all frequented his small confectionery which was an amalgamation of general store, bistro and pawn shop. Tony also had the concession rights at the Chatham County Jail, which was located next to his building's back door on Habersham Street.

"Are you sure everything's all right?" Bill asked, as we sat in Yatro's having a beer.

"What'cha mean, Bill?"

"Well, for starters, you've been moody as an old mule lately. Every time we've had a conversation, you seem to be somewhere else. I wasn't gonna say anything, but a few other folks have noticed it also — they say you haven't been the same since that lick on your head. Frankly, I'm worried about you, too."

I thought about it for a moment, then said, "Bill, I don't think the injury has anything to do with it. Doctor Hood said I only had a mild concussion; he didn't even take an x-ray. I appreciate your concern and apologize for being so distracted. I've had a lot of heavy crap on my mind lately."

He fished a cigarette from the pack in his shirt pocket and lit it. Then he hesitated, looking me straight in the eyes. "This ain't none of my business, but I'm gonna ask you anyway. Are you and your wife having problems?"

"Not any more than usual. Why?"

"I thought that might be the problem."

"Bill, you know what this is?" I asked, changing the subject.

"Looks like a bullet," he said examining the object.

"It is. You recall a couple of weeks ago, you sent a lady down to the yard with a piece of gunwale molding."

"Yeah, I think so — was she wearin' red high-heels and had those humongous knockers that bounced when she walked?"

"That's the one, brother! Robbie Bright dug a couple of these slugs out of that piece of wood."

An amused look came over his face. "Must have been a gun fight to see who was gonna board the broad first," he laughed, and handed me the bullet back, saying, "She was driving a new Ford Mustang with Florida plates."

"Right, with the Miami one suffix," I replied.

Bill shook his head. "I remember now; she asked for you specifically when she came in that office." He paused a moment, then grinned. "Bobby you know that broad, don't you?"

"No, not really," I replied. "But, I'm gonna make one hell of an effort to find out who Carmen, the mystery woman, is."

"Yeah, I'll bet you will," he added as he lit another Camel.

I smiled and said, "Well, what kind of resolutions are you gonna make this year, you old Irish Goat?"

He flicked ashes on the floor, nodded his head, and thought for a moment. "Only one — to get me a pistol, so I can walk these friggin' streets at night without a bodyguard."

"See that gentlemen over there in the dark suit and sunglasses talking with Tony Yatro. He can get you a bazooka or anything else you might need."

"Who the hell is he?" Bill asked.

"Ken Whitaker, the agent-in-charge of the local FBI," I said as I fanned cigarette smoke from my eyes.

"Hey, I'm serious. You walk from that mill down Liberty Street after dark like I do, and you'll know what I'm sayin' is the truth. These young jitter-bugs will hurt you if you let 'em — a gun is my only New Year's resolution."

I sat in silence for a moment, then said, "Bill, I hate to leave good company, but it's been a long day. How 'bout goin' out to the truck with me?"

As Bill and I walked out of Yatro's, I stopped and wished Tony a happy and prosperous 1969.

I opened the glove compartment and handed Bill a box of cartridges and a chrome-plated .38 snub-nosed Smith & Wesson. "Here's a little belated Christmas present, brother. Be careful and don't point it if you ain't gonna use it," I said.

He put the cartridges and pistol in his pocket. "God bless you, boss-man," he said warmly, putting his arm around me. "Bobby, whatever's bothering you, you can talk to me. Happy New Year, son."

"Thanks, Bill. You're a good man and I appreciate that. See you in the morning."

Sergeant Norton and I traveled to Fort Benning on the 3rd of January as planned. But it would be nearly a year before I had any memory of the trip and the two parachute jumps I made that same weekend.

"Now, tell us about the television show, "Second Tuesday," that aired January 7th, 1969," asked attorney Fred Clark.

"I think it was the Tuesday prior to my leaving for Cuba that I saw the program. Castro had allowed the NBC television network to interview some of the Americans who were in Cuba. In particular, I remember an interview with a young woman from Atlanta who had joined his revolution. It turns out that she had attended high school in Savannah, Georgia. The reporter asked her, 'Would you kill an American, one of your fellow countrymen, for the revolution?' She said, 'I would, because I believe that capitalism is the great exploiter of mankind. In our struggle for freedom against the imperialists, our battle cry must be — Create two, three...many Vietnams.'"

"What was your reaction after seeing this on television?" Clark asked.

"It upset me. How could a young girl feel so passionately about Communism? Where was this country's sense of patriotism? Why were we tearing this nation apart — student uprisings, war protests and civil rights riots. No! It angered me."

"What intention did you acquire as a result of this?"

"I didn't..."

"All right, let me ask you this. Would you testify that any one particular act set you off more than any others to cause you to take this trip to Cuba?"

"No, I don't think so."

"Now, prior to your taking this trip, had you been building a boat?"

"Yes, I had."

"Tell us how long you had been working on it."

"Several months."

"Did you finish it before you left?"

"Yes, and the reason I built the houseboat was because my father-in-law had been shot during a robbery at his store and was paralyzed from the waist down. He loved the water as much as I did. I thought it might be good therapy for him."

"All right, what is this paper I just handed you?"

"An order for the bookstore at Fort Bragg, North Carolina."

"What did you order from the bookstore?" asked Clark.

"My Senior Wings and the new subdued uniform patches, which are being used in Vietnam."

"Did you also send for lesson plans for future drills? By future drills, I mean after January 11th?"

"I did, because our S3 shop didn't have the training manuals I needed for the 15 to 20 hours of instruction that I was scheduled to give on cold weather training at Fort Drum, New York, in February."

"Had you intended on going to this training?"

"Yes, I had."

"Your Honor, we're going to offer this receipt in evidence."

"Now, do you recall Saturday, January 11th, 1969, the day of this event?"

"Yes sir, I do...."

The morning was clear and bright when I arrived at the Savannah Planing Mill that Saturday morning, the 11th of January. Bill McGuire was sitting on the front porch steps smoking a cigarette and holding a styrofoam cup of steaming coffee.

"Boss-man, you're almost late and that's unusual," he said, as I opened the door and turned the ADT alarm system off.

"Yeah, I had to go and pick up these jump boots I had repaired on Waters Avenue. You know Flipper, the high-yellow fellow who owns the cobbler shop? Anyhow, for years I've noticed a picture of a black man who appeared to be in a military academy tunic hanging on his wall. Curiosity got the better of me and I asked who the man in the photograph was. Flipper told me that it was his grandfather who had been the first African-American to graduate from the United States Military Academy at West Point. It just awed the shit out of me how a Negro could overcome those kind of odds.

"Hell, I just got carried away with the conversation and the time slipped by."

Bill laughed, "Boy, you love anything to do with that military stuff, don't you?"

Saturdays were usually pretty routine at the mill. Since we were only open from eight a.m. until noon, we only needed a small number of employees.

Bill and I normally worked the front office together. On that particular Saturday, I worked filling customers' orders on the yard because I was a man short. About 11:30 Bill sent word for me to come to the sales office. Upon entering the building, I recognized the woman standing at the counter. The black cashmere sweater she was wearing clung to her like a wet tee-shirt, and Bill seemed to be in a near-trance, watching her every move.

"This lady says you have something for her," Bill said, smiling wide, enjoying the moment.

Walking with her in the direction of the lumber shed, I tried to weave a logical fabric from threads of confused thoughts ... the CIA, Alpha 66, now this mysterious woman, again. My mind raced back to that muddled night in Washington.

She sat there for a moment, examining the piece of molding, "Bobby, you've done a beautiful job of matching the old molding."

I took a deep breath, trying to compose myself. "Lady, it's time you and I had a little talk."

Her eyes opened wide. "What do you mean?" she asked.

"I mean, you didn't come here for any molding. You and I have met before ... you're either CIA or some anti-Castro origination. And I'd bet my ass you know a guy named Merlin."

The coloring drained from her face. She blinked as though I had struck her. "Maybe we should talk."

"Good!" I said, looking at my watch. "Why don't you go over there and check that houseboat out while I close the mill," pointing to a boat under the distant shed.

She nodded affirmation.

I went back to the sales office. "Wild Bill, after we close, you drive my truck down to Yatro's. I'll be there in a little while. I have some unfinished business waiting for me down on the yard."

He grinned, shaking his head. "O.K. boss, I'll be there. Don't let me down."

It was a Saturday ritual when Bill and I worked, to go to Tony's and unwind. When Carmen dropped me at Yatro's, Bill was on his usual stool, in deep conversation with Tony.

"Boss, you look a little peaked. That unfinished business must have really strained your monkey," he remarked.

"Old man, you got'cha mind in the gutter again. But, I do have a headache — it ain't nothin' a cold Budweiser can't cure."

Bill looked at Tony and said, "Give my boy a headache powder and a cold Bud, please, sir."

"Just the beer, Tony. The lady gave me something for a headache a few minutes ago," I said.

"Yeah, I'll bet she did," Bill grinned. "Before I forget, your neighbor, Bob Brookfield, called and asked me to remind you of the plywood you're supposed to bring when you head home."

"You know what he's gonna do with that plywood?" I asked.

"No! Because you got some crazy fuckin' friends."

"The man's got twenty-five Eastern diamondback rattlesnakes in a wire cage in his backyard and he wants to build 'em a bigger and better home."

"Man! He'd be the one huntin' a home if he lived in my neighborhood. What the hell is he gonna do with all those snakes?"

"Milk 'em." I said.

"Shit! What kinda milk do you get from a rattlesnake?"

"Hemotoxic venom. The kind that sells for big bucks. Bill, this guy is no bullshit artist. At one time he did contract work for Ross Allen in Central America. The man has milked the fer-de-lance, the pit viper called the 'eyelash' snake. If one bites you — your ass is dead before it hits the ground"

"That what I said, you got some crazy friends."

"Well, the headache ain't gettin' any better and I've still got to go back to the mill and pick up Brookfield's plywood."

"Yeah, go on home and get some rest, you look bushed."

I nodded, then said, in a low voice, "Bill, do me a favor and don't ever mention that woman if anybody should ask. I've torn the shop ticket up ... no record, you understand?"

He looked at me, puzzled. "I got'cha boss, you don't have to worry about me. Are you sure you're all right?"

"Yeah, I think so. I'll see you Monday, Bill."

After dropping off the plywood at Brookfield's, I arrived

home at approximately 5:30 in the afternoon. I went directly to my room and picked up a briefcase. I then walked into the den where my wife and children sat watching television.

Suddenly I experienced a sharp pain over my right eye. Then I felt as if I were standing next to myself observing what was happening in a dreamstate.

"Angelyn, I need to talk with you," I said softly.

"Now, were you aware of the plans that you and your wife had made for the evening?" Clark asked.

"Yes, sir, we had planned for the Brookfields to come over."

"Based on that, would it be correct to say that you expected them to be at your home later that evening?"

"Yes, sir," I said as I looked at the jury.

"All right, after you got home, tell us what you did."

I watched Angelyn's expressionless face as I told her that I was part of a CIA assassination plot to kill Fidel Castro.

"After I've landed in Cuba, you'll receive a quarter of a million dollars from Ken Whitaker. He's the agent in charge of the local FBI office."

I knew she didn't believe any of the story. But for a moment her eyes did brighten when I mentioned the money. Because I didn't want one of her howling inquisitions in front of the children, I asked her to drive me to a service station on Drayton Street, a block from the home of Captain Tommy Close, who had agreed to take me to the airport.

"How long are you gonna be gone, Bobby?" she asked.

"If everything goes all right, I should be home in three to four months," I said opening the car door.

"Suppose it doesn't?" she asked.

"Then pray for me, Angelyn."

I watched as she drove away in the dark of the night.

The walk from the service station to Captain Close's house took less than five minutes...

* * *

FBI Report, January 1969

Two days later, on January 13, 1969, Thomas M. Close, voluntarily appeared at the Savannah Office of the FBI, advising that he had information concerning Robert M. Helmey, an individual in Close's Special Forces Reserve Unit, who had allegedly hijacked an airplane to Cuba. Close then provided this signed statement:

I, Thomas M. Close, a Captain in Company E of the 11th Special Forces Unit in Savannah, GA., make the following free and voluntary statement to SAC K.W. Whittaker, ASAC Thomas D. Westfall, and SA William P. Lawler, JR., who have identified themselves to me as Special Agents of the FBI in Savannah, GA.

On Saturday night, January 11th, 1969, at approximately 7:30 PM, I received a telephone call from a friend, Sergeant Robert M. Helmey, of the above Reserve Unit, who is also known to me as "Reds." He asked me to give him a ride to the airport. He said he was at the service station his father owns which is behind the Savannah Theater on Drayton Street, which is in walking distance from my house at 122 East Oglethorpe Avenue.

He came over and came into the house and I gave him a beer. We rode to the airport, and on the way he opened his briefcase, which was all he carried, and said, I want to show you a revolver. Being interested in weapons, I looked at it. I believe it was a Model 1918 Double Action Army manufactured by Smith and Wesson, but these revolvers are similar to those manufactured by Colt.

He said, "I put our friend Curtis Harper on the plane before he left for Vietnam, to go over there and fight communism." Then he said, "You are going to put me on the plane to go fight communism in Cuba."

I was amazed, and he then said, "I am going to highjack a plane to Cuba and assassinate Fidel Castro on Wednesday." He also said, "I am in a conspiracy which is headed by the FBI and CIA, and they have given me permission to tell you this story so that you can assure my family that I am not a communist and in case I fail in my mission, they would know their father did not highjack because he was a communist but instead, that he was going to Cuba and take part in this conspiracy because it is important to the Johnson Administration that Castro be assassinated and Cuba be freed before Johnson leaves office."

I dropped him off at the airport, at which time he said, "Come on in with me and have a beer." We went to the Delta counter and he purchased a ticket with cash on Delta Flight 411 leaving Savannah at 8:11 PM to Jacksonville, Fla., where, according to his ticket he was to change planes and catch a National flight from Jacksonville to Miami, Fla.

He went on to say that there was probably a CIA man in the room right then, "having a fit" because he was drinking a beer and talking to me. He was not drunk when he got onto the plane. He said, "After 11 P.M. tonight I will be in Cuba, and then you can tell anyone that I am part of history." He implored me not to say anything to anyone about the assassination plot because they would kill him in Cuba when they found out. He said, "After it is all over with, Ken Whittaker will contact you as he knows about it. You have to believe this is true." I told him I believed him, but at no point did I actually believe him ... I talked to his wife and found that he had told her the same story, which she did not believe either at that time."

I have read this statement, consisting of this page and two other pages, initialed each page, and now sign it because it is true.

Close advised that he had no idea who might possibly be involved in this alleged conspiracy to kill Castro. He stated that at first he completely disbelieved Helmey's story; however, inasmuch as he actually was on the hijacked airplane and was possibly the hijacker, he thought he might just be crazy enough to try and kill Castro. Close stated that if he received any additional information he would immediately provide it to the FBI. Witness: William P. Lawler, JR., Special Agent, FBI, Savannah, GA., 1-13-69.

Part Eight

LIFE AND DEATH

Any life...is made up of a single moment —
the moment in which a man finds out...who he is.
Jorge L. Borges

Life and Death

"Now, tell us what you and Captain Close discussed at the Savannah Airport prior to your flight?" my attorney asked.

"We talked about our friend, Curtis Harper. I told him as much as I could about the plot to kill Castro. And that I was authorized to detour an aircraft to Cuba. Just before boarding the flight from Savannah, I handed him my Scottish Rite ring and asked him to see that my son Kerry got it."

"Now, tell us what happened on the flight in which you diverted the plane to Cuba?"

After a stopover at Jacksonville for a carrier change, I prematurely boarded the Boeing 727 after discovering that the flight line boarding gate was unattended and unlocked. As I entered the aircraft, two flight attendants were engaged in deep conversation. Holding up my boarding pass, I walked between them and said, "Excuse me, ladies."

"Sir, you may be seated anywhere in the first class cabin," said one of the stewardesses nonchalantly.

I chose a forward window seat on the left side of the aircraft and placed my briefcase under it. I noticed there was only one other passenger, a woman, in the forward cabin.

As the aircraft's forward door was being closed, a man in civilian clothes exited the cockpit compartment and took a seat directly across from me. The seat belt sign came on, the pilot announced the continuation of United's flight 459 to Miami and the 727 taxied for take-off. It was 10:35 p.m. as the jetliner, with a capacity of 150 passengers, lifted from the runway with only twelve and a crew of seven.

After the 727 leveled off, the man seated across the aisle turned and remarked, "I guess you're headed to the Super Bowl?"

"No, but I hope the Jets can pull it off," I said, reaching under the seat for my briefcase.

"Yeah, so do I. Willie Joe Namath is a talented and lucky son-of-a-bitch. If he has a good day, it's possible."

After removing the concealment capsule I placed the briefcase back under the seat and went to the lavatory. When I returned, the chatty gentleman asked, "What time do you have, friend?"

Glancing down at my wrist, I said, "10:58."

"Thanks ... I'll be glad to get to Miami," he mumbled, as he lay back and closed his eyes.

I leaned over to him and in a low voice said, "You mind going by way of Havana?"

His eyes popped open, "No sir, I sure don't."

I took the unloaded .45 caliber revolver from the briefcase, walked to the cockpit and tapped on the door. It was opened by the flight engineer.

"Do you mind taking me to Cuba?" I asked calmly.

"No, sir, come right in," he replied.

I sat in a jump seat on the left side of the aircraft directly behind the pilot.

"Do you have enough fuel to get to Cuba?" I asked.

The co-pilot and engineer answered in unison, "Yes."

"How about the weather ahead?"

Pointing at the pale green glow of the radar screen, the pilot said, "There's a squall line far to the east. We won't have any problem getting around it."

"Will there be a problem with the North American Defense people — I mean, a scramble or some kind of confusion?"

"No trouble at all," the co-pilot answered.

"Are you familiar with the runways at the Jose Marti International Airport in Havana?"

"Everything is all right," he assured me.

"If for any reason this aircraft should not go to Cuba, you can land at Key West, or Miami."

I handed the flight engineer my pistol and told him to have the stewardesses check on the passengers and then have one of them bring me a Jack Daniels and water.

While the engineer held the gun, I asked the co-pilot if he would "Radio Havana and tell Fidel that *El Rojo* is coming!"

"Now, what was your mental state during the hijacking? Did you realize what you were doing?" asked Fred Clark.

"At times I felt like I was seated next to the person who was doing it. I knew that I wasn't myself. And without a shadow of doubt, I believed that I was on a CIA mission."

"Now, one moment. Judge, the next part of the examination is going to be very extensive. Do you think we should break or go on and complete it?" asked my attorney.

For a moment Judge Lawrence stared at Clark pensively, then said, "Well, we'd better break now. I'm going to finish this case, this afternoon, Mr. Clark."

With 10,000 tons of raw sugar, crated cargo, and passengers, the Cuban freighter *Commandant Camilo Cienfuegos* pointed her bow north and sails from the port of Matanzas, Cuba.

At the last sea buoy, a bar pilot wearing combat fatigues scurried down a Jacob's ladder with a Czech submachine gun swinging wildly from his shoulder, jumps onto the pitching deck of a pilot boat and vanished over the southern horizon.

For a moment I had the most incredible sense of freedom, but when I looked up and saw a black "Hammer and Sickle" affixed to the crimson stack of the vessel, I was reminded where I was and the euphoria melted away. I knew the waters ahead could be as turbulent as those I had just survived.

The months of solitary confinement had left me weak and thin. But time had given me the opportunity to discover more about myself. All the things that I had learned growing up about heroes and honor were now on trial. The near death experience had changed me. It had taken a big jolt to open my eyes, but I wanted another chance at life.

I shared an aft deck cabin with two Cubans who both spoke English. While in port, it had been almost impossible to get them to talk, but that night, when the ship hit international waters, things changed. One boasted that Fidel Castro had personally arranged for him to be reunited with his family in Puerto Rico. The other gentleman humbly explained that because of his advanced age, Castro had allowed him to visit his daughters in Canada, whom he had not seen in almost ten years.

Now that the ice had been broken everybody appeared to be starving for conversation. I told them how I happened to be aboard the ship. To my surprise, both had seen me on Cuban National Television the night I arrived in Havana. They seemed to know more about my sojourn on their Communist island than I did.

The next morning, in the gray light before sunrise, I stood on the ship's starboard deck watching the lights from a distant shore move closer. At daybreak, I recognized the multistory hotels of the South Florida coast. The *Cienfuegos* was slowly riding the Gulf Stream's current north. Then I realized, from the address printed on the cargo crate and the conversation that I'd heard the night before, that our next port-of-call would be Canada.

Later that morning, as a United States Coast Guard cutter slowly cruised alongside, I was tempted to jump ship. But the thought vanished when the elderly gentleman, Mr. Raul Bobes Cueruo, staggered up and gently placed his hand on my shoulder. From that point in time, the trust between Mr. Bobes and me gained momentum.

During the entire voyage the octogenarian was never quite able to build any viable sea legs. I became his support, and he, my interpreter and confidant. Several times during the voyage he cautioned me against walking the decks after dark. When I'd ask, "Why?" the answer was always the same, "You might get washed overboard, *Rojo.*"

On May 1, the captain made it mandatory that all off-duty crew members and the fifteen passengers report to the galley at 1900 hours to observe the 52nd anniversary of the "Bolshevik Revolution." When Senor Bobes and I arrived, the gathering of comrades was celebrating with the intensity of a company of drunken Cossacks. The Captain and First Mate seemed extremely nervous as they handed out Cuban cigars, while three glassy-eyed stewards liberally poured vodka and rum for the thirsty bunch.

After the 'Internationale' played over a scratchy PA system, my friend and I found seats at the table where most of the English-speaking passengers were gathered.

The two husky black men who had gotten on the ship in Matanzas were seated directly in front of me. One of them turned and introduced himself as Donald. Removing his Mao cap, he leaned forward and rested his elbows on the table, and in a low voice, said, "Comrade, is it true that you were once a Green Beret?"

I nodded my head slowly, taking in his dark look.

He gave me a hard stare. "Which is the better weapon, the Soviet Kalashnikov Assault Rifle or the American M-16?"

I leaned toward him and replied, "I prefer the M-16, but ultimately the person who has the fastest trigger finger and aims straightest will be the final judge of that."

"First wisdom, then wit. I like that in a man." He lifted his glass, grinning, then asked, "Where ya from, Comrade?"

"Savannah, Georgia."

"I went to college in Atlanta."

"Georgia Tech?" I asked.

He shook his head. "Not hardly — Morehouse College. You ever heard of it?"

"Yeah, I've heard of it," I answered without smiling.

Later that night after the rum kicked in, he boasted about military training in Cuba and other Communist bloc countries. He was knowledgeable about urban warfare, automatic weapons, explosives, and a wide variety of other paramilitary subjects.

I asked if he had ever served in the U.S. military. "Not even the motherfuckin' R.O.T.C., Comrade!" he said, grinning smugly and looking closely into my eyes. After that I understood my Cuban friend's advice about not walking the decks after dark. My presence aboard the *Ceinfuegos* caused a few others the same paranoia — they had obviously been told that I had chosen to return to the United States and face air-piracy and kidnapping charges. Knowing this seemed to puzzle them as much as it did the Cuban G2 who kept me in solitary confinement.

The "May Day" celebration ended prematurely when high winds and heavy seas suddenly started pounding the ship. Everything that wasn't lashed down began to move. The hull squeaked and banged from the strain as the North Atlantic unleashed its fury.

Early the next morning as the vessel labored with thirty foot seas and gale force winds, Mr. Bobes and I lay talking as our roommate struggled with seasickness in his berth.

"Old friend, I watched you when the 'Internationale' played. You're not a Communist, are you?" I remarked.

"Oh! *Rojo* can tell an old man's political ideology by watching his facial expressions. But you're right, I am not a Communist. I am a Roman Catholic and a Cuban. My children were born there, as were my father and his father before him. One day, if God be willing, my body will rest in the sacred soil of a free Cuba," he said proudly.

"Then I guess you're not gonna return to Cuba after your visit to Canada?"

"I am! And why wouldn't I?" he replied sharply.

Before I could answer, he sat up in his bunk and with a

stern look on his ancient face, began telling me the story of his life: his childhood spent on a sugar plantation near Santiago de Cuba, the social evils he witnessed in his early years. The one-room thatched shacks with dirt floors and open fires for cooking, no doctors or dentists; forced to work at hard labor from the age of five; using his savings as a laborer to buy a small plot of land, planting sugar cane and banana trees, then using the profits to purchase additional land.

Eventually he had become a successful planter and was able to send his children to private schools. One son had attended a Jesuit boarding school in Santiago de Cuba, becoming a close friend of Fidel Castro, and was now in Fidel's inner circle.

He ended his memoirs with a short discourse on how he lost his life savings when he took a stand against the United Fruit Company. He attempted to export bananas directly to the States instead of selling in Cuba at their fixed prices. Several large shipments arrived in New York City, rotten after being delayed on railroad sidings in Florida. He was convinced that the company and the railroad had conspired to sabotage his attempt to market his produce in the United States.

"Financially, they broke me, but I learned an important lesson about greed and power. Before Castro, the peasants of Cuba were no more than beasts of burden, harnessed to the yokes of U.S. companies and their Mafia methods."

I didn't say anything for a moment. "Your life kinda sounds like my Grandpapa Helmey's. He came from the school of hard-knocks, too — lost his life savings when an unscrupulous broker friend sold him thousands of dollars of worthless stock, and then had the balls to charge an exorbitant broker's fee. No disrespect, but I don't think greed and power have international borders.

"In this world, the good and the bad folks are all mixed together. Papa Helmey always said, 'Let a smile be your umbrella, because you're gonna get soaked anyway.' I don't know whether his logic was right or wrong, but I do know this, I will be damn glad to get back to where people are free to say and think what they like. Castro is a dictator who loves to hear himself talk, and if you don't agree with his atheistic, Communist horseshit, your ass is grass. Mr. Bobes, that's why I thought you wouldn't return."

He studied my face for a moment, then said, "Maybe that's true, but if Fidel is such a tyrant, why is he letting you return to the United States?"

Suddenly a hard knock jarred the cabin door. "Omar. I need to talk with you," someone said when I asked who was there.

"Just a minute," I answered. But first I told Mr. Bobes not to get out of his bunk until I returned because it was too dangerous for him to walk with the ship pitching about. "I'll bring you and Louis something back from the galley."

"I don't think Louis will appreciate food. Be careful, my friend, and hurry back," he said, smiling.

As I left the cabin, Omar motioned for me to follow him. He led me to an empty cabin on the deck above.

"My name isn't Omar, it's Carl Davidson and I also hijacked an aircraft to Cuba," he said nervously.

"Then you weren't in the Hados security prison on bogus counter-revolutionary charges?"

"Yeah, I was. But let me explain...."

"So what's this got to do with me?" I asked.

"Man! I've heard you're gonna turn yourself in when we get to Montreal — is that true?"

"I thought you told me this ship was going to Spain or Russia," I replied, grinning.

He hesitated, putting his cigarette out. "Helmey, I been watchin' you since we got on this boat. You've been helping that old Cuban around like he was ya daddy. I also know his son is tight with Castro. You keep a smile on your face, like you're on some kinda all-expense-paid sea cruise. I don't think that's normal for a man facing a possible death sentence. You're either CIA or crazy as a motherfuck and I don't believe that."

"Carl, if I were CIA, what could I do for you, and what could you do for me?"

"I wanna cut a deal. I need money and the charges dropped in exchange for intelligence information. My wife and child were on the aircraft — she had no prior knowledge of the hijacking. It was strictly solo on my part; I don't want her implicated."

He stopped and nervously lit a cigarette. "My wife witnessed beheadings and other atrocities at Camp America where she and my child were held. Eldridge Cleaver is going to meet with a group of Black Panthers in Madrid. I know the story about the four other American passengers, and believe me they ain't tourists. There is also a female KGB agent aboard," he said in a jittery voice.

"Carl, you can cut your own deal after you turn yourself in — you don't need me."

"The hell I don't. The minute this ship docks in Montreal and you tell Canadian Customs that you're a hijacker, the shit's gonna hit the fan, and my family ain't gonna be able to get off this boat. Look, I'm gonna turn myself in, but I need a couple of weeks to take care of business. Man! Let me and my family clear the boat before you do what'cha gotta do."

I looked at him for a moment before nodding. "So, how will they be able to contact you after Montreal?" I asked.

"I'll get in touch with you," he said.

I removed one of my shoes, pulled the arch support up, took out a small piece of paper, and said, "Call this number and ask for Ken Whitaker."

"Who's he?" he asked.

"An FBI agent."

"No! I wanna deal with you."

"That's impossible. I will promise this: when I get back to the States, I'll pass on your proposition to the right people. The rest is up to you."

"Good, I'll be in touch with the man." A broad smile spread

across his face. "Watch your ass — they'd love to see you get washed overboard."

For three days, the North Atlantic tossed the vessel about like a toy boat in a bathtub. Many of the crew and passengers suffered severe seasickness, including the two who most wanted me to disappear.

On May 4th, the *Commandant Camilo Cienfuegos* entered the Gulf of St. Lawrence and calmer waters.

The communications officer sent for me to come to the radio shack. "Holmey, the Canadians hab requested nonresident pasaporte passenger gib dare intended destination in Canada."

"You mean — where I'm goin' when we arrive in port?"

"Si, si!" he answered sharply.

"The American Consulate!"

He then told me to go to the purser's office, where I was given back my Cuban passport and the International Certificate of Vaccination. The Purser explained that I wouldn't have any problem getting off the ship if I didn't mention the air-piracy charge to the Customs officials who would be coming aboard in Montreal.

My eyes narrowed. "You mean, I shouldn't let it be known that I'm wanted in the United States?" I asked.

"Si, if jew wanna get off. This ship is goin' to Russia after Canada." he grinned, pleased at the shocked look on my face.

"Not with me aboard," I said, shaking my head.

"Good, jew understand," he said.

I didn't say anything, but I knew what I had to know.

The frigid Canadian air slapped me in the face, like the punch from a Chinook wind. The heavy cotton undershirt that Mr. "B" had just given me helped as I watched the *Cienfuegos* being docked in Montreal.

We stood in the rear of a line awaiting Customs to process the passengers.

"*Muchas gracias, Rojo.* I'm glad our paths crossed and I was able to meet the man who told Fidel he was coming. Your kindness on the voyage will not be forgotten."

"Thanks, Mr. Bobes. I hope you and your family have a good reunion, and you're able to locate all the parts it's gonna take to get that '50 Packard Clipper going again. If I get back to Cuba, we'll take that 'Cherry' for a spin. We can check out those Hemingway hideaways you talked about."

An amused look came over his face. "*Rojo*, that automobile is like me, old and battered," he said. "The time for us grows short. And soon we will know, for whom the bells toll'."

Then I watched him disappear down the gangplank.

The Customs officer became very upset when I told him that I was not staying aboard. "Mr. Helmey, the only way you can leave this ship is by a stopover in the Montreal jail. Later you'll be given a hearing, and those things take time."

"Sir, that's fine! I don't have a problem with that!"

"Good," he nodded.

On the trip to the jail, my thoughts were filled with the realization of what lay ahead. I knew I would be asked many questions in the days

Calling from the Montreal jail, I identified myself to a U.S. Marine officer who answered the phone at the American Consulate. I requested to speak with the charge d'affaires as soon as possible because I had classified information.

"The Canadians have jurisdiction over you now. There's no staff at the Consulate on Sunday, but I will pass this information on and someone will be in touch with you in a day or two," he said, his words laced with official sarcasm.

That cold dismal day stretched into one of the longest I could remember in my thirty-six years of life, and for the first time I felt totally confused and abandoned. The following morning, I was taken to the Canada Immigration Centre in Montreal and given a hearing. I requested to be sent back to the United States as soon as possible. I told them I would surrender myself to the proper authorities.

The deportation order read:

On the basis of evidence adduced at the inquiry held at Canada Immigration Centre, on May 5th, 1969, I have reached the decision that you may not come into or remain in Canada....In that you admit having committed a crime involving moral turpitude, namely, hijacking an aircraft of United Airlines, and your admission to Canada has not been authorized by the Governor-in-Council.

Shortly after the hearing, two Royal Canadian Mounted Police Officers transported me to the U.S. border where I surrendered myself to the FBI. I was then taken to the Clinton County jail in Plattsburgh, New York. Later that day I was brought before a United States Commissioner, who advised me that I had been indicted by a Federal Grand Jury at Miami, Florida, April 30, 1969, on two counts: kidnaping and aircraft piracy.

I informed him that I had discussed this matter with my attorney, H. Sol Clark, of Savannah, Georgia, and that I would like to waive my preliminary and removal hearings in order to return to Florida as soon as possible.

"Mr. Helmey, you are ordered held on $250,000 bail for appearance in the U.S. District Court in the Southern District of Florida," said Commissioner Kelly.

It took two and a half weeks, five county jails, two state penitentiaries, and three Federal detention centers for U.S. Marshals to move me the 1500 miles in unmarked cars to the Dade County jail so that I could be arraigned before a federal judge in Miami.

I was asked by a talkative marshal to compare U.S. prisons with Cuban, and I had to laugh. "In the U.S., prisoners have to diet not to get fat — in Cuba, you got to lie down and not move a finger so you can get up. The food is too much to die, and not enough to live. After what I've seen, America looks like a dream world, even in prison," I said, thinking how blessed I was to be alive.

While in the Dade County jail I was interviewed by the FBI and CIA. I voluntarily gave them what I considered to be classified information on American citizens who had received training in Cuba, and were a threat to our national security.

After being arraigned before Judge William O. Mehrtens, my attorney filed a motion requesting that my trial be held in Savannah rather than Miami, "for the convenience of the parties involved, because it would not be any less convenient to the government and in the interest of justice."

The judge granted the request and ordered me transferred to Savannah where U.S District Judge Alexander A. Lawrence would determine the date of trial.

When I arrived at the Chatham County jail the following day, Sheriff Carl Griffin came to my cell. "Reds, it's good to have ya back in Savannah. I'm gonna let 'cha have a visit with your family this afternoon up in my office. Can ya handle a T-bone steak, son?" he asked, grinning.

"Sheriff, this world is a better place because of people like you. Thanks, and God bless you," I said shaking his hand.

Fred Clark, my attorney's son, who had recently joined his father's law firm, visited the jail and advised me that they had filed a motion with the court to have my bond reduced.

"Bobby, we want you released before the August court term so that we can prepare your defense. Tomorrow you'll be taken for a government psychiatric evaluation," he said.

"Didn't Dr. Brandt give me a clean bill of health?"

"Yeah, but now Dr. Center has to have a shot at ya."

"Ain't that a bitch — I've learned that most psychiatrists don't listen as long as you make sense," I said.

"This traditional right to bail before conviction permits the unhampered preparation of a defense, and serves to prevent punishment prior to conviction ... the defense in this case will be temporary insanity and that he was acting under a delusional psychosis. He had actually sustained three mental concussions over a period of three and a half years. The young man actually believed that he had been sent to handle this matter in order to assassinate Castro at the behest of a government agency which had to be done before Lyndon Johnson went out of office. Such a statement was, in fact, made to the Federal Bureau of Investigation in their investigation of the matter by the man who had driven Bobby to the airport.

At the trial itself we expect, of course, to bring in other evidence to support the fact that this was a transitory delusional psychosis. We wish to put witnesses on the stand and although it is with some reluctance that we selected a former partner of Your Honor and the reason we selected Frank 'Sonny' Seiler is because he has known Bobby all his life, and not because of the reason he had been formerly associated with Your Honor," Clark said, in conclusion.

"Is this on the reduction of bail?" asked the judge.

"Yes, Your Honor. The father, who is willing to stand his bond, will testify to his financial worth and that he cannot meet the requirement of $250,000."

"And wouldn't I look good? He could take another plane while on bond," Judge Lawrence said.

"Your Honor, I am satisfied that following the treatment that he will have, plus the improvement in his mental condition, there will be no fear of that."

"All right, put the witnesses up."

Pastor J.R. Cumley, Jr ... Frank Seiler ... S.M. Helmey ... all testified.

"Has the Government had a psychiatric examiner at all?" the judge asked Mr. Greene, the Assistant U.S. Attorney.

"The only one that the Court ordered examined him yesterday. Dr. Brandt is the only other I know of," Greene said.

"No, I mean Dr. Center, Mr. Greene."

My attorney interrupted, "And I must disagree with the view that Bobby was not cooperative. He was willing to talk with Dr. Center, but he was not willing to discuss the details of the hijacking itself. I am certain that Dr. Center understood under the assignment that it dealt with whether or not he was presently competent to stand trial," he argued.

"Well, I am going to get another expert view point on that. I'm ordering the United States Marshal remove him to the U.S. Medical Hospital at Springfield, Missouri. I want him sent away from these local influences. Now, that leaves the motion for reduction of bail undisposed. Nor will I rule on the question of my discretion whether or not bail should be permitted at all. This case is a capital offense punishable by death," Judge Lawrence said, picking up his gavel.

"It'll work out," I said, looking at Mr. Clark.

After 26 days and every test known to modern medicine, six doctors unanimously agreed.

"It is our opinion that he was not sane at the time of the hijacking. It was the blow from a logging chain that struck his forehead and pushed him over the edge. He apparently underwent a psychotic break immediately prior to the hijacking and did not know what he was doing when he forced the plane to Cuba. He just wanted to do something to alleviate what he felt was an immediate danger to his country," said Dr. Harold Fain, Assistant Chief of Psychiatry, U.S. Medical Facility, Springfield, Missouri.

My thoughts were fixed on my family that hot morning in July when two U.S. Marshals picked me up in Springfield. After stopping for gas in a small Missouri town, one of the officers offered me a Coca-Cola from a coin-operated machine. After drinking it, I did the usual — looked at the bottom of the bottle.

"You won't believe this," I said, holding the empty coke bottle out of the car window.

The marshal looked at it, "S-A-V-A-N-N-A-H G-A. Damn! The possibility of this is a million to one, Helmey."

"Yeah, and I hope it's a good sign?"

"Houston, Tranquillity Base here. The Eagle has landed." At almost the same moment in time that Apollo 11, astronaut Neil Armstrong told that to Mission Control, I was walking out of the U. S. Commissioner's office in Savannah. The Eagle had truly landed — my father and a friend of my mother's family put up $750,000, worth of property as security.

When I walked from the Federal Building, Angelyn was waiting in the car. At first we didn't say anything — it was like I had just stopped at the post office to mail a letter. "I missed you, Bobby," she said, smiling.

"And I missed you, too, Angelyn," I said, placing my hand on her leg, and gently rubbing her thigh.

"It's hard to drive with you doing that — we'll have plenty of time for that later. Right now, everybody is down on the dock waiting for us," she said, pushing my hand from her leg.

"Who's everybody?" I asked.

"You'll just have to wait and see."

When we arrived at an empty house, I wouldn't take no for an answer. We made love hurriedly, but with unrestrained passion. It was more than sex. It was a release of everything. It seemed Angelyn's sexual inhibitions at last had vanished. We showered, and headed for the reunion.

A few days later, my attorney called and informed me that the judge had scheduled the trial for November 17th. "Bobby, how do you feel about another psychiatric evaluation? We need another opinion. Dr. Brandt has suggested his friend, Dr. Corbett Thigpen who is one of the nation's leading psychiatrists and the co-author of the famous book, *The Three Faces of Eve*."

"That's fine with me."

"O.K., I'll see if I can arrange it."

The Cleckley-Thigpen Psychiatric Associates
August 21, 1969.
Dear Mr. Clark:

... I put him in the hospital for several days' observation. I also had some neurological examinations run on him and an examination by a neurosurgeon. All tests (electroencephalogram, brain ECHO, and brain scan) were negative. A pneumoencephalogram run by Doctor Pomeroy Nichols also was negative. Doctor Nichols was of the opinion that he had no brain damage or at least none that could be revealed by usual examinations.

I do not believe that Mr. Helmey was mentally competent at the time he hijacked the plane. I believe that he was under the delusion that he was carrying out an act of true patriotism and at the direction of the CIA and FBI. As a matter of fact, I am concerned that he still may entertain such ideas, though the rather fearful experience that he underwent is very apt to deter him from taking any similar steps in the future.

I would like to know if you have any objection to my submitting this testimony to *TRAUMA*, which is a professional medical-legal journal. There have been only three cases in my career which I have testified that a defendant was insane at the time he or she committed a crime. I believe that these cases are so rare that they are worth reporting ... Helmey still holds his belief in a 'CIA Plot.'

Sincerely, Corbett H. Thigpen, M.D.

So much had happened in those few weeks since I'd been home that Angelyn had neglected to give me the letters from Curtis Harper that had been mailed from Vietnam months earlier. At the same time, she gave me newspaper clippings about the hijacking and other related stories from different papers around the country.

> 1st LT. Curtis Harper
> 173d Airborne Brigade
> APO San Francisco 96250
> Friday, 7 Feb., 1969.

Hi Reds,

Well how's things back in the world? Cold I bet. Believe it or not I have really froze my ass off for about a week! I guess Judy told you about me getting hit! Man, that was a close one. It was 8:35 at night on the first of February. I was laying up under a poncho shelter behind my foxhole about to go to sleep when an AK-47 opened up. It started chewing up the ground about two feet to my right. I was scrambling my ass off to get to the hole when I got it.

At first I thought I had been shot because it burned real bad. The next thing I knew, I was in the hole holding my head and blood spurting between my fingers. I never heard the grenade go off. I had to spend the rest of the night in the field because the Dustoff chopper couldn't come into the LZ, it was too hot! I'm going to Quin Nhun tomorrow for a week as the 173rd's Liaison Officer. Then back in the field on the 15th.

We operate about one-third of the time without tracks. Boy, I really like those things. We have been in real heavy contact with the NVA five times — you can really get scared at times. I need Sgt. Norton's address at the Armory, I'm gonna try to get an advisor's job when I get back. Well, I better go for now, write me soon, and hold the home front down. Your friend, Curt.

"When did Curt find out that I was in Cuba?" I asked Angelyn, after reading the letters and newspaper clippings.

"Around the first of February, Judy called to tell me about him being wounded. While he was in the hospital, she said he read your story in the *Stars and Stripes*."

"I've gotta get a letter off to him in the next few days. Fred is going to try and get him out of Vietnam. He says we need him as a witness."

"What about those newspaper stories?" she asked.

"Most of them are bullshit! Fred has requested that the president of United Air Lines produce the cockpit tapes. The whole hijacking episode was recorded. Let those tapes tell the story of what went on in the cockpit of flight 459."

As the trial date neared, Fred Clark and I met daily. At first I mistook his unpretentious nature as insincerity. But after a few "head to head" sessions I realized that he was a skillful lawyer who did have my best interests at heart. I remembered clearly his father's easy going manner when Joyce and Angelyn accused Nick and me of infidelity — Fred was a chip off the old block.

"Bobby, I don't think we're going to need Sergeant Norton as a witness," he said.

"That's good, because he's back in Vietnam."

"How'd you learn that?" Fred asked.

"I went by the Reserve armory to find out why I'd been discharged while I was in Cuba. And that's what I was told."

"No problem! But don't get distracted worrying about a discharge — we'll cross that bridge later. Understand?"

"Yeah, I understand. But it ticks me off to think they washed their hands of me so fast."

"Bobby, who's *they?*"

"I wish I knew."

Fred looked away as if he were not paying attention. "Remember this, we have the testimony of nine doctors. Six of which are U. S. Government employees and they unanimously agree that you were temporarily insane at the time of the hijacking — head injuries. Let's just leave it at that."

"You're right!" I said, pointing to a scar above my right eye.

Fred nodded, then handed me a letter with the United Air Lines logo. "Read it, and tell me what you think."

Fred S. Clark, Esq.
Brannen, Clark & Hester
140 Bull Street
Savannah, Georgia 31402

November 10, 1969

Dear Sir:

Please be advised that I have caused search to be made for the tape requested in your letter of October 24, 1969. As I mentioned in our phone conversation of November 6, 1969, it was my understanding that the cockpit voice recorder tape, the tape requested, retains only the final 30 minutes of flight and erases automatically all that goes before. That is what happened in this instance so that the tape requested was erased on the trip back from Cuba ...

As an additional result of our conversation, I checked with United's Stewardess Training Center to see, as was your understanding, if this tape had been used in any training session for stewardesses. I received another negative response from the personnel in charge of the training center. No such tape has ever been used in any Stewardess training session. It is my understanding that you will take steps to recall the subpoena issued to Mr. Keck and, if that fails, will not in any event require his presence at the trial ...

I sat for a moment, not saying anything. Fred studied my face curiously. "You don't believe the letter?"

"No, I don't! There's no doubt that the stewardess who told Tommy Close about hearing that tape played in Miami didn't know what she was talking about. Besides, the captain had to know the importance of that tape. The electronics on a Boeing 727 are pretty sophisticated. I can't believe he didn't have the option to save more than the final 30 minutes or possibly even the entire cockpit voice record," I said, shaking my head.

"Bobby, why would they wanna do that?"

"To cover their asses. If you'd read the *Miami Herald* the day the crew returned from Cuba, I think you'd understand."

"What'd it say?" he asked.

"Some of the crew who were interviewed said I was far more belligerent than hijackers usually are. I'm supposed to have tried to jump out at 10,000 feet because I was convinced the plane had landed. They also claimed that I kept the stewardesses busy bringing Jack Daniels. Fred, so help me God, it didn't happen that way. And the tape would prove it."

"Didn't you say that you weren't yourself at the time?"

"Yeah! But I didn't suffer from amnesia on that flight." I paused. "Fred, I don't deny the seriousness of the charges and I'm not blaming the crew. In fact, I hope I have the opportunity to apologize to each of them personally. But, all I needed was a ride to Cuba."

A broad smile spread across Fred's face. "Bobby, let's forget the tape and move on."

"I wonder if the crew received overtime for the flight?"

* * *

Judge Lawrence ambled slowly into his courtroom. Everyone rose and stood reverently as he cleared his throat, shuffled some papers, then brought the court to order. He then read the indictment, "Two counts of air-piracy and kidnapping, which carries a possible death penalty."

The Government attorney told the prospective jurors that I was of sound mind when I hijacked the aircraft to Cuba. "His scheme to kill Castro was a well-laid, well thought-out plan that backfired," said U.S. Attorney R. Jackson B. Smith.

Fred told them he intended to present a defense of temporary insanity.

"Helmey was motivated by love of country and patriotic zeal," he went on. "He was also influenced by a television story that was filmed in Cuba by CBS. The program was about Americans who had joined Castro and his Communist revolution. It included a young woman who said that she'd attended a Catholic high school in Savannah, Georgia. When asked by the television journalist if she would be willing to kill her fellow countryman, she replied, 'Yes! For the revolution I would even die'," Fred said, as he looked solemnly at the prospective jurors.

After lengthy questioning by both attorneys, the eight-man, four-woman jury was seated.

Over the next two days the prosecution presented its witnesses.

"Helmey could not have been more calm or controlled," said the pilot. He also testified that I threatened to kill the copilot several times.

The stewardesses all recounted that I was drunk and that I had "manhandled" them. The only other prosecution witness was a passenger whose wife was a stewardess for United Air Lines.

After their testimony, two government psychiatrists testified. "It is our opinion that he was not sane at the time," said Dr. Harold Fain, assistant chief of psychiatry at the United States Medical Center in Springfield, Missouri. "He wanted to alleviate what he felt was an immediate danger to his country."

"It was the blow from a logging chain which the medical center staff feels pushed him over the edge," said Dr. David Hubbard, a teaching consultant for the government. "Helmey considered himself a man of destiny and a man with a mission."

When the prosecutor asked Dr. Fain if my actions might have been caused by drinking, the doctor replied, "I rather doubt this — I could not state to a certainty unless I knew how much he drank."

Following their testimony, the government rested the prosecution's case.

Captain Thomas Close Jr. was the first defense witness. He said he had driven me to the airport on January 11th, and that I had outlined the plan to hijack the plane. He said I claimed that I had been chosen by the CIA to assassinate Fidel Castro, but that he didn't believe any of the tale at the time. He also testified that I had acted "strangely" in December after having sustained head injuries.

Several other fellow reservists offered similar testimony, including my unit commander Major Logan B. Dixon, Jr., who described me as a "good soldier and quite patriotic."

My wife testified that I knew the gun used in the hijacking was broken and unloaded. She also told of my head injuries and that I had complained of headaches and dizziness on the day of the hijacking. She described the story about the plot to overthrow Castro as "a little fantastic."

My father testified that I had always been "a good son, a real good son," he added. "Bobby expressed an interest in the military at an early age ... I tried to get him to give up the Reserve because I felt it was taking up too much of his time."

In a signed deposition to the court, Dr. Corbett Thigpen said that the blow from a logging chain "may have set off an emotional flight ... I do not believe that Mr. Helmey was mentally competent when he hijacked the jet to Cuba. When I insisted that the plan was ridiculous, the more defensive he became about it and it became plainer and plainer that he still believes that there was a plot to kill Castro.

"I finally asked him if he got the assignment to go again, would he go? He looked at me and said, 'Yes, I would go if I thought I really could get to kill Castro.' He probably has had a paranoid character for years and views himself as a knight in shining armor who wishes to rescue the nation and perform heroic acts. He may still entertain a patriotic paranoia."

The press coverage about a possible CIA plot to assassinate Fidel Castro had obviously attracted some pro-Castro and anti-war people to the trial. Every day the courtroom was filled to capacity. Many of the faces I had known most of my life, but the majority I had never seen.

At home that night, the phone rang and the voice on the other end said in a taunting tone, "Helmey, you'll be the first hijacker to receive the death sentence. You're the sacrificial goat. Not only are you a fanatical nut, but you're a stupid bastard — that's why Fidel released you." Then he slammed the receiver down.

"State your name and address for the record, please," my attorney said.

"Robert M. Helmey, Route 2, Box 19 A, Savannah, Georgia."

I remained on the witness stand for five hours during direct examination, then almost two for cross examination. When the prosecutor finally said, "I have no further questions," I knew my fate would soon be in the hands of twelve people.

That night I received another phone call. "Helmey, they should give you an Academy Award for your performance on that witness-stand today, but you're still going to die."

"If I do die, I'm comin' back and hauntin' your draft-card burnin' ass!" I said, hanging up the telephone.

The next morning in closing arguments, Fred said, "Testimony should cast reasonable doubt as to my client's sanity during the hijacking. He's lived a reasonably normal life for 36 years and then for six hours of his life, he had this mental break."

In rebuttal, U.S. Attorney Smith said, "Helmey was of sound mind ... he fully expected to come back to this country a hero, but the plan backfired."

In charging the jury, Judge Lawrence told them their task was to decide whether I was sane on January 11th. "Under the law, anyone who is insane cannot form the wrongful intent necessary to the commission of a crime. Specific intent must have been proved by the prosecution in order for a guilty verdict to be returned."

At approximately 11:45 a.m. on Thursday, November 20, the jury retired to consider the charges. Before Fred and I could finish our lunch, two U.S. marshals came rushing into the restaurant directly behind the Federal Courthouse, and one said, "Judge Lawrence wants both of you back in the courtroom immediately."

The moment we returned, the jurors walked out of their room and the court was called to order. The Judge asked the foreman if they had reached a verdict.

"We have, Your Honor," he replied.

"Hand the verdict to the marshal," the Judge said softly.

There was a breathtaking silence in the room as Judge Lawrence examined the decision. When he handed the piece of paper back to the marshal, I had to remind myself to breathe. As I turned to face the jury my eyes automatically searched the faces of the twelve.

"Read the verdict!" the judge ordered.

"Innocent by reason of temporary insanity on all counts," echoed the marshal's voice through the room.

A mixture of euphoria and relief swept over me. I grabbed my attorney and hugged him, then rushed over to the jury box.

"It didn't take us long to make up our minds," said Herb Schafter, the jury foreman, shaking my hand.

The last juror out of the box was an elderly gentleman. "I

consider myself a pretty good judge of character. I realize you weren't yourself the day you hijacked that airplane. But the sad fact is, what this country needs is more men like you. God bless you, son."

I stood there speechless for a moment, then broke into tears as he slowly walked away.

Once the jury was out of the courtroom, I found my wife and embraced her.

Later, outside the courthouse, a reporter asked, "How do you feel about the verdict, Mrs. Helmey?"

"The Lord was with us," she answered.

"Where do you go from here, Reds?" he asked.

"Back to work, back to my family and back to being a good citizen."

"And away from airplanes," quipped my wife.

Part Nine

THINGS DO CHANGE

The essence of true friendship is to make
allowance for another's little lapses.
David Story

Things Do Change

I sat reading the news accounts of a sailing disaster off the coast of Great Britain. "A violent Atlantic storm struck when the race yachts were in the Irish Sea between Land's End and the Fastnet. Eighteen persons lost their lives. The race was won by Ted Turner of the U.S. in the *Tenacious.*"

As I read the story, my thoughts went back to the storms of the '70s. It had been ten years since Cuba. The race seemed a perfect metaphor for my life during that decade. Angelyn's decision to leave didn't come as any surprise. I had known for a long time our marriage was over, if it had ever existed.

The rickety cypress boardwalk to my father's dockhouse on Talahi Island extended over the tidal marshes of Bull River at the juncture of St. Augustine Creek. The wooden lean-to building at the end always reminded me of what Salzburger outhouse architecture must have looked like. But its location more than made up for the flaw of human design. It had always been my favorite spot when my world seemed to wobble. This time it was more than a place of balance; it was my new home.

Since Cuba, this was my first serious attempt at taking control of my life. I didn't want to make the mistakes of the past. I kept remembering those days and nights in solitary confinement, when I would kneel for hours and beg God for one more chance.

A prisoner was being dragged through the narrow corridor in front of my cell. His pleas rang in my ears — the language was foreign but the terror in his voice was universal. When the faint muffle of gunfire echoed in the night, cold-ass fear gripped me. I prayed, my God, my God, help me...

Now I wasn't sure He even existed. I wanted some answers, but I didn't know who to turn to or trust. I'd seen enough of so-called Christians to know that I didn't want any guidance from that bunch of hypocrites.

One Sunday morning during a rainstorm, I turned on the television. I couldn't find anything but religious stuff; so I got a beer and decided to kill time until the rains let up.

Two of the preachers I heard that day were Charles Stanley and Jimmy Swaggart. It seemed strange that both Stanley, a Baptist in Atlanta, and Swaggart, a Pentecostal in Baton Rouge, would preach from the same scripture. It was as if they had gotten together with God to remind me of a deal I'd made with Him in Cuba.

After Swaggart preached his last words that morning, the sun came out. I felt it was no coincidence that the two men both had the same message. Both sermons touched my heart and made more sense about life than anything I'd ever heard. I thought of my Grandmother, the hymn 'Amazing Grace,' and wept like a child.

Later I was ashamed to tell anybody that I had watched the television preachers. I wanted to forget that morning, but I couldn't.

As I stood watching the golden sunset dance across the waters of Bull River, I could see the silhouettes of three people coming down the long walkway. I could hear them before they were close enough to recognize.

"Reds, I brought you a couple of housewarmin' gifts." There was no mistaking the Greek's voice.

I couldn't tell who was holding up whom. Nick was in the middle of two long-legged, high-heeled women. How they'd made it to the dock house without breaking their necks or falling overboard was a miracle.

"Hey, brother, I'm lying — I didn't come to give you a house-warming. I came to take your ass back to civilization with me."

"Nick, it ain't so bad. Kinda like campin' out."

"Man, fuck campin' out. You've done enough of that for a lifetime, big boy."

For the next couple of hours we drank wine, talked trash, and watched the sunset. The girls were so caught up in the romantic setting of the moment, they suggested that we all get naked and go for a boat ride. Nick and I thought it was a bad idea, but when they called us chickenshit, our male egos kicked in. We all stripped and left our clothes at the dock. The only thing that Nick refused to leave behind was his .38 snubnosed pistol. As we boarded, Nick was wearing only his shoulder holster. He looked over at me and said, "I ain't naked as long as I'm packin' this piece, Reds Baby."

"Nick, that's a short barrel you got there," I said.

"I wouldn't say too much, Bubba. Your barrel ain't much longer." The girls cracked up.

When we passed under the Bull River Bridge with both girls riding on the bow of the *Wild Thing*, you could see the glow of tail lights as the cars slowed down.

After we pulled over in a creek and fired the ole snubnose a few times, we headed back to the dock. Before we got back, Nick had persuaded me to move in with him. Nick always knew exactly how to cheer me up. He was like the brother I'd never had. I didn't know how to say "no" to him. In so many ways, our lives had paralleled, even our preference in women.

As we were putting our clothes on, one of the girls said, "Nick, instead of Reds' moving in with you, you oughta move in with him. This place reminds me of Key West, the hippest place in the world. Where else could you live so close to nature, drink wine, and go naked?"

"That's the problem with you fuckin' dreamers. This winter when the North winds blow and you're freezin' your ass off, you'll be singing a different tune. Besides, girl, your ass is too fine for frostbite, ain't that right, Reds?"

"Yeah, Man!"

"Girls, pack this crazy motherfucker's bags before he changes his mind. I need to get to my bar and check up before they close."

"Nick, I can't move tonight. I've got to be on the job at six in the morning, and I can't be late."

"That's another thing I wanna talk with you about."

"Hey, I've got to make bread to live, Nick."

"I know, but you don't have to kill yourself doin' it."

I didn't need a U-Haul-It for the move to English Oaks Apartments. My worldly possessions now could fit into a couple of brown paper bags, with the exception of my workboots, which I carried over my shoulders.

Joyce had divorced Nick two years earlier.

Living with Nick was an adventure that only the lionhearted and virile could survive. If I had to compare it to something, it would be Airborne Jump School. You definitely had to be in potent physical shape, and slightly insane.

I found out that working my day job and running with him at night just wasn't working.

"Nick, I love you, man, but there's no way I can run the streets at night, and then cover pipes all day."

"Then stop coverin' those fuckin' pipes. Asbestos is gonna kill ya if you don't. Besides, you can work for me."

It was hard convincing Nick that being a union asbestos worker didn't mean you were up to your ass in the stuff every day. I tried to explain the safety requirements and equipment used on different jobs. But I knew he really didn't understand. He'd been raised in the food and beverage business, and it was foreign to his ears. I appreciated his brotherly concern because at the time nobody else seemed to give a damn about my health. It was just my paycheck that interested them. However, since I now had a union card, and as long as I paid dues, I could always find a job. I decided to try it the Greek's way.

* * *

"Reds, you're gonna need a pistol. So here's a present." He handed me a new Smith & Wesson .38 snubnosed Detective Special.

"What do I need a gun for, Nick?"

"Because you just need one, that's why. Hell, ain't nothin' like it used to be. Nobody does what's honorable anymore. Instead of duking it out, they shoot it out," he said, handing me a box of .38 caliber cartridges.

"Maybe you're right, Nick."

"Ain't no maybe about it. You said that like you didn't believe me. Hey, you're the one that's always talkin' about reality. You know what reality is to me — it's what I see right before my eyes. Believe me, if you run these streets at night, it's your best friend."

Nick was managing The Other End, a well-known bar on River Street at the time. He was a little vague on my job description. But it turned out I was to be his chauffeur, gofer and bodyguard. I was also about to add a new life experience to my resume.

"Reds, you know Walter Matthau?" Nick asked.

"Yeah, he's a captain down at Atlantic Towing Company. Why?"

"No! he's not a tugboat captain."

"Well, then, who in the hell are you talkin' about?"

"I'm talkin' about the actor."

"What does he look like?" I asked.

"You know — the guy who's got a mouth like a catfish."

"Oh yeah! He's a hell of an actor."

"So, you wanna be in a movie?"

"What's the pay?"

"All the beer you can drink," Nick said.

"Hell, I'm already gettin' that."

Nick explained that a casting director had been in The Other End earlier in the week. "He was here the night you duked it out with that motorcycle bad boy. He said that he'd never seen Hollywood stage a better fight scene."

"Man! The guy pulled a knife on me. I was just takin' care of business."

"Yeah, I know, but I laid some heavy shit on him. I wanna get you a job in Hollywood, big boy. I told him about you being an ex-Green Beret, and how ya hijacked a 727 to kill Castro. That didn't seem to impress him near as much as seeing you beat the man's ass, then pick him up, help him back into the bar and buy him a drink while you doctored on him. He said he'd like to meet you and offer you some kind of a part in the movie, 'Hopscotch'."

"Where's it gonna be filmed?"

"Some of the scenes, right here in The Other End."

I met the casting director a few days later and accepted his offer. I never quite understood just what an extra was until I had the opportunity to be one. The scene that I was in lasted less than ten seconds, but in reality it had taken more than six hours; in it I was seated at the bar facing Walter Matthau and another actor during the entire filming that day.

Matthau later described me as "The pissin' extra," and said, "If Academy Awards were given for imbibing beer, that son-of-a bitch would win, hands down."

However, I knew after the filming that day my acting career was over. I'd agitated the director by calling 'cut' when I had to make head calls. "We would have come out much better paying Reds, than furnishing his suds," the casting director joked at the 'can party.' It was ironic that the movie was about a CIA assassination plot, with a comic twist.

Just after my bit part in the flick, "Hopscotch," I played a real character in an actual shoot-out.

Nick always liked to stop at the Plantation Club and talk shop with John Steed before he called it a night. This particular night we had just ordered a drink at the bar when a woman came running in the front door screaming, "There's a gun battle in the parking lot!" A bullet had grazed her leg as she walked from the club.

"Nick, let me hold your pistol," I said in a soft whisper as I came off the bar stool.

"Hey, where's yours?"

"I ain't got it, man!"

"Then stay the fuck out of it."

When I opened the front door to look, a bullet hit the jamb just above my head. I instinctively dropped and lunged forward, landing outside the building. I could see one man kneeling in front of a car firing at another. They had to be the worst shots in the world because as close as they stood to each other, they could have pissed in the other's pocket.

I rolled between two cars and started crawling on all fours thinking I was getting away from the action. Instead, I'd crawled up behind one of the shooters. He had started turning towards me when I grabbed him from behind and wrestled the gun from his hand. It fired as it hit the ground between my legs.

Nick and an Army Ranger came running from the building and held the man while I searched for the gun. They said the other shooter had jumped the fence and was long gone. It was then that I recognized the guy they were holding. Nick and I had known him for a while.

"Ernie, what's goin' on?" I asked.

"The motherfucker owes me money, and he tried to kill me."

"Hey, the way you two bastards were sprayin' bullets, it's a wonder you didn't kill a bunch of people. Here's your gun. Now get out of here before the police get here!"

On the ride home that night, Nick was in a mellow mood. He hadn't called me 'Bobby' in years.

"Bobby, you must be tryin' to kill yourself. That was a dumb-ass thing you did tonight."

"Hey, you're one to talk, Zorba the Greek."

"I know, liquor fucks us both up, brother. We need to find a couple of those 'lifters' you're always talkin' about."

"I know that's right, Arthur."

"Man, don't call me that."

"You stop the 'Bobby' bullshit, and I stop the 'Arthur'."

"You got it, brother."

One night just before Thanksgiving, 1979, Nick called the apartment and said, "Hey, I've got somebody here that wants to see and talk to you."

"Bobby, how's things?" the familiar female voice asked.

"Maxine, it's good to hear your voice — I've thought about you a lot lately. How's things?"

"Fine. Nick told me about you and Angelyn splitting."

"Hey! What can I say?"

"You don't have to say anything."

"How long are you gonna be at The Other End?"

"As long as it takes," she said in a low voice.

"I'm on the way, lady."

I hadn't seen Maxine in a couple of years. The last time we'd talked, she appeared to be happily married. I'd always thought of her as a lady who had her head screwed on right. She had that rare gift that seemed to be missing in most of the women in my life: she was a good listener. She also had all the physical attributes that I loved: the tall body of a ballerina, blonde hair and sexy green eyes that seemed to brighten as I talked.

"Maxine, it' good to see you," I said as I hugged her.

"Bobby, how long have you had the hair and beard?"

"Girl, are you makin' fun of my new look?"

"No, it just seems funny not to see your head shaved and you lookin' like G.I. Joe."

"Yeah, I know. I was a little radical back then."

"Hey, I love the new look." She smiled, then said, "Let's ride down to the beach and catch a sunrise."

"Sounds good to me. I'm tired of these barrooms."

On the way to the beach she said that her marriage was over. "Hey, you don't have to explain anything to me," I said. So we agreed not to waste time talking about our past. But that's exactly what we did as we walked the beach waiting for the sun to rise on a new day.

"So, where do you go from here, Bobby?"

"I don't know Maxine, but not back to where I've been."

My decision to return to union work was a quick fix to a dilemma that I didn't want to deal with. I was totally burned out with Nick and the night life. As much as I loved him and enjoyed his capricious style, it was killing me.

"Nick, my business agent called and offered me a job in West Virginia."

"What'cha tell him?"

"I told him yeah."

"Bobby, you know that asbestos shit will kill you."

"Nick, you're always givin' me advice, and I appreciate it. But what the hell do you think this way of life is doing to us? You can't fool me. You're livin' like there's no tomorrow. Since you and Joyce split, you haven't been the same. I'm tellin' ya like a brother, get out of the whiskey business before it's too late. I don't have the answers, but I do know this — there's a better way of life than runnin' these streets all night chasin' something that doesn't exist."

"What can I say, brother?"

"Don't say anything. Let's go have a beer."

"You got it, man! Enough serious shit for one day."

The weather was cold as a bitch when Short-Man Corley, Kurt Drescher and I arrived in West Virginia; it didn't seem like such a wild and wonderful place to us. Our job was to insulate a smokestack at an electric power plant on the Ohio River. The stack was over 200 feet high and the wind chill factor on the river was minus 10 degrees.

"This place reminds me of North Korea, Reds," Short-man chattered as he looked out over the terrain from high atop the scaffolding.

"I don't know what the fuck it reminds me of. But in this trade, you're either burnin' or freezin' your ass off. There must be a easier way of killin' yourself."

"Hey! Where are those duck feathers comin' from, Reds?"

As I looked up, feathers swirled all around the icy stack and scaffolding.

"Yeah, somebody must have shot a mallard over the river, and the wind has carried them up here."

"I guess you're right, Short-man. At this altitude, we couldn't hear the shots, even if they were firing at us."

It was then we discovered that I had leaned against a hot pipe, and melted a hole in the nylon fabric of my parka, causing the goose-down filler to be released into the air with my body movement. "Hot damn! Let's dog-it-off, Short-man! I've had the lick! I might be able to patch this fuckin' feather blanket up after a hot shower and a drink of your Irish Whiskey."

The ride back to our Point Pleasant hotel took an extra hour because of the icy road conditions. When I walked in the lobby, the manager told me that I had a long distance message.

"Nick, you called?"

"Yeah, Bobby, I wanted you to know that my dad died during the night," Nick said with a heartbroken voice.

"Man, I'm sorry. I know how much you loved him. I remember the last time I visited him in the hospital: 'Red, you get me outta here, I donna like dis place. If you fall asleep, maybe you donna wake-up,' he said, holding my hand tightly. 'Mr. Nick, you gonna be all right. These pretty nurses will take good care of you.' 'Red, you need'a your eye fix. Ain't no pretty nurse here, only da big anna fat ones. Find'da pretty one, maybe I stay'.

"Nick, I love ...if you need me, I'm on the way."

"No, Bobby, I just wanted you to know. Oh yeah, Maxine called a couple of times lookin' for you. Should I give her your number there?"

"Yeah, that's fine — I'll call her right now."

As soon as I hung up talking with Nick, I called Maxine. She had already heard about Nick's father. She asked if there was anything she could do.

"I'd appreciate it if you'd send flowers for me."

"Bobby, how long are you going to be in West Virginia?"

"I don't know. But I really wanna see you. Why don't you fly up next weekend since we're both off and you've never seen this wild and wonderful state."

"Allegheny Air's Flight 211 from Atlanta will be approximately fifteen minutes late due to weather conditions," the announcer said.

As I walked back to the lounge, I spotted a little brown teddy bear hanging in a gift shop window. I went inside and bought it. It was then I realized that this was my first sincere act of courtship since my failed marriage. "What the hell am I doing?" I asked myself. It frightened me to even think about becoming serious with anybody.

I'd just finished my Irish coffee when the announcement was made that Flight 211 had landed and was disembarking passengers at Gate Three. I didn't know why I was so nervous standing there waiting for her. It could have been that I felt pretty awkward holding a teddy bear or maybe just apprehensive about the whole idea of trusting a woman with my feelings.

"How was the flight?"

"Terrible. I think James Brown was flying that airplane. Bobby, I need something to settle my nerves."

"We'll stop at the lounge," I said, laughing.

The flight hadn't affected her physical appearance. She looked as if she'd just stepped out of a fashion magazine. I helped her remove her long wool cape and white beret as we walked in the lounge. Her beige skirt fit snugly around her trim hips and stopped just above her knees. Her long legs seemed to be even longer in boots. She looked fabulous.

As we sat at the bar, I thought, then said, "Mama, you sure look foxy."

"Don't call me that. I'm not your mama," she laughed.

"Bartender, bring this lady a double shot of your strongest libation. She needs something to soothe her frayed nerves."

"Bobby, you're crazy, but that's what I love about you."

"Hey, don't say that. My last wife said the same thing, and when I tried to change, she thought I was a bore."

"That's certainly where our similarity ends."

"You'll have to explain that later."

It was like meeting somebody for the first time. Even though we'd known each other for years, and though we both had heard the gossip about our relationship being more than platonic, we had never spent more than a couple of hours together as friends. The little town of Point Pleasant where the Ohio and Kanawha Rivers run together seemed a perfect place for our first date. That weekend our spirits ran together like those two waters.

It wasn't long before I was making excuses to go back to Savannah. St. Patrick's Day was just a few weeks away, and I knew Short Man wouldn't be hard to convince.

"Short Man, let's go home for St. Pat's Day?"

"Shit, Reds, your head ain't in West Virginia. If you don't watch what you're doing, your ass is gonna be six feet under. You can't walk these fuckin' scaffolds with your mind somewhere else. Gravity ain't easy, but it's the law. Let's go home before I have to pay a union death assessment for ya."

I did a lot of soul searching on the trip back to Savannah. Where do I go from here? I didn't want to move back in with Nick. I knew where that road would lead. I wasn't able to make any kind of a serious commitment to Maxine even if she were willing. One of the biggest problems was how to survive financially. There just wasn't enough union work in Savannah to make ends meet. Here I was, forty-seven years old. People just naturally didn't want to hire an old airline pirate. Yet I was determined to overcome, even if I had to shovel shit for a living.

* * *

Sinatra was belting out, 'I did it my way,' on that dreary afternoon in February when I walked into the Other End. Nick and a familiar face sat at the bar. I knew they were pretty deep in the sauce.

"Hey, Reds, baby! Good to have you home. You remember Roy, my old buddy from Atlanta?" Nick asked as he hugged me.

"He should! You loaned him my brand new cashmere jacket to get past the maitre d' at the Brave Falcon."

"Yeah! He had to punch out a guy that was trying to move in on Angelyn. Hey! I got the blood out and you still made me buy you a new jacket — so what'cha bitchin' about," Nick wise-cracked.

"I ain't bitchin', Greek. Reds is my fuckin' hero. He can have anything I got," Roy said grinning.

"Robin, hand me that bottle of Cutty, we gonna party down."

"No, Robin," I said, standing up. "Nick, I've got to get some rest — I ain't closed my eyes in two days, brother."

"Man! You've been with those 'hillbillys' too long. Give me a few days and I'll get you back in shape, Rose Eye Reds."

"Whatever you say Greek. But right now give me the keys to your apartment," I said.

"Catch you later, Reds," Roy said as I walked away.

The next morning when I awoke, Nick and Roy were seated at a table in the living room counting a sizeable stack of money.

I yawned, and wiped the sleep from my eyes. "Damn, you two guys must have robbed the First National Bank."

"Sit down, before you fall down. How about a hot cup of coffee?" Roy asked.

"You think we should cut him in on the deal?" Nick said winking at Roy.

"How much cash can you put your hands on, Reds?" Roy asked as he picked up a handful of hundred dollar bills.

"I don't know, why?"

"Reds, you knew Roy managed the first Whiskey-A-Go-Go Club, in Atlanta. He's rubbed elbows and made some friends with, let's say, 'syndicate people'! Now one of them wants to give Roy a chance to invest in a deal that could make him and us some serious money — explain it to Reds," Nick said.

Roy straightened up in his chair and lit a cigar. "Reds, can you put your hands on five thousand dollars?"

"Maybe, but I'd like to hear more about it before I say I could or couldn't."

"Reds, I met this man during my nightclub days. He would invest money for folks who had a little extra cash and didn't want the government to get it, mostly show business people. He's made millions for himself and others."

Roy tapped his temple with his index finger and said, "Brains, Reds, brains. It's volume. He'd take ten, fifteen, twenty thousand, whatever, from let's say a hundred investors, now he's got a few million to lend certain entrepreneurs who can't get it from the regular institutions. That's the same shit banks do, except they take the 'little man's' money and lend it to the 'big boys.' Selling money, it's a fuckin' racket," he looked at Nick and smiled.

"Man! What kinda people borrow money like that?" I asked.

"Who gives a shit? There's an old saying, 'The buyers and the sellers are no different fellers.' Believe me, nobody defaults him but once — your money is safer than with the FDIC."

"Reds, Maxine would back you. In a couple of months, you could make $30,000 back on a $5,000 investment," Nick said.

"Yeah, but it sounds like a hell of a risk," I said.

"Hey, life's a fuckin' gamble any way you slice it. You wanna wear that hardhat the rest of your life," Nick said.

"How much time have I got to get it together?"

"A couple of days, but don't screw around because a few others want in," Roy said.

"Reds, that ain't nothing but walkin' around money to the Max — she'd do anything for you," Nick laughed.

Roy leaned forward and handed me a fifty dollar bill. "Reds, go have your beard trimmed. We're goin' to Florida next week and meet the man — I want you to drive us down."

As I looked at the Mall's marquee trying to find "Maxine's Hairstylist," I wondered if she'd be as happy to see me as I was to see her. I should have called her.

"Could I help you, sir?" asked the attractive young receptionist.

"Yes, you may. I'd like an appointment with Maxine."

"Sir, she's booked up today," she said looking down at a book. "How about tomorrow at ten?"

"How 'bout you tellin' her *El Rojo* wants a trim today, honey."

The young lady stepped back from the desk with a perplexed look on her face. "Excuse me, El who?"

"*Rojo.*"

"Maybe I'd better go get her," she said nervously as she disappeared toward the back of the shop.

After a few minutes she came back with one of the biggest smiles I'd ever seen and said, "Mr. Row-hoe, she wants you to have a seat and she'll be right out."

"What are you doing in Savannah?" Maxie said, hugging me.

We stopped by a Thunderbolt seafood market and bought a dozen blue crab, five pounds of shrimp, and a couple of bottles of white wine.

The sun was setting in the western sky as we drove over the Lazaretto Creek bridge. The grayish-green waters of the Atlantic reflected the tiny speckles of light from Hilton Head like a giant mirror across the ocean inlet.

"Bobby, you can turn at the Spanish Hammock sign, the house is only a half-mile away."

"Maxine, how long have you had this place?"

"Not long. I bought it as a weekend getaway. But now I've fallen in love with the place," she said handing me the front door key.

"I can understand that — this view is beautiful. The glow from that old lighthouse and the smell of the marshes cast a spell on you. I wouldn't go back to Savannah if I were you."

"Bobby, don't tempt me. If it weren't for making a living, I wouldn't."

"That's one of the things I love about you. Your head is beautiful and it's screwed on tight. You're the most sensible and sensitive woman I've ever met. I love you, lady."

She sighed softly and touched my hand. "It's the wine and candlelight, but I love it," as flames danced in her eyes.

That night I shared things with her that I had never shared with another living soul because I trusted her — something I'd never been able to do with many people, especially women.

The next morning, when I opened the bedroom blinds, all I could see was the icy glaze that covered the window. During the night, a strong cold front had swept into the area and come down like an iron hand covering everything with sheets of ice. The radio and television called it the "Alberta Clipper." They warned that all bridges to the beach were iced over and motorists should not attempt to cross them.

Whether it was fate or just one of those things, I'll never know, but I will always believe that some power bigger than the weather kept us together those two days.

During our sequester that weekend, I mentioned to her that Nick and Roy wanted me to go in with them on an investment deal in Florida.

"What kind of deal are they talking about?" she asked.

"Roy has this friend that's an investment broker. He makes large, short-term loans to people that deal in quick turnover, and pay high interest on your money."

"Are you gonna invest?"

"I'd like to, but the truth is I'm a little short. Maxine, the dogs have been snappin' at my behind lately. I just can't get it together."

"That doesn't sound like you ... you've always been the eternal optimist," she said, smiling sweetly.

"Hey, baby! Nowadays, I laugh to keep from cryin."

"Bobby, how much money are you talking about?"

"Roy says, five thousand will get me back thirty in about two months."

"Do you need the whole five thousand?" she asked.

"Yes,' I said softly.

She said she would loan me the money. She also suggested that I move into the beach house until I could get on my feet financially. It seemed like the perfect solution to a lot of my immediate problems.

When I offered to do some repairs on the dock until a job opened in Savannah with the union, she insisted that I didn't have to do a thing to her property except, "Keep the dogs from snappin' your ass, because that belongs to me, now."

The following Friday afternoon, Nick, Roy and I traveled to Jacksonville Beach for a meeting with Mr. Big. But Mr. Big couldn't make it down to Florida. Instead, he sent his right-hand man, who turned out to be a one-armed shrimp boat captain, who according to Roy would only deal with him.

After a few questions and a lot of butterflies in my stomach, I handed Roy the five big ones. He assured Nick and me that it was a done deal. He explained, "The less you know, the better off y'all be."

The only thing I knew about the deal was that it was nautical in nature and Lloyd's of London wouldn't have touched it with a ten foot pole. Months later, Roy told me he had gotten a telegram saying the boat had been lost between Jamaica and Columbia.

The French have a phrase for it: The more things change, the more they remain the same. The next two years seemed to corroborate that saying.

Maxine's unconditional love was the only thing that hadn't changed during those two years. The feeling that she was the best thing that ever happened to me was even stronger. Through a heart attack, being diagnosed with asbestos in my lungs, and the Florida investment fiasco, she never lost faith in me. So, I decided to try and make it a permanent partnership.

Maxine and I sat on the back deck, drinking coffee and watching the tide rise in Chimney Creek; white clouds drifted lazily in the morning sky. Spring seemed near as the warm ocean breeze rippled the waters.

"Maxine, what do you think about us getting married?"

"Bobby, is that a proposal?" she asked.

"Yes, and I'm not very good at this kind of thing. I've never loved another person in my life like I love you, Maxine."

"Bobby, I don't know what to say," she said as tears filled her eyes and she tenderly put her arms around me.

"Hey," I said in a soft voice. "I should be the one crying for you. I thought you'd have better sense than to get mixed-up with a crazy guy like me."

"Bobby, I haven't said yes, yet."

"Well — will you?"

"You know I will," she smiled.

On April 3rd, 1982, Maxine and I exchanged vows and became man and wife. Following the wedding and a Zorba-style reception, we skipped out aboard our 28-foot cabin cruiser.

Our three day honeymoon was spent anchored in the secluded waters off Beach Hammock in Wassaw Sound. The old Broadwater that Max and I had rebuilt from the keel up had become our escape machine. She loved the ocean and boating as much as I did.

"Max, I'm promoting you to First Mate of this vessel."

"Hey, who made you the captain?" she responded as we stood in our birthday suits fishing from the stern of *Amazing Max*.

"Girl! You know a female can't command a ship in the Navy."

"Whose Navy?"

"*El Rojo's.*"

"I thought we were partners, Admiral."

We started laughing when all of a sudden, she grabbed a

towel and ran for the cabin. A Coast Guard helicopter had caught us by surprise and was hovering directly overhead. A crewman leaned from the door of the chopper and spoke over a loud speaker: "Is everything all right down there, Captain?" I sheepishly gave him a thumbs up, and they continued their flight.

Maxine came from the cabin laughing and said, "Captain, I'm sure they understood everything was o.k. when you gave them the thumbs-up and pecker-down signs."

"If you don't start showin' the captain more respect, he's gonna put you on the rack until you get it right."

"Promises, promises," she said as she dropped her towel.

It was hard for me to imagine that a man and woman could have so much fun just banging around on a boat for three days. However, we did have a few serious moments when we shared our thoughts on our future, our children, and political issues. Religion seemed to be the only subject that we had any real difference of opinion. She said that she was a born-again Christian, and it was the devil that was snapping at my ass and not the dogs. I told her that I had no problem believing that God was real. But I didn't believe the devil called any of the shots, and there was no such place as hell except on earth, and I'd been there.

"Maxine, the trouble with most born-again Christians is that they're even bigger pains in the ass the second time around."

"Bobby, I can't argue that, but it doesn't give you the right to categorize all Christians as hypocrites. I'll admit there are some self-righteous fanatics that turn people off to God. Hey, God is about love and understanding."

"Max, I've always heard that you weren't supposed to discuss sex and religion."

"Yeah, that's exactly why most folks don't know a damn thing about either," she answered, then kissed me.

"I love ya, girl ... we're just different. You're such a damn conservative. If you were a man, you'd wear a belt and suspenders. I'm a bleedin' heart liberal — I'll agree with anybody who agrees with me," I said smiling.

There was a long silence before either one of us said anything. "Bobby, tell me something — why do you call Nick, 'Zorba'?" she asked with this puzzled look on her face.

"He reminds me of the character in that movie."

"I personally don't think so, but remember the last scene where he and the Englishman were on a beach and Zorba says, 'You need a little madness to survive,' and the Englishman says, 'Zorba, teach me to dance'?" she asked dramatically.

"Yeah, I remember. I loved it when Anthony Quinn and him got up and danced. That's when the Englishman finally understood Zorba's madness and was able to set free his own demons."

"Bobby, you're Zorba, not Nick. You've lived your life with the zeal and passion of a gladiator. And a few times it's gotten you in a whole lot of trouble, hasn't it?"

Before I had a chance to respond to that statement, a thunderstorm hit with high winds, causing white caps in Wassaw Sound. I rushed to the bow and pulled anchor while she cranked the engine of the *Amazing Max*.

"We'll talk about this later!" I yelled from the bow.

The honeymoon was officially over as we headed for Chimney Creek and safe harbor.

Maxine's comparison of me and Zorba didn't really ruffle my feathers. But the question of whether my "zeal and passion" had gotten me into a lot of trouble did cause me to reflect on my past errors of judgment.

I promised myself I was going to be open and honest with Maxine when I attempted to answer that question. She had never mentioned Cuba or the hijacking, but I knew that's what she was referring to when she remarked that my passions had caused me a lot of trouble.

A few weeks after our marriage, I was in Doc's Bar on the beach and I ran into my old friend, Dr. Charles Usher, Jr.

Charlie had been a Combat Engineer in both Europe and the Pacific during World War II. We always enjoyed each other's company and seemed to find a myriad of things to discuss over a few drinks.

Regardless of how long our conversations lasted, Charlie always ended by asking, "Reds, did you really go to Cuba to kill that son-of-bitch?" My answer was always the same, "Doc, if I think my country's right, I'll go tonight." And he would always say, "You got it, brother!"

This time he ended by asking, "Reds, you wanna go to the Republic of Haiti with me?"

"Man! They drink chicken blood and do that voodoo dancing."

"Yeah, I know," he laughed.

"Charlie, I just got married and besides, it's too damn close to those Communist bastards."

"Before you say no, let me give you the scoop."

He went on to explain that he was a member of a medical team that volunteered its services in various parts of the world. The group needed both lay and medical personnel for this particular mission to Haiti. He said that another ex-Green Beret was considering going with them. "We really need good security," he added. "That would be right up your alley."

"Charlie, 'Papa Doc' is as crazy as a shit-house rat, he might decide to keep ya, and make a zombie out'ya ass."

"That's why we need you, Reds. Besides some pretty nurses are going."

"Why didn't you say that in the first place, Charlie?"

"Like you said, you just got married."

"After I talk it over with my wife, I'll call you."

"Reds, did you really go to...?" he asked, grinning.

* * *

Sunday mornings had become our tete-a-tete time. Maxine was a firm believer in people talking things over, a practice I wasn't accustomed to, especially with a woman.

Since our marriage she'd come to believe that most of my health problems were related to asbestos and alcohol. She thought that I should change my vocation as soon as possible, and cut back on the booze even sooner.

"Honey, I've already started the process. I've mailed out resumes and have an appointment with Billy Mills at Backus Cadillac-Pontiac next week."

"How about your drinking?" she asked.

"One step at a time, sweet darlin'."

After our chin sessions she always turned the television on to Christian programs.

"Max, I've got a job at Backus; it'll be a few weeks before I start." I had decided that the trip to Haiti could be a sabbatical from the demon rum. I figured this would be the perfect time to get her blessings and travel with Charlie.

"Are you crazy? Why in the world would anybody in their right mind wanna go to Haiti?" she asked.

"Security for a medical team. Dr. Usher has always been a good friend. Besides, it's only for a couple of weeks, and it might open some doors of opportunity."

"Bobby, everybody's your good friend. What you need to do is close some of those damn doors."

Silence.

"Is that a yes or a no?" I said, with a big smile.

"I wish I didn't love you so. Sometimes there's a little boy in you that I can't say 'no' to."

"It's a good cause, Max."

"Yeah, I know, you've got those rose-colored glasses on again," she said and shrugged her shoulders.

A couple of days before the team was scheduled to leave, Charlie had a problem come up and was unable to make the Haitian mission. However, after going through the orientation and training required for membership in MEDIC, I committed to go, regardless.

The chartered bus ride from Savannah to Miami was my first chance to get acquainted with the other members. Charlie's assessment of some 'pretty nurses' turned out to be correct. But he failed to tell me about the couple of Pentecostal sisters who would accompany us.

My seven-hour ride to Miami was spent drinking beer and listening to conversations. It was one the most diverse groups of people that I'd ever been with.

At the Miami Airport, the physician in charge of the team gave me the responsibility of transporting the two plastic jugs he described as the "wonder drug" through Haitian customs.

"These must get to Haiti, Reds," Dr. Jimmy Metts had said.

The pilot announced that the island of Cuba could be seen from the right side of the aircraft. I looked down from 30,000 feet on the isle that I once believed would be my grave. My thoughts went back to my wife, and the questions that I'd left unanswered: the mystery of Cuba and why I'd hijacked the aircraft. I knew that she'd heard all of the convoluted bullshit over the years. I vowed to myself that I would unravel the puzzle for her on my return.

* * *

On a hot, humid day in early August, 1982, I looked up at the cloudless blue sky of Haiti one last time, before I boarded a DC-10 and thanked God for His amazing grace. I leaned against the headrest as the aircraft lifted from Port-au-Prince and closed my eyes. I began to go back over the last twelve years of my life — most of it etched in my consciousness as clearly as though it happened yesterday.

Now I wanted to share it with my wife — I owed her that.

"Bobby, there's something different about you," Maxine said as we sat having coffee the next morning.

"I guess I lost some weight. I felt guilty every time I picked up a spoon on that island — there's such poverty."

"No, Babe, I don't mean physically, I mean there's a peace about you that I've never seen before."

"Maxine, something happened to me in Haiti," I said as tears streamed down my face and the lump in my throat grew. "I don't want to hide any part of my life — no secrets."

"Bobby, you don't have to do this, we love each other and that's all that matters."

"I know, but I've got to get it off my mind. While I was in Cuba, I made a promise to God, and I haven't kept my end of the bargain. I wanna clear up some of the rumors I know you've heard. Then I'll tell you about Haiti."

She had heard most of the gossip around Savannah, especially the story about my father's spending hundreds of thousands of dollars for my release from Cuba, and even more for my legal defense.

"The truth is, nothing was paid to Castro or anybody else for my release. If that had been possible, I'm sure he would have gladly done it. But the fact is, that never happened. Nor did he spend a fortune on the trial. The trial cost less than $20,000, and Savannah Planing Mill paid it. My father didn't have enough capital to post my bond. When he asked a brother-in-law, who could have easily helped but chose not to, that seemed to upset him more than anything at the time.

"An old friend of my mother's family, Joe Hobbs, put up all his properties as security so that I could be released prior to the trial."

"Bobby, from everything I've read and heard, you had a slam-dunk case — even the government doctors testified that you were not sane at the time of the hijacking. So why was it so important that you be released on bond?" Maxine asked.

"Honey, from where I was sitting, it didn't look that way. When I went to Cuba, I believed without a shadow of doubt that I was part of an assassination plot. But, after gettin' back to the States and being treated like some character out of a 'Looney Tunes' cartoon by the FBI and CIA, I wasn't sure of anything. But, to answer your question, my attorneys needed time to prepare a defense. And believe me, it's not easy to convince a jury of temporary insanity."

"Bobby, if you didn't work for the CIA, how in God's name did you ever get reinstated in the Reserves?"

"Thank God for 'due process'. That was a hard battle that lasted almost two years after the trial. Finally, a good friend, Mr. Clarence Williams, who worked for us, wrote his friend, General W. C. 'Childs' Westmoreland. Shortly after they corresponded, I was given a hearing before the Army Discharge Review Board in the Pentagon. This is the letter Mr. Williams received from General Westmoreland."

UNITED STATES ARMY
The Chief of Staff

16 March 1972

Dear Clarence:

My sincere apologies for this belated reply to your 5 January letter. As you can appreciate, the press of official business keeps me extremely busy, and I spend much of my time on the road. My staff, however, has been keeping track of Robert's appeal.

By now you know that Robert appeared before the board. The board made a detailed and impartial study of all available evidence ...

The board's recommendation was approved by the Secretary of the Army and forwarded to the Commanding General, Reserve Components Personnel ... In the near future Robert will receive from the agency a form to be signed and returned. His records will then be annotated to indicate his eligibility to apply for a waiver to reenlist in the Army Reserve ... However because of length of time he has been out of service, his grade will have to be determined if he is accepted by a unit. Just because the waiver is approved does not mean that he will be able to reenter the Army Reserve at his prior grade.

While this does not resolve Robert's problem to everyone's satisfaction, I do believe an equitable solution under the circumstances has been reached. Many thanks for bringing the matter to my attention.

With best regards,

Sincerely,

Childs

Maxine smiled after reading the letter. "Go on," she said.

"While in Washington for my hearing at the Pentagon, I was approached in the Hotel Washington's bar by a man who identified himself as a reporter for the *Washington Post*. He said he'd heard about my Cuban ordeal and that he was very interested. He asked if I would be willing to give him an interview. I politely told him that I was doing my best to put that part of my life behind me, and I wasn't interested. He then told me that Senator Frank Church was heading up an investigation of possible assassination plots against Fidel Castro, and that my name had been mentioned for a subpoena. I again told him I was sorry, but no interview.

"A few days after I arrived back in Savannah, I received a letter from Ira Rosen in Jack Anderson's office. In the letter, he requested that I call the office, and stated that Mr. Anderson had deep pockets — if I was willing to do an interview. I called my attorney, Fred Clark, and gave him the reporter's name and asked him to talk with the man.

"Several days later, Fred called and said that he had taken care of it. When I asked what he had told him, he said, 'I told him that you'd had a nasty head injury and suffered a psychotic break immediately prior to the hijacking, and there was no assassination plot. Mr. Anderson would *need* deep pockets if he bothered you again.'"

"Bobby, was it really the head injury?"

"Maxine, I've asked myself the same thing. I'll get back to that after I clear up some of this other stuff."

"Whatever happened to your buddies, Harper and Prince?"

"Both made it home from Vietnam. Lt. Col. Curtis Harper is now a special operations officer, somewhere in Germany. Sergeant Major James E. Prince is living out his dream, turning boys into men at Parris Island. Man! I love those two guys. We all believed that we could make a difference."

"Bobby, before we go on, let me make another pot of coffee and go to the bathroom."

"All right, Honey! But I wanna answer all your questions and finish this confession today," I said anxiously.

"Now, why did the mill close?" she asked calmly, while pouring another cup of coffee.

"My dad didn't own the property the mill was located on. The only thing that belonged to him was the ancient equipment that he inherited when he bought the company. And the lady who owned the property was my father's ex-partner's mother-in-law, and she wouldn't renew the lease. I guess it was her way of getting back at my dad for buying out his trifling ex-partner. She figured my dad should have carried her son-in-law the rest of his life. A strange vendetta ... but, nevertheless, true."

"What happened to your marriage after that?"

"Intensely disjointed — one thing piling on top of another. We couldn't talk about anything without getting into a shouting match. After we lost our home, she was miserable, I was miserable. I think we were both tired of living the lie."

"O.K., please explain this to me: head injury or no head injury, CIA or no CIA, how could you have possibly thought you could get close enough to kill Castro by hijacking an aircraft?"

"I'm gonna answer that hypothetically. If I told you that you could conceal a plastic suppository, which held a device so deadly it killed almost on touch, would it be possible?"

"Maybe, but you'd have to describe the device and give me

the odds of Castro being at the airport at that precise time. And most important — the escape clause," she said.

"What if I said the device has a clear plastic outer ring that slips over the finger — almost invisible to the eye. That a small reservoir is attached to the ring and is concealed under the finger in the palm. When the safety tip is removed from a small needle at the bottom of the lemon-shaped reservoir, a person can be injected with a highly lethal poison by applying almost imperceptible pressure; the victim dies minutes later of what appears to be natural causes.

"Castro routinely visited Jose Marti Airport, especially late-night flights, and always interviewed the hijacker. If then, everything else fails, there's an 'L' pill in the suppository for the ultimate escape."

"What kind?" she laughed.

"A lethal pill."

"Bobby, if I used your hypothesis, I'd have to believe that you were a major player in a failed assassination plot. But what really concerns me, after reading Liz Rich's book, *Flying Scared*, is where she quotes a psychiatrist who interviewed a hijacker named Sam, who in reality is you. According to this Dr. Hubbard, 'Sam had a death wish ... if he hadn't attempted to kill Castro, he would have vented his anger at the real target, his father.' Bobby, please explain that," she said calmly.

I thought about her questions for a moment. "Maxine, have you ever talked to a psychiatrist?"

"Not as a patient."

"Well, all I can say about Hubbard's Freudian supposition is, I first met the man at the Federal Medical Facility. I spent a total of two hours with him and several other psychiatrists and psychologists who asked questions about everything from my childhood to whether I preferred masturbation or intercourse.

"The only thing that I said about my father was that he thought you should be able to read his mind and that it was his way or no way. Hell, Dr. Thigpen asked me to tell him about some of the things I remembered as a youth that angered me. I told him about an incident that happened when I was twelve: I'd seen a white man almost beat an elderly black man to death with an axe handle, and I couldn't do anything about it. Another time, when I'd seen movies of the emaciated bodies stacked in Nazi death camps, it made me ashamed of my German heritage.

"After the interview he surmised that I'd probably had a paranoid character for years and that I viewed myself as a knight in shining armor who wished to rescue the nation and perform heroic acts. I can't explain it, I suppose they all see inside your head differently."

"Did your dad really write a letter to Fidel Castro like the newspapers reported?"

"According to my father, he never wrote any letter. However, he claims to have talked with Fidel Castro personally."

"How could that be possible?" she asked.

"He's supposed to have gotten Castro's personal telephone number from a Mexican friend of the Brookfields' who worked in the Cuban Embassy in Mexico City. I know this sounds like a lot of horseshit, but I'm gonna tell you anyhow. He said that when he talked with Castro, he explained that I had been hit in the head and wasn't myself when I hijacked the plane to Cuba. He asked him if he would please allow me to return to the United States. He went on to say that Castro spoke good English when he said, 'I will consider your request, Mr. Holmey.'"

"Bobby, do you believe that really happened?"

"I think my father believes he actually talked to Fidel. The strangest thing about the whole thing is this: I confirmed with the Brookfields that they had given my father the number of their friend in Mexico City and shortly thereafter the friend traveled to Cuba and never returned to Mexico. I guess the only way we'll ever unravel that mystery is by asking Fidel."

She looked puzzled and said, "Bobby, before you continue, I've heard for years how caring your dad is supposed to be. But since I've been in this family, I've seen how insensitive he really is to you and your mother, and I've certainly changed my feelings about him — he treats strangers better than family."

"Maxine, we're gettin' off the subject. I can't figure how anyone, including a psychiatrist turned philosopher could reason that I subconsciously wanted to kill my father. Not once did they mention the possibility of an assassination plot. Dr. Thigpen was the only one who questioned that, and he concluded that I had kept my belief in the CIA plot. This is just my opinion, but most psychiatrists would make a hell of a lot better fortune-tellers than they do physicians. They only listen to you as long as you don't make sense."

"Bobby, I love you, baby. I'm glad this is all delusional and hypothetical stuff," she said, grinning broadly.

"Now I'll tell you what happened in Haiti."

* * *

After a two-and-a-half hour flight we touched down at Francois Duvalier International Airport in the Republic of Haiti.

Watching Haitian Customs at work reminded me of a scene from a Western movie. The Indians had just raided a wagon train and were ransacking their victims' booty. They seized anything they wanted without an explanation. Most of our medical supplies were confiscated by the Tontons Macoutes, the Secret Police, who seemed to rule with an iron hand. Fortunately, we were able to slip the wonder drug through without detection.

Our tap-tap ride (the colorfully decorated little buses made from Japanese pickups) to our overnight destination took us by Cite Simone, the shantytown built on the mud flats of Port-au-Prince Bay where 200,000 people live in some of the worst poverty on earth. The stench of burning rubbish and rotting offal filled our nostrils. Tiny shacks made from anything that would stand or lie flat, packing crates, plywood scraps, cardboard, and tin from a million cans seemed endless.

Long lines of children and old people stood in the blazing sun with plastic jugs and anything else that might hold water, waiting their turn at a single spigot.

As we traveled up towards our stay-over in the mountain suburbs of Petionville, the palatial homes with their high walls and broken glass embedded in the tops, overlooked Port-au-Prince's grim poverty below. Perhaps nothing better demonstrates the abyss between poverty and plenitude so swiftly and graphically as does the short trip up that hill.

The beautiful blue stucco dwelling that housed World Harvest for Christ was also used as an orphanage, clinic and rest spot for other groups who volunteered their services.

Charlie had neglected to tell me that we'd be hosted by a group of women missionaries. That didn't present any serious problems. However, I didn't want them sermonizing or praying over me. On the entire flight from Miami, two sanctified sisters in particular had kept their eyes glued on me and prayed every time I got out of my seat. I was determined to stay as far away from them as possible without hurting their feelings.

Miriam Fredricks, the Missionary/Director gave a brief orientation upon our arrival. "Tomorrow we'll be traveling to the village of Zetoit. It's located in the bush about 100 miles west of here. If the rivers aren't flooded, it won't be but an eight-hour trip. Anyone who would like to go to Port-au-Prince this afternoon, see Sister Mavis immediately."

Mavis didn't exactly fit the mold of what I thought a missionary would look like. Her dress was very conservative with a high collar and long skirt, her hair was pulled back in a bun and she wore no makeup. But none of this concealed the fact that she had the body of a young nubile women. I found it difficult to call her Sister.

In the back of a crowded Toyota pick-up, I listened as Mavis talked about everything from voodoo to vitamins. She'd been on the mission field for a couple of years and spoke the Creole language fluently. It was obvious from the things she said that she had a deep love for the Haitian people.

"Mavis, does voodoo still exist in Haiti?" I asked.

"Voodoo is now and always has been Haiti's most important religious tradition." We bounced around in the truck. "Most Haitians have never seen a contradiction between Christianity and voodoo. It was forced underground during slavery and, they say, merged with African, Christian and Indian spirits. I'll tell you about some strange things that's happened to me since I've been in Haiti. But I'll wait until we're in the bush, Brother Red."

"Mavis, it sounds like you believe it's real."

"Oh, it's real, all right. But it's the devil, not voodoo."

"Sister, you sound like my wife," I said grinning.

In Port-au-Prince the parks were weed-grown and littered, and the statues of heroes were oxidized with pigeon shit. The only thing clean was the Presidential Palace of "Papa Doc" Duvalier. The next morning, while Metts and Mavis went to replace the confiscated medical supplies, the team loaded the motorized phaeton that had been chartered for the land portion of the expedition.

The name placard above the windshield of the oversized tap-tap was 'The Concorde'. The mix of voodoo and Christian symbols that ornamented the multicolored carrier must have been achieved by a witch-doctor and a drunk preacher.

Going west along the coast, we were stopped at three military checkpoints and were questioned at each. The information on our passports was laboriously copied by soldiers who held the pencil stubs as though they were holding a snake by the head.

The first river we came to after running out of paved road was on a goat trail about 50 miles and six hours out of Port-au-Prince. "No problem, mon, dis ting blest," announced the pilot of the Concorde. After unloading passengers and luggage, everybody waded through the waist-deep water to the other side. We watched the driver back the bus up, race the engine, and then floor-board the Concorde and literally sail it over the river. We then reloaded and continued the journey.

Someone started singing, 'Shall We Gather at the River,' and everybody joined in. "The beau-ti-ful riv-er..."

After repeating that same scenario at two other rivers, we finally reached Petit-Trou-De-Nippes, a small fishing village on the Gulf of Gonave, where a boat had been waiting to take us on the last leg of our trek to Zetoit.

It was now one in the morning and a near gale-force wind was blowing. Dr. Metts, Miriam, the boat Captain, and I met to make the decision whether or not we'd go now or wait until the weather lifted.

Miriam and the Captain conversed in Creole as Metts and I stood silent.

The Captain also was the pastor of the small mission church in Zetoit. It was apparent to me from his body language that he was anxious to get the show on the road. His facial expressions signaled a state of near panic.

"Pastor Shalom says that, since his announcement that American doctors were coming to the village, people from other villages had come to Zetoit expecting miracles. There's sickness and disease everywhere and the local witch doctor is itching to start trouble. Even some Tontons Macoutes are there. He believes it's important that we leave at once. Also, he would like for us to show more faith and let him worry about the weather," Miriam said with a look of affirmation.

"How ya feel about that, Reds?" Metts asked.

"Doc, today we've jumped three rivers in a wreck named the Concorde. So I don't see any problem with us makin' it to Zetoit in a boat that looks like the *Titanic*. However, I highly recommend that you get those sisters busy praying."

The night was weird. As high winds and a rough sea continued, members of the team rushed to load the small Haitian craft. After the supplies were aboard and the last person stepped on the pitching deck, the winds suddenly ceased and the sea calmed, a thick fog surrounded us. Within ten minutes, it had lifted and the stars were shining.

I'd spent a great deal of my time on the water and had seen a lot of weather, but nothing to compare with this. It was eerie.

As the Captain cranked the engine, he pointed to the North Star and said something to Mavis in Creole.

"What'd he say, Mavis?" I asked.

"He said: Polaris was watchin' the night he was born," she shouted, "and it will be watchin' the night he dies!"

At daybreak the new light turned the sea from black to blue and the mountain shadows from a ghostly grey to green.

As we neared the rickety little pier, a couple of 12- to 15-foot boats sat swayback on a mud bank. Their hulls had been eaten by rot. I could see daylight through their sides. Dugout canoes and small sailing craft were beached all around the cove. In the distance you could see the palm-thatched huts that dotted the hillsides. People stood peering down on us with smiles on their faces.

The children were the first to come, then it seemed everybody, young and old, came to help.

It was after we had walked up the hill to the only cement block building in the village, that I understood the urgency the captain had shown earlier.

There are some moments that hang forever suspended in time. That day was one of those. The village, which was perched on the shore of Haiti's impoverished Southern claw, was a jumble of people. The clearing near the uncompleted cement block building was crowded with the sick and ailing.

Children with bloated bellies, many with the reddish tinge to their hair, a sign of malnutrition Mavis told us, lay corpse-like on the ground. Men and women of all ages sat with glazed expressionless faces waiting for a doctor to work his magic. While unconcerned children played in the foot paths, an old woman rode on a donkey, other women with bundles on their heads walked gracefully past as goats grazed nearby. A young man caught my eye, "*Kouman ou ye?* How are you?"

"Good," I answered as he grabbed my rucksack.

"My name Solidad," he replied as we walked into the half-roofed building. He claimed great powers as a guide, translator, purchasing agent and porter.

"Solidad, why do I need your services?" I asked.

"I am a Christian," he said with a big grin.

"How much?" I asked.

"Two American dollars, one day."

"All right, but see me later and we talk."

The rest of that day, the nonmedical team members worked to set up a makeshift clinic, as Dr. Metts and the four nurses began seeing the critically ill. It had been a long day; Miriam asked Pastor Shalom to announce that the doctors needed sleep and the infirmary would be closed until sunrise.

Before daylight, I was awakened by what sounded like an anemic rooster choking to death. Solidad lay munching a mango with his eyes fastened on me. During the night, more sick had come to the village and many had found shelter in the same crude structure in which we were housed. The entire dirt floor was strewn with people and medical supplies, sleeping bags, water bottles, and the straw mats of the newly arrived.

Jimmy Metts and Mavis were either aroused by the same sick chicken or hadn't slept. By a Coleman lantern light, they were feverishly operating on an infant with a large goiter protruding from her neck.

As Mavis held a plastic airway down the child's throat, Metts worked with a large syringe extracting an amber-colored fluid from the cantaloupe-sized tumor. The mother stood near with voodoo beads in hand and fear on her face. I listened as Metts explained what could have happened if the mother had waited another hour. "The child was literally being choked to death by the cyst as it filled with fluid," Metts explained.

"Doc, won't it happen again if it's not removed?" I asked.

"Yes, it's a relatively simple procedure, but it can't be done here in the bush."

I watched as Mavis handed the child back to the thankful mother and I thought to myself, it's just a matter of time.

I motioned for Solidad to come to me as I grabbed a towel from my rucksack. It was as if he'd been reading my mind.

"*Merci beaucoup, Rouge,*" he said pointing to the door.

The sun was just coming up as I stepped in the dugout canoe. He paddled us out in the middle of a small lagoon and pointed to the water, "O.K. *Rouge*, you wash now!"

I removed my clothes and dived into the clear blue water. It was my first opportunity for a bath since we'd left the States and it felt great. When I pulled myself back into the swaying dugout, he handed me the towel.

"Where're my pants?" I asked, when I didn't see my clothes. He held up a plastic bag and grinned, "My wife wash good for you."

"O.K. Solidad, but I've got to have them to wear back to the village."

He didn't seem to understand so I wrapped the towel around me, and he started paddling. I rushed back up to the mission and got a change of clothes, then stepped behind a tree to dress, not knowing that half the village was watching.

That afternoon Solidad told me what an old Haitian man had to say: "I never see a white mon naked till I glimpse at dat banana tree. Dat white mon got balls big as ya fist, wid red feathers growin' on 'um." He said, "Dat old mon never laughed so much in he life. *Rouge*, you funny mon, wid chick'n feathers on da nuts."

It seemed ludicrous that an area which had every appearance of a Garden of Eden could possess so much human misery. Diseases that modern science had either eradicated or developed immunization against seemed commonplace.

"They're plagued with infectious diseases. Measles, diarrhea, and tetanus are major child killers. Two hundred fifty out of every thousand children die before reaching the age of five. Over fifty percent of these deaths could be prevented if something was done about the water." Mavis's face reflected her frustration as she held an infant suffering with severe amoebic dysentery in her arms.

"Mavis, what could be done about the water?" I asked.

"Right now the only good water in Zetoit is being brought over that mountain from Obus," she said as she pointed. "What they need is a well in Zetoit. If not, they're gonna continue to drink from that dirty cistern at the bottom of the hill."

Later, Jimmy Metts confirmed that unless something was done, the health problems wouldn't get any better. I'd seen enough to be convinced that both knew what they were talking about. Every time the thunder clapped or a dark cloud appeared, people grabbed plastic buckets or anything that would hold water and stood waiting for the rain. I also watched as animals drank and walked in the same cistern that the village used as its main water source.

Solidad's expertise as an entrepreneur was nothing short of genius. His imagination was only limited by the depth of the cash flow. It seemed incredible that he could speak three languages, French, Spanish, and English.

"Solidad, it's hard to get any sleep in that mission building. I need a quiet place — can you find me one?"

"No problem, *Rouge!*" he shouted as he disappeared down a footpath.

A burly mulatto, standing next to a brightly dressed black woman, motioned to me. There was no mistaking the chrome plated pistol wedged in his belt. As I stood trying to interpret his broken English, Solidad reappeared. He and the man exchanged words in Creole. Then Solidad pulled me off to the side and said in a low voice, "Dis mon a Tontons Macoute. His woman need doctor, bad pussy."

"Tell him, he'll just have to wait his turn."

"*Rouge*, dis a very bad mon — jew tell him," he said in a low voice.

I immediately escorted the man and his friend to Dr. Jimmy Metts.

Solidad found me a palm-thatched hut overlooking the lagoon, and for five bucks a day he included fresh mangoes, limes and a bottle of rum. "I look out for *Rouge*! I Christian, I like yew much!"

That night after clinic, he brought me the rum and mangos. At first I was hesitant because fruit-flies were circling the bottle. So, I handed it back and told him to take a drink. When he didn't fall over, I tried a swig — it wasn't bad at all.

Later that evening, I was awakened by the sound of drums and tambourines. After the cobwebs cleared my mind, I realized it was Wednesday night prayer meeting that Mavis Woods and Jean Waters had invited me to. I couldn't go back to sleep, so I decided to visit another Medic member who also was keeping his distance from the sanctified sisters.

Fred's sleeping accommodations were in the rear of the structure where the services were being held. When I entered the room, he was leaning against the cement block wall reading Dostoevsky's *Crime and Punishment* by the light of a lantern.

"Reds, I'm sure glad you came over," he said, removing his ear plugs. "Pull up that box and have a seat."

"Sounds like the sisters got the choir and rhythm section fired up tonight," I said, handing him the bottle of rum.

Fred shook his head and laughed cynically. "Yeah, I don't doubt they can be heard all the way back to Port-au-Prince."

"I can tell by your brogue you ain't from Savannah."

"That's right, Reds — I'm a transplanted Yankee."

After several drinks, Fred and I decided we might as well join the revival, since there was no escaping the call of Gabriel's trumpet, drums and tambourines.

When we entered the half-roofed part of the building, the

only place to sit was directly in front of a makeshift podium. The mix of languages didn't veil the rhythms of 'Amazing Grace'.

"Listen for one more moment," Miriam Fredricks said, after preaching in the Creole tongue. "If by chance you're still with me, I beg of you not to judge the oil and the wine by the flawed female vessel delivering it. All of us desperately need prayer, but the Holy Spirit is real and perfect. God forbid! To allow the greatest message in the history of the world to be cheapened and distorted by preachers who use people to build bigger sanctuaries and feed their own greed.

"Two thousand years ago a blind begger cried out, 'O thou son of David.' Millions of blind beggars are still crying out. All of our worldly ways, all of our talents and abilities can't slake the thirst of one such thirsty soul. Only Jesus can, and if we fail to introduce Him to a dying world we have utterly failed in what God has set before us."

She then looked at me and said, "Before I close, I have a word of prophecy for someone in this room. You've cried out to God and He has given you a second chance at life. But you're like the person who keeps God locked in the trunk of his automobile until the road of life becomes so crooked he no longer can steer. Then he unlocks the trunk and let Him in the driver's seat just long enough to straighten out the curves in his life. Then back in the rear He goes. Give up, and let Jesus make a way that is straight and good for you."

I was moved and convinced by her message and revelation. I had been led to believe that it was a sacrilege for a woman to even be allowed in the pulpit. She blew my theology.

The night was hot and humid in the village, so I walked up the hill that overlooked Zetoit. A fresh breeze was blowing as I sat staring up at a zillion stars. I knew I was the person in Miriam's parable, and, looking back over my life, I realized the only time I ever cried out to God was when I was in need — most of the time I totally forgot Him.

The next morning during sick bay, a hysterical woman came running in and handed me an infant that had been scalded after turning over a pot of boiling water. The skin on the left side of her body had been melted away. Amazingly, the baby wasn't crying and seemed more upset at her mother's wailing than her own pain.

"I don't understand, why she didn't cry," I said after Dr. Metts and Mavis did everything possible to save the baby.

"Reds, first- and second-degree burns are extremely painful, but third-degree, like this child had, usually hurt very little. The nerve endings which send pain impulses to the brain are damaged. Maybe it was God's way of showing mercy after the Tontons confiscated our pain medication," he replied emotionally.

Over the next few days, I was aware that something was happening inside of me, and I needed answers. Why were these people, whose only sin seemed to be that they were born poor and black, have so much misery? And yet they appeared to have such a hunger for Godly and spiritual things. I remembered watching the fear-ravaged mother of the scalded child clutch tightly to a voodoo charm and a rosary.

"Mavis, you promised to tell me about the weird things you've seen, since being in Haiti."

"I also remember telling you it was the devil and not voodoo, then you said, 'Sister, you sound like my wife.'"

I gave her a surprised look. "Okay, you do remember. So, you believe the devil is real and he's behind it all?"

"Sure, don't you?"

"Mavis, it's hard to believe that some supernatural hobgoblin calls all the shots on who's gonna catch hell and who's gonna be happy."

"Oh, you're right! He doesn't call the shots, unless God allows him to — he's real and supernatural. If the devil doesn't exist, how can you believe God does?"

"I just don't swallow all the supernatural, holy ghost, tongue-talkin' stuff," I said.

There was a pause. "Brother Reds, please don't be offended by what I'm about to ask you — are you a Christian?"

"Yes! I'm a confirmed Lutheran."

"Did you know Luther was so convinced the devil literally existed that he threw an ink bottle at him, then turned the religious world upside down when he said, 'We are saved by grace through faith.' That quote in Romans changed his life, and became a rallying cry of the Reformation. Reds, how often do you read the Bible?"

"Not much, I leave that up to a man-of-of-the-cloth."

Her face turned serious, then she said in a quiet voice, "Reds, when you come face-to-face with God, do you think a man-of-the-cloth will be with you?"

"No, I don't believe that at all," I said slowly. "The truth is, I don't know why we're even having this conversation, except that I haven't been able to get the picture of God, locked in a trunk, off my mind since Miriam's sermon."

She smiled hesitantly. "Maybe the Holy Ghost is trying to tell you something."

"Maybe, but I haven't heard any voices lately."

"But, you have heard them," she countered.

"*Touche!*" I said.

She smiled patiently, ignoring my cynical swipes at her Pentecostal theology. "Reds, do you know what it means to be born again?"

"Mavis, I've heard that saying most of my life. But no, I don't know what it means."

"It means a complete change in your life. Born again is not reforming. Reform is from without, conversion is from within. You completely surrender to Jesus. It's the willingness to do what he wants you to do. Unless you surrender and do His will it means nothing. You can be reformed a thousand times and have your name on fifty church rolls; that doesn't mean you're saved."

"I thought all of us were born with a free will; how can you possibly know what God wants in your life?" I said.

"Before you can know God's will, you have to know Him."

"Mavis, how can anyone know or comprehend Him?"

"Spiritually. If you can pray this prayer and mean it in your heart." She paused, bowed her head, "Dear God in heaven, I come to You in the name of Jesus. I accept You as my personal Savior. Amen. Reds, I can't explain it, but it's real."

I gazed at her silently for a moment. "Mavis, tell me how a woman with your credentials winds up in a place that only Mother Teresa could appreciate."

When she didn't respond, I just looked at her with a playful grin. "Honey, you've got looks, personality and a few other things, but here you are in this beautiful hell."

After I finished, she broke into a broad smile. "Reds, I'm gonna share a few things with you. I was born an Air Force brat. Before I was twelve, I'd lived on three continents and been exposed to more cultures than Zsa Zsa Gabor. At sixteen, I ran away from home and traveled all over the States. Later, I joined the Peace Corps and worked in Africa and the Middle East. While I was in the Middle East, I was drugged and coerced into a sheik's harem. So, I think it's fair to say, I've been around the block a few times myself, but..."

I interrupted her. "Mavis, I'm sorry, I didn't mean to sound so blunt. I know you're for real and you believe that God has called you to this place."

She interrupted, "Reds, please let me finish."

"Please do," I said apologetically.

"...there is no way I could return to that life style," she said with tears flowing down her cheeks. "Reds, would you pray the salvation prayer with me?"

I was silent for a moment, then said, "Mavis, I'm no theologian and I don't profess to have the answer, but there has to be more to salvation than a few words."

"You don't have to understand it or explain it. Accept it and let God do the rest. The people who try to figure God out will probably be the smartest people in hell. Reds, you ever heard the words of the hymn, 'Amazing Grace'?"

"Sure, many times. And not always in church."

"Remember these words, 'I once was lost, but now I'm found, was blind, but now I see. How pre-cious did that grace ap-pear, The hour I first be-lieved..'."

I shook my head and said, "Mavis, how 'bout these words, 'Oh! the games peo-ple p-l-a-y, now! In the name of hu-manity; they talk about you and me, our pride and our van-ity. La-di-da, and la-di-da-da. Then they sock-it to you, in the name of the Lord'."

I awoke perspiring. Outside I could hear a deep voice chanting in the Creole tongue. I immediately rolled out of my sleeping bag, grabbing a flashlight and a machete. Coming out of the hut, I spotted the silhouette of what looked like a giant chicken. At first it was so macabre I thought the 'monkey rum' had caused me to hallucinate. But as the beam of light hit the poultry shape, I saw that it was a black man wearing a cloak made from feathers, and a cap shaped like a rooster's comb. He was holding a voodoo talisman in one hand and a long forked staff in the other.

I shouted loudly, hoping to wake someone, "Man! Get your chicken-feathered ass down the road, before I use this machete!"

When I shined the light in his glaucous eyes, he began shouting and trembling like a person having a seizure. After a few seconds, he did a 'bossa nova' step, let out a demonic howl that split the night air, then vanished down the footpath.

The only person that responded to my distress call was Solidad. "*Rouge*, what de matter, mon?"

"Some guy with glowing eyes, wearin' a bunch of feathers, came by the hut and did a wild dance."

"Dat been the 'Houngan Mon,'" he said excitedly.

"The who?" I asked.

"Voodoo root doctor — he from Obus, he think all white

mon is devils," Solidad said, as he reached into his pocket and handed me a small cobalt blue bottle. "*Rouge*, throw dis water on de mon if he com back."

"What is it?"

"Mon, dis holy water, de bad spirits hab to go."

"Thanks, Solidad, but I don't need it, we're leavin' tomorrow. Come in the hut, I've got a few things I hope you and your family can use."

I emptied out my rucksack and seabag, keeping only the clothing and toilet articles necessary for the trip back to the States.

As he gathered-up the clothing in his arms, Solidad seemed more impressed by an old tattered red, white and blue jersey with an American flag and a Budweiser logo, than all the other gear.

"*Rouge*, why ya wanna do away wid Fidel?"

"Man, who told you that?" I asked.

"Da say — jew jack-off de aeroplane and tell de mon to tell Fidel dat yew on de way to get'um," he said grinning.

"Solidad, you can't believe everything you hear — anyway that was long ago and I wasn't myself," I said, pointing to a scar over my right eye.

Then he gave me this curious stare, "Oh Gawd, *Rouge*! I glad jew don't kill de mon 'cause he help de por folk."

The next morning, as I loaded gear aboard the old battered sailboat, Mavis stood holding an emaciated child close in her arms. "Reds, are you coming back and help us in Zetoit?"

At first, I didn't answer. I continued as if I hadn't heard her, but when Solidad said, "Sister Mavis, *Rouge* a good mon, he com back and help us get de water."

It was like I had no control over what I said next. "Mavis, as soon as I get back to Savannah, I know this guy Bogie Worth, who's one hell of a water expert — I promise, you'll see me again."

"Praise Jesus," she said softly. "God's gonna bless you, Brother Reds."

"Mavis, hand me the baby and get in the boat. I've got to talk with you before we leave for Petit-Trou-De-Nippes.

"Mavis, I know God is real. If He didn't exist, there would be no rules for life. I don't understand salvation or the 'born again' stuff. You'll probably laugh at what I'm about to tell you. I've heard God whisper my name and tell me to quit playing games. I've used my own hypocrisy to accuse some Christians of what I'm most guilty of — calling on God only when I need Him, then forgettin' He even exists when things are going my way. I'm tired of myself. I'm tired of taking the same old streets and fallin' in the same holes."

"Reds, God loves you unconditionally, you don't have to understand it. It's so simple, just believe in your heart that Jesus died for you and ..."

I looked up into the oval silver sky with tears flowing down my cheeks. "Mavis, I've had this spiritual emptiness for a long time. Marian's sermon helped me realize what a phony I've been. I do believe ... say the sinner's prayer with me."

* * *

"Maxine, as soon as the words came out of my mouth — a feeling of peace flooded over me like I'd never known before."

"I knew there was something different about you the moment you stepped off that airplane. Bobby, I hope this is real in your life."

Over the next few years I returned to Haiti four times. Each time it was a voyage of transformation by trials and revelations. I found myself reevaluating beliefs I'd held since childhood. At times the events of my life — such as Cuba and Castro — were still a painful reality that manifested itself with questions that I could not answer. I knew the world wasn't divided into good and evil people. Rather, good and evil coexist in every human heart.

* * *

In 1995 I wrote the editor of the Savannah *Morning News.*

Dear Editor:

As I was channel surfing not long ago, I stopped on C-Span to hear an address at the Abyssinia Baptist Church. At first, I thought it was a recent convert giving his testimony to his new belief. Amen, I was hanging on every word the preacher was preaching.

It was a gospel that I had heard many times before. There was a difference this time in the messenger, not the message.

The preacher wore olive drab combat fatigues. He spoke in Spanish and was translated into English. His pulpit was the Abyssinian Baptist Church in the heart of Harlem. 'Amen,' 'Amen,' 'Preach it brother,' echoed all over the church. He seemed to mesmerize his audience.

There was no doubt that this man didn't believe he was called by an ideological belief that was greater than any one individual. The message was politically provocative and spiritually arousing. The speaker was president of the only Communist country in the Western hemisphere, Cuba's Fidel Castro.

He quoted the Bible with the passionate rhetoric of Jimmy Swaggart. 'If I would have had a pastor like yours to guide and encourage me in my youth, maybe my ideas would be different today,' he said, as he turned to look at the Baptist preacher behind him.

Was I witnessing a man's transformation of ideas, or had I completely missed in my earlier assessment of this man? Was he the greatest snake-oil salesman of the 20th century, or the most misunderstood, a real patriot of everything that is good in man, or just another phony politician?

Will history absolve him of his unwavering, tenacious beliefs that the Cuban Revolution was just and necessary for Cuba to survive as a free and Democratic people? Maybe even Fidel Castro can be 'born again.'

After hearing his oratory, I still had doubt. I remembered the night we landed in Havana and I saw an old Soviet missile. Obviously it had no military significance now, because it was mounted on cement blocks and had a jumble of girders and cables holding it up. It stood about sixty feet tall, at a slight angle that seemed to be pointed toward the United States of America. I know the Cuban missile crisis is history, but I will always believe Fidel Castro would have pulled the trigger if the Russians had not controlled the missiles. Now Kennedy and Krushchev are dead, but Castro and the missiles still survive.

Occasionally I'll pass the American Legion Post where the Lemon Dances were held. My thoughts always go back to ghosts of the past and I recall the song:

> *The lemon tree is very pretty*
> *And the flower is sweet,*
> *But the fruit of the lemon*
> *Is impossible to eat.*

As I saw what happened around me, I became aware of something happening inside of me. For all my blunderings and failures, I ask forgiveness.

Reds

Notes

Documents

Canadian deportation order of R. M. Helmey, May 5, 1969.

Excerpts from the reduction of bail hearing held in the United States District Court, Savannah, Georgia, June 19, 1969.

Excerpts from deposition given by Dr. Corbett H. Thigpen, The Cleckley-Thigpen Psychiatric Associates, Augusta, Georgia, August 21, 1969.

Excerpts from testimony in the trial of *The United States vs. Robert M. Helmey*, United States District Court, Savannah, Georgia, November 17 - 21, 1969.

Statement by Thomas M. Close to Federal Bureau of Investigation, Savannah, Georgia, January 14, 1969.

Newspapers

Savannah Morning News
Savannah Evening Press
Miami Herald

Books

Red Star over Cuba, Nathaniel Weyl, The Devin-Adair Company, New York, 1960.

Small Arms of the World, 12th edition, Edward Clinton Ezell, Barnes & Noble Publishers, New York, 1993.

Flying Scared, Liz Rich, Stein & Day Publishers, New York, 1973.

The Three Faces of Eve, Corbett H. Thigpen, M.D., and Hervey M. Cleckley, M.D., McGraw-Hill Book Company, Inc., New York, 1957.

Letters from Earth, Mark Twain's unpublished works which were published by Albert Paine, date unknown.

Church Hymnal, Tennessee Music & Printing Company, 1951.

The Holy Bible, King James Version, published by Holman Bible Publishers, Nashville, Tennessee.